ISBN: 9781527230781

First published in 2018

Cover design by Anton Pshinka

Book design and production by How2Become Ltd

Author photograph by Janet Penny

Chapter illustrations by Kitty Kevan

Disclaimer

This book is intended to provide helpful information on the subjects discussed. The information is provided for educational purposes only and should not be taken as medical advice. This book is not meant to be used, nor should it be used, to diagnose or treat any medical condition. For any health issues seek medical advice before making a change to your regimen. The author and publisher are not responsible for any specific health or allergy needs that may require medical supervision and are not liable for any damages or negative consequences from any treatment, action, application or preparation to any person reading or following the information in this book.

Keep Your Health and Fitness for Life

Don't let age be a barrier

OLDER FITTER
DON'T LET AGE BE A BARRIER

sturoberts@olderfitter

This Book Is Dedicated To All Those Who Want To Live Their Life In The Best Possible Health And Are Prepared To Take Responsibility For Achieving It.

Acknowledgements

This is a book that I have wanted to write for a long time. There's not space to thank everyone but first of all I'd like to thank all the people I've worked with over the years who have made amazing strides in their fitness. There's nothing more rewarding to me to see people transform their health and fitness, and see the positive impact it has on other aspects of their lives. Of course, I would not have been able to help these people without the amazing teachers and mentors who have shaped the way in which I view ageing and health and fitness.

The work of nutritionist and educator Patrick Holford in leading at the forefront, bringing the latest research and breakthroughs in nutrition to the public was instrumental in inspiring me to become a nutritionist. His nutrition magazines were the first things that I read that opened my eyes to the incredible possibilities for humans to live long and healthy lifespans free from disease. He continues to be an inspiration to me and studying with him introduced me to Lawrence Plaskett and Michael Colgan.

Professor Lawrence G Plaskett inspired me to become a naturopathic nutritionist and my training with him showed the incredible abilities of the human body to self-heal and to attain levels of wellbeing in middle and older age that are still thought in broader society to be at best, fanciful. This truly exceptional yet incredibly modest man with years of experience as a biochemist has a truly encyclopaedic knowledge of nutrition and numerous other therapies that can be used in combination. This is where I first really appreciated the power of synergy and the fact that you can't have true health without it.

Dr Michael Colgan was one of the world's top sports performance research scientists for over 30 years. His books and training courses made me realise that you can combine nutrition, naturopathic principles and unique forms of exercise to achieve fitness levels and abilities that are quite extraordinary. I attended his training camps in Canada when he was in his mid-sixties. The exercises he demonstrated and his level of fitness was awe inspiring – he's a true role model.

Dr Cory Holly who worked closely with Michael Colgan, developed a comprehensive sports nutrition course for the Canadian Health Food Association, which I found really empowering. His uncompromising vision and drive to educate on human potential for peak performance at any age was very inspiring, coining the phrase "age is not a barrier, only an excuse"

Rick McMunn is a friend and was a work colleague for many years in the Fire Service before moving on to set up and grow an outstanding, award winning online publishing business. I was so fortunate to have him as my mentor.

Rick's inspirational example of determination and persistence, together with his amazing in-depth knowledge of publishing online have helped to drive me forward and complete this book.

Kitty Kevan is an amazing artist and has created some brilliant illustrations for this book. Kitty was a joy to work with and we had many fun hours discussing ideas. Her drawings have helped to bring each chapter alive and imbue a sense of fun, which is crucial as optimising our health and fitness shouldn't be seen as a chore!

The last person I wish to thank for being my inspiration and the catalyst for all that I have achieved with my own health and fitness as well as helping others is my wife Susan. She is someone who has always been open to new concepts and been willing to try new ideas, even if they seemed implausible to others. Susan has been invaluable in proof reading the book and has used her extensive experience and knowledge as a personal development coach to contribute significantly to the last two chapters. She has been unwavering in her encouragement and belief in what I was looking to create in this book.

CONTENTS

About the author

Growing up watching loved ones at the mercy of debilitating illnesses Stuart became passionate about transforming people's health, helping them attain boundless energy and maintain their fitness whatever their age.

Being a Fire Fighter for 30 years Stuart was lucky to have a job that required him to keep physically fit. Early on his career he qualified as a Fire Service Physical Training Instructor and did this for 25 years until he retired.

Learning about the power of nutritious food in transforming his own health, he studied nutrition for 6 years and qualified as a naturopathic nutritionist. His methods are based on the importance of making changes that are easy to implement, sustainable over the longer term and that fit into busy lives without denying people the pleasure of their favourite foods.

In 2004 he built on his experience supporting Fire Fighters with their fitness and qualified as a Coach and Instructor in a completely new and revolutionary exercise program developed for athletes which could be adapted and used by anyone. He learned from mentors who changed what he thought was possible with respect to health and fitness at middle age and beyond.

Introduction

Hello and welcome to **Keep Your Health and Fitness for Life**

This book aims to provide you with the means of maintaining a level of health and fitness for the rest of your life that many would consider unattainable.

It looks at how pre-conceived ideas and commonly held perceptions about ageing and health can unwittingly convince us to expect significantly declining health and physical fitness as we get older.

Whilst age will have some impact on our health and fitness, we can greatly increase our chances of remaining physically active and healthy to the end of our lives, and avoid the illness, pain and infirmity often seen as inevitable. It is therefore my aim to provide you with some fresh perspectives that will take your fitness and well-being to a whole new level.

Combining the latest research with fundamental principles about how the body keeps healthy, I wanted to make this an accessible and pragmatic guide whether the concepts covered are building on what you already know about ageing, nutrition and exercise or whether, if you're like many of my clients, it's a complete paradigm shift.

To make it as practical as possible, throughout the book there are simple tips and suggestions to implement changes easily to get you started and move you forward. That said, this book is not a "quick fix". Instead it's about making incremental changes and investing in your health over the long term so that you benefit throughout your life.

At the same time, I'm sure you will be amazed at how quickly your body responds and your health improves. I've certainly found that as people start to experience the positive changes to their wellbeing, these provide extra momentum for creating more new habits. Of course, it's completely up to you as to how much you want to integrate into your lifestyle.

This book is not about preaching from some self-righteous vantage point! It's about providing you with a practical tool kit, so you can make informed choices about what feels right for you, whether you're looking to work on your fitness, eat more healthily or improve the way your body digests and absorbs the foods you eat. I'm fully aware of the challenges of making changes and the demands of 21st century living so the last two chapters focus on stress and keeping motivated.

My Five Health & Fitness Principles

Over the years I noticed that there were some key themes that stood out as being vital for people to achieve their health and fitness goals and maintain long term success. From these themes I developed five principles:

Principle 1: Don't underestimate what your body is capable of

Principle 2: Synergy & balance

Principle 3: Do what you love .....consistently

Principle 4: Listen to your body – be in tune with it

Principle 5: Less is more

Whilst the principles originated from my approach to exercise I soon realised that they applied to all areas of health and fitness whether it was the food we eat, how we support our digestive system to how we minimise stress.

These principles underlie the philosophy of this book and I hope will help you to achieve your goals, whether it's making some minor improvements or transforming your health and fitness.

Principle 1: Don't underestimate what your body is capable of

As you will see in chapter one, the human body is capable of incredible things. Unfortunately, social conditioning inhibits many people who have consciously or sub-consciously been influenced by the broadly negative view on ageing in society in general. It perpetuates the erroneous belief that maintaining great health and fitness for life is impossible after a certain age. This book aims to give you the means to prove this way of thinking is outdated.

Principle 2: Synergy & Balance

A concept that applies to each chapter and that underpins the whole philosophy of this book is synergy. I was first introduced to the importance of synergy by Doctor Lawrence Plaskett, when training to be a nutritionist. It is defined in the dictionary as *"increased effectiveness or achievement produced by combined action or cooperation".*

Combinations are always better than singular actions and what never ceases to amaze me is the incredible results you can achieve through making many small and seemingly insignificant changes. Making big changes like becoming vegan overnight when you love a bacon sandwich and your favourite meal is steak is going to be pretty challenging. Conversely, making small changes like drinking one extra glass of water a day, getting to bed ½ hour earlier each night and having one meat free day a week is likely to be far more manageable and the benefits you reap will probably encourage you to make some additional tweaks. The synergistic power of using a wide range of resources and making small changes gradually cannot be underestimated.

We all know how important it is to have the right balance in our lives. Work/life balance, for example, can be challenging to achieve and yet when we get it right our energy and sense of fulfilment can really soar.

From a nutrition perspective we soon feel the effects of eating unhealthy food too frequently, or perhaps a stressful time in our lives has led to relying more on alcohol to help us switch off. This book is not about denying the simple pleasures of a glass of wine or a favourite bar of chocolate, it's about balancing the food we eat in favour of healthy options so our bodies are strong enough to deal with the odd indulgence.

In fitness it's easy to get into the habit of focusing on one form of exercise. I've known people who get such a high from running they don't bother with other forms of exercise such as flexibility and resistance, which can lead their bodies to get out of balance. Integrating some stretching routines and weight training can help them to maximise the effectiveness of their cardiovascular fitness.

As you work through the chapters it may be useful to collate tips and suggestions that you could easily implement. Keep a journal of when you started and note down any changes you notice to your sense of well-being and vitality.

Principle 3: Do what you love .....consistently

The only way to ensure continuing success and establish great habits is to find out what really suits you. This runs through every chapter, from finding ways to exercise you enjoy, selecting recipes you love to cook and eat to choosing fun techniques for reducing stress. As you read through, it may be useful to jot ideas that resonate with you.

Principle 4: Listen to your body – be in tune with it

It is so important that we learn to read the signs and symptoms that our bodies continually give us. We often ignore the odd twinge and wait until we are in excruciating pain before we take action. The ability to interpret the subtle nuances in the way our body reacts to different stimuli tends to be forgotten in our revved up, fast paced society. This is a skill that is vital to master if we want to achieve our very best health and well-being for the rest of our lives. I hope the chapters ahead will give you some extra 'antennae' to help you to be in tune with your body's needs.

Principle 5: Less is more

Achieving outstanding health and fitness for life does not require a huge amount of time. Once the fundamentals are in place, you will see that it is the quality rather than the quantity that wins every time.

~~~~~~~~~~~~~~~~~~~~~~~~

So, before we get started, I want to wish you every success in continuing to enhance your wellbeing and in doing so, inspire your family and friends to do the same!
~~~~~~~~~~~~~~~~~~~~~~~~

Chapter 1

Challenging the Concept of Ageing

OUR PERCEPTION OF AGEING

It is fascinating how ageing is viewed by different cultures and societies around the world, and the corresponding impact this social conditioning can have on health.

For the vast majority of people in western society, getting old is viewed as an inevitable decline in mental and physical ability. Many of us start to get a taste of what's to come in middle age when we feel a bit stiff getting out of bed in the morning and get those painful twinges in joints and muscles. This can engender a fear of ageing and a passive acceptance of the inevitable.

We are surrounded by information that promotes this negative perspective on getting old. Studies have shown that the language we use for youth is far more positive that the words we use to describe older people. The media is full of stories of the ageing population and how society will not be able to cope with so many old people in hospitals and nursing homes. Such stories compound the message that being old means being infirm.

Adverts on television and in magazines are full of equipment to help us get out of our chair, get upstairs and help us get in the bath. My mother-in-law was told recently by a friend that she should start thinking about getting a stair lift now that she was in her seventies – not because she was injured but because of the number of birthdays she had had!!!

So many people I know have been told by their doctor that their symptoms are to be expected at their age. Even friends and family inadvertently disempower us with socially conditioned remarks such as:

"You can expect to put on a bit of weight as you get older".

"My running days are over"

"I'm not as young as I used to be"

"What do you expect at your age?"

It's no wonder that people feel so down at the thought of getting older!

WHY I'M PASSIONATE ABOUT HELPING PEOPLE TO OPTIMISE THEIR VITALITY AS THEY AGE.

As far back as I can remember, my father suffered from health problems.

Dad had suffered from ulcerated ankles since he got an infection from an insect bite whilst in the Royal Navy many years before. The ulcers never seemed to heal and as a result of this his long-term health suffered as he was not able to exercise properly. Having a sedentary office job and lifestyle also didn't help, leading to an underactive thyroid and a life-threatening operation to graft arteries to improve the circulation to his legs, which nearly killed him and left him in hospital for months following an infection.

Dad was also very traditional. He placed the responsibility of his health solely with doctors, following their advice to the letter. He dutifully took whatever medication was prescribed even though he never experienced any improvement in his health. Over time Dad became convinced that as the doctors could not make him better then all his problems were simply because he was getting older. As a result of this accepting attitude he aged prematurely and spent the rest of his life in increasing pain.

The experience of witnessing my father's problems dominated my thinking about health and fitness as I went through my teens and into adult life. I always made sure that I exercised regularly and took part in athletics and rugby at school. After leaving school my desire to stay healthy never diminished as Dad's continuing health issues proved to be a powerful motivator.

When I was 24 I joined the Fire Service and this gave me a career that enabled me to maintain my fitness. After a few years I became a fitness instructor in the service and gained further external qualifications in my spare time.

However, it was not until I reached the age of 35 that I discovered one of the most vital factors in helping to maintain health and fitness as we age. I decided to study Nutritional Medicine, and the next six years proved to be nothing short of a revelation to me.

It opened my eyes to the amazing potential of the human body to stay healthy, active and disease free if it was nurtured in the correct way. This was the first time I really became aware of the many different factors that prevent us from retaining optimum health and fitness as we age.

Once I'd qualified as a Nutritionist, after 6 years of intensive study and practice I was so keen to apply my knowledge to help Dad. Despite his growing list of ailments and adverse reactions to the cocktail of pharmaceutical drugs he was taking by then, he was reluctant to adjust his diet or take nutritional supplements in case they interfered with his prescriptions.

Dad had an unwavering belief that there was only one way to deal with illness and that his continually deteriorating health was an inevitable part of getting old. I wish at this point I could say that I was able to change Dad's view. Unfortunately, I could not and he eventually died at the age of 77 after many months of pain and suffering in hospitals and hospices.

This obviously had a huge impact on me and is why I'm so passionate about helping people to be aware of the different resources available to them to optimise their health. Understanding the power of our mind on our health is paramount.

CHRONOLOGICAL AGE, BIOLOGICAL AGE AND PSYCHOLOGICAL AGE

Our physical health is affected on a daily basis by how we feel as the mind and body are intrinsically linked. If we become stressed and feel down, tests have shown that all our systems are negatively impacted. The digestion and immunity are prime examples and are particularly susceptible. If these two systems are underperforming for prolonged periods it can accelerate the ageing process and make us more prone to illness and disease.

On the other hand, if our thoughts are happy or positive, for the majority of the time (nobody is perfect) then the function of our immune system and digestion is greatly improved.

Tests have consistently shown that when we laugh or watch a happy film the positive physical effects on our body are truly profound.

You can literally think yourself old if you have a pessimistic, negative view of the ageing process. But this can also be reversed and was demonstrated by an amazing ground-breaking experiment that was carried out in America by Professor Ellen Langer of Harvard University in 1979.

Professor Langer wanted to research whether changing old people's mind-set could really have direct positive physical effects on their well-being. To do this, she took a group of men in their late 70's and 80's and told them that they would be taking part in a week of reminiscence. They were not told that they would be taking part in an experiment on ageing.

She then split them into two groups and whilst one group did indeed spend the week reminiscing about 1959 the other group was put in a carefully constructed time warp environment for one week. They were surrounded with sights, sounds and all the sensations that they would have experienced when they were younger. They were not helped with any of their day to day tasks and had to manage as they had back in 1959. There were no aids or gadgets designed to help older people. They discussed news of the time in the present tense, watched films and listened to the music of that year.

Professor Langer took physiological tests before and after the experiment and found the improvements after completion of the experiment to be significant.

There was a measurable improvement in their blood pressure, speed of movement, gait, dexterity, arthritis, cognitive abilities and memory. Amazingly, their eyesight and hearing had also got better in the one week of the experiment. Both groups showed improvement but the group that was in the 1950's environment showed the greatest improvement.

Professor Langer believes that because the men were encouraged to be more independent and no longer thought of themselves as old, their bodies began to respond to their new younger mind-set and started to become physiologically younger.

"My own view of ageing is that one can, not the rare person but the average person, live a very full life, without infirmity, without loss of memory that is debilitating, without many of the things we fear." Professor Ellen Langer

A repeat of Langer's study was undertaken for a BBC program in the UK in 2010 which took a group of ageing celebrities in their seventies and eighties and this time put them back into an environment from the 1970's. The same protocols were used and the results were the same; measurable improvements in the physiological factors that are widely supposed to inevitably decline with age.

INSPIRATIONAL ROLE MODELS WHO CHALLENGE THE WESTERN VIEW ON AGEING

If you search the internet there are numerous examples of older people who are fabulous role models. I have selected seven who truly inspire me.

When you read about these people, think about how you feel. Many would look at these examples and think that these people are a bit freakish and just exceptionally lucky to enjoy such longevity and health. They are currently the exception to the rule, but they shouldn't be!

These people are prime examples of what can be achieved with the right state of mind. Yes, there are many other factors that need to be in place for this degree of health and vigour to be achieved, which I will talk about in the rest of this book. However, the main attribute that they all have in common is a powerful underlying belief that they can continue to be healthy and active, and proof that you can be chronologically old yet psychologically and biologically young!

Yuichiro Miura

Miura has a history of scaling Everest, climbing the peak in his 70th and 75th years before reaching the summit on 23 May 2013 at the age of 80 years 223 days, the third time he has held the record. He is also an extreme skier and has skied down the tallest peak on all seven continents including Everest.

He is quoted on his expedition's website *"It is to challenge my own ultimate limit. It is to honour the great Mother Nature."* He said a successful climb would raise the bar for what is possible. *"And if the limit of age 80 is at the summit of Mount Everest, the highest place on earth, one can never be happier."*

Tao Porchon-Lynch

Based in New York Tao is currently recognised as the world's oldest practicing Yoga teacher at 99. On her website, the strapline of the homepage reads THERE IS NOTHING YOU CANNOT DO. And to view the pictures and videos of this incredible woman doing Yoga you believe her. She can still achieve even the most difficult of Yoga postures that a lot of people a quarter of her age would not be able to do.

Tao has practiced Yoga for over 70 years which complements one of her other great passions in life, ballroom dancing, for which has won world class awards.

Don Pellman

Don took up athletics late in life when his son told him about athletics events for seniors. He holds many American track and field records for athletes who are over 90. Amongst these are long jump, high jump, discus, 100 metres, javelin and triple jump, all when 96 years old. He also holds a number of world records. He says he uses common sense with his health, never having smoked. He rarely drinks alcohol and thinks that most people don't exercise enough. Don would always take the stairs rather than the lift and does some sort of exercise every day. *"You need to stay active."* One of the best habits Don says is to push yourself away from the table when you have eaten sufficient and not to over eat.

George "Banana" Blair

George Blair was an extreme water skier who learnt to ski barefoot at the age of 46. He then continued to ski barefoot and snowboard up until he was 92! One of his party pieces whilst skiing barefoot was to hold the tow rope in his mouth. His nick name was given to him by friends because he always seemed to have a peeled banana in his hand ready to eat.

Faukja Singh

Now aged 107 Faukja is the world's oldest distance runner and has just retired from running but still distance walks every day and for charity at 106 years old! He took up distance running in his eighties and holds numerous world records including the marathon and other shorter distance events for the over hundred category. Many of these over 100 categories did not exist as no one had attempted them before Faukja. He attributes his good health and longevity to a vegetarian diet, avoidance of smoking, alcohol and drinking plenty of water, much of it with ginger. He also takes time to walk every day.

Sam Heggessy

Sam, who has just turned 100 is Britain' oldest gym member and has been a member of his local gym for 20 years where he does Pilates, Yoga and Tai Chi once a week with his wife Doris who is 83. Sam has always exercised and swam for one hour three times a week when he worked. Sam and his wife are also keen walkers. He eats sensibly but has no special diet; however, he avoids red meat and alcohol (except for half a glass of champagne once a week).

Johanna Quaas

This amazing lady born in 1925 is in the Guinness Book of Records as officially the world's oldest competing gymnast at 93! She is quoted as saying that she has always been sporty and coached gymnastics when younger. When she was 57 she took up gymnastics again and competed in competitions.

~~~~~~~~~~~~~~~~~~~~~~~~~

These people are truly inspirational and demonstrate what is possible. Wouldn't it be great if they were the rule rather than the exception? Whilst you may not want to run a marathon when you are 100 or bare foot water ski at 92 I do hope that these people inspire you to make the changes in your life that will lay the foundations for your health in the years to come.

My aim in the following chapters is to provide you with a comprehensive tool kit to help you optimise your health, whether you want to make transformational changes or small enhancements, and in the process, remain psychologically and biologically younger than your chronological age!
~~~~~~~~~~~~~~~~~~~~~~~~~

Chapter 2

10 Ways to Immediately Improve Your Health

10 Ways to Immediately Improve Your Health

We live in a society where speed seems to be paramount, we want everything fast and our lives are often dominated by this. When we set ourselves health and fitness goals it is only natural that we want to see improvements as soon as possible. However, in health and wellbeing, we need to be patient and consistent to get meaningful and lasting results.

Thankfully, there are exceptions to this rule; there are certain things that you can initiate immediately that will prove to be a great investment in your long-term health and you will notice the results quickly. So, in this chapter we will look at 10 key areas that will give you a great start on your road to optimum long-term health and fitness:

1. Get enough quality sleep
2. Drink enough quality water
3. Skin brush
4. Practise deep breathing
5. Avoid pollution
6. Meditate
7. Have a passion
8. Reduce the amount of time you spend sitting down
9. Oil pull
10. Test homocysteine levels

You can choose to incorporate any of these into your daily routine and each will be of benefit. To get the greatest effect, I would recommend that you try to use all of them so that you will benefit from their combined synergistic effects.

1. GET ENOUGH QUALITY SLEEP

Sleep is one of the cornerstones of good health. We all recognise that we cannot get by without it but it's easy to underestimate how absolutely vital it is for long term health. It's not just about the number of hours we spend asleep it's also about the quality of the sleep we get. Psychological factors such as stress, anxiety, worry or simply having too much on our minds when we go to bed are common causes these days of poor sleep. The tips that follow later in this section will help you to address factors that can prevent us from having a refreshing and revitalising night's sleep. First of all, let's look at the benefits of a good night's sleep as well as how our body ideally likes to fall asleep and how it prefers to wake up.

Our bodies are light sensitive. As light fades the pineal gland in the brain produces a hormone called melatonin. Hormones, as you may know, are chemical messengers that are manufactured by your body and their role is to give instructions to your cells to carry out certain functions.

Melatonin's job is to communicate with your cells and prepare it for sleep. It has a relaxing, calming and sedative property which helps you to get to sleep and promotes restorative sleep.

Once asleep, your body diverts energy that is used during the day for physical movement, mental processes, digestion and other metabolic activities to carry out essential maintenance and repair of systems and organs. It releases hormones that:

- ☺ promote tissue growth and repair, which accelerates when you're asleep
- ☺ help boost the immune system
- ☺ are in involved in restoring energy levels
- ☺ play a role in balancing appetite.

These are processes that your body does not have the opportunity to do properly when you are awake, so it is vital that adequate time is provided for it to do this. Anybody who has had a series of late nights or perhaps stayed up all night, will know how jaded and below par you can feel. It's easy to rely on stimulants such as caffeine and/or sugar to get us through the day. All our faculties suffer; examples of symptoms of sleep deprivation (either lack of or poor-quality sleep) include:

- ☹ less patience
- ☹ poor concentration
- ☹ depression

☹ frequent colds and infections

☹ weight gain

☹ loss of sex drive

☹ lack of co-ordination

In order to wake you from sleep, your body begins to produce and increase levels of other hormones such as cortisol which start to rouse you from your slumber. These hormones are as a consequence of rising light levels which pass through the eyelid and stimulate a nerve pathway from the retina into a part of the brain called the hypothalamus.

The human body has evolved over hundreds of thousands of years to have these exquisitely controlled chemical reactions to light and darkness. If we allow ourselves to follow these natural evolutionary rules, then our sleep would be much improved. But much of the time we don't; we have artificial lights which allow us to stay up all night if we wish. This disrupts the natural sleep cycle and commonly results in poor sleep.

Unless we address this imbalance, the short and long-term consequences for health can be serious. Sleep deprivation is so effective at messing up our health and making us feel awful that it is frequently used as a very efficient method of interrogation!

In fact, sleep deprivation is increasingly being recognised as one of the main factors in the development, especially in later life of chronic conditions. This is thought to be caused by the disruption of the delicate hormonal balance of the natural sleep cycle, especially over long periods of time. Long term sleep deprivation or insomnia can not only make our lives miserable but can prematurely age us and in the worst cases make them considerably shorter.

I had first-hand experience of shift work in my previous career in the Fire Service that required me to do night duties and I did these for 30 years! I certainly saw so many of my colleagues pay the price with long-term health consequences who did not realise how necessary it was to re-balance their sleep deficit.

Whilst it's not always easy as life inevitably gets in the way, I endeavoured to be very careful to ensure that I took steps to offset the negative effects of disturbed sleep patterns through nutritional support and getting plenty of rest in between and after night shifts.

Let's now look at ways to ensure that your sleep is consistently of the best quality. We will look firstly at the best ways to get to sleep easily, then talk about how to ensure that you stay asleep and finally the best way to wake yourself up.

Getting to sleep

Do you ever envy those people who seem to be able to sleep anywhere? They just seem to decide that they are going to have a nap and they are off, asleep, within a few seconds! I have never been able to do this and so, over the years I have developed ways to ensure that I can consistently get quality sleep when I go to bed.

To enable you to easily drift off into peaceful sleep and wake up feeling refreshed and full of energy the following tips may be useful to you.

Do:

- ✓ Try to establish a routine leading up to bedtime which will help you prepare for getting a good night's sleep. You can try incorporating some of the suggestions in this section into your routine.
- ✓ Having a relaxing bath or shower before you go to bed is a great way to relax and soothe away aches, pains and stresses of the day and prepares you for sleep. Placing one or two drops of lavender or camomile oil in your bath or on your pillow can also help you sleep as they have sedative properties.
- ✓ General stretching or practising yoga just before bed are fabulous for relaxing your body and you will find that combined with the deep breathing used in yoga, you will get into bed beautifully calm and relaxed. Yoga can be done after bathing, which is great way to warm your muscles and prepare your body for stretching.
- ✓ Do some physical exercise during the day or the early evening as this can help to promote sleep. A fitness class or a brisk walk, for example, can help to get rid of the stressors of the day and the energy it uses can help to stimulate sleep once it's time for bed. However, if it's too late in the day and the exercise is too vigorous it can fire you up and is unlikely to promote rest so low impact exercise early evening at the latest is likely to be the most beneficial.

- ✓ Try to make sure that you get to bed at roughly the same time as often as you can. This will help the body to establish a more effective sleep cycle. Ayurvedic medicine has been practised in India for over 3,000 years. It is a natural healing system and is the oldest medicinal system in the world. According to Ayurvedic medicine, the best times to sleep are between 10pm and 6am.

  During this time the sleep hormone melatonin is at its highest and provides you with the greatest health benefits, not only in terms of restorative sleep which provides the right environment for repair and growth, detoxification and recharging of systems such as the adrenals, but also as a supreme antioxidant and immune booster.

- ✓ Melatonin occurs naturally in certain foods so eating these foods in the early evening (preferably no closer than 3 hours before bedtime) can help increase the blood levels of this hormone and help you get to sleep.

  The tart cherry variety known as Montmorency has been found to have the greatest amounts of melatonin. Porridge also contains melatonin and can also help with getting to sleep.

- ✓ Herbal teas can also be useful sleep aids. For example, Valerian and Passionflower are calming teas that soothe stress and are an excellent aid to sleep. Camomile tea contains glycine, which relaxes nerves and can act as a mild sedative and in the process, can help to reduce stress and anxiety.

- ✓ Play a subliminal CD which is designed to induce sleep.

- ✓ Soft background music can help you relax, a little classical music can help, alternatively, there are many CDs with sounds from nature that can be very calming and help to induce sleep including rainfall, waterfalls and my personal favourite a thunderstorm! (It sounds a bit strange but helps me to sleep every time)

- ✓ At least half an hour before going to bed soften the lighting in your home. Bedside lamps that can be dimmed help the body to release the natural sleep inducing hormones.

- ✓ Reading in bed; make it something that you really enjoy and nothing that requires too much brain power. You may think that this would stimulate rather than prepare you for sleep but I have found that it puts me in a relaxed frame of mind and before long I find myself doing an impression of a nodding dog and know that a good night's sleep is on the cards.

Besides, I think that reading in bed is one of life's great little luxuries! When our bodies feel nurtured we're more likely to feel tranquil and relaxed. Just try to make sure you read something pleasurable, books on conspiracies or contentious newspaper articles are probably not a good idea!

- ✓ Wearing socks. Poor circulation shows up in the feet first and wearing socks can help to reduce night time waking. Plus, it's a great look!
- ✓ If you live in an area where there is a lot of artificial light you may want to invest in heavy curtains or blinds that block out external light that can not only prevent you from getting to sleep but wake you up during the night. You want to ensure that your bedroom is completely dark as even the smallest bit of light can disrupt your sleep hormones. Sometimes this may be difficult if you live in an urban area or your partner goes to bed at different times to you. In this case, you may want to think about trying an eye mask.
- ✓ Also, if you get up to go to the toilet in the night, try to avoid putting on any lights at all as any form of artificial light will disrupt your body clock and fool your body into thinking that it's time to get up.
- ✓ Eating a high protein snack a couple of hours before going to bed can help to boost levels of the amino acid L-tryptophan which is used in the production of sleep hormones. Eating a small piece of fruit will help get the L-tryptophan into the brain where it is needed to make these hormones.

<u>Try to give up, avoid or reduce</u>

- × One of the most obvious inhibitors of sleep is the stimulant caffeine, so this needs to be avoided too close to bedtime. That cup of coffee after a meal out is often regretted when we are still awake in the early hours! Coffee, tea, energy drinks and anything else containing caffeine should not be consumed at least 5 hours before you go to bed. Caffeine can also be found in many food products, especially processed confectionary and in some medications so it's best to read the labels.
- × Try to avoid getting involved in work that over stimulates your brain before

you get to bed. A classic example of this would be bringing work home and working on the computer late into the evening. This will mean that your mind will still be buzzing when you get to bed and it can become a vicious circle as the more you try to get to sleep the more frustrated you are likely to become.

- There is some evidence from studies that exposure to electromagnetic fields (EMFs) may affect the quality and length of your sleep. EMFs are produced by any electrical appliance, especially televisions and computer screens. It is therefore not a great idea to have a television in the bedroom or electrical appliances near your bed such as mobiles, clock radios etc. Although it is an indulgence to watch TV in bed and you may fall asleep watching it, it may well affect the quality of your sleep and if you are waking up feeling un-refreshed, this could well be a factor. Also, try to avoid watching TV in general just before you go to bed as this can be too stimulating and has been shown to disrupt the function of your pineal gland.
- Try to avoid drinking alcohol within a couple of hours of bedtime if you can. It's easy to believe that it promotes sleep as it can make us feel sleepy. Whilst it may help us fall asleep, we are more likely to wake up through the night and therefore the length and quality of our sleep will be affected. This is because alcohol has a number of sleep-impairing effects which include the release of adrenaline. It also impairs the manufacture of the hormone serotonin which makes melatonin, which, as you will recall, helps prepare your body for sleep.
- Try to avoid eating for at least 3 hours before bedtime, especially large meals. Eating too late will increase your metabolism and make it more difficult to get a good night's sleep. It prevents your body carrying out effective maintenance and repair work as energy is diverted to digestion. At the same time your digestion suffers as it cannot be as efficient and complete as it would be when you're awake as your body is trying to rest!
- Avoid using over-the-counter sleeping pills. Whilst they may be of help in the short term they can cause significant problems with long term use as they can become addictive with numerous side effects that interfere with normal sleep patterns. This can lead to a cycle of taking the drug to induce sleep that is itself disrupting the normal sleep cycle. This results in waking up tired and commonly resorting to caffeine to kick start the day which then further worsens the insomnia.

- Try also to avoid all non-prescription drugs if possible because they can have side effects that are counterproductive to health; a common one is disturbed sleep patterns.
- Don't have your bedroom too warm. This can disrupt sleep and studies have shown that it is best to have a cooler environment (less than 70 degrees). I prefer not to have any heating in the bedroom at night and have a small window open which I find helps me to sleep very well. It can be a bit cold when you get out of your warm bed in the winter, but it certainly wakes you up!
- Avoid any sugary snacks or drinks as well as grains before going to bed as these can upset your blood sugar levels and lead to a disturbed and poor night's sleep.
- Try to avoid eating foods that you may be sensitive to. (e.g. grains, dairy, sugar). These can cause symptoms such as nasal congestion and digestive discomfort (bloating, cramping) that can disturb sleep.

During Sleep

Many people find that although they can get to sleep relatively easily, they suffer from interrupted sleep through the night. It is important to try to ensure that this does not happen as it disrupts the hormonal sleep cycle and prevents you going through the different stages of sleep that are required to maintain optimal health.

Here are some tips to help ensure this does not happen:

- ✓ Ensure that your mattress is good quality; buy the best that you can afford as this is an investment in your future health and wellbeing. This investment will not only ensure better quality sleep with fewer disturbances but will also provide proper support for your back. Poor quality or worn mattresses increase the likelihood of developing postural problems.

  Mattresses can last for up to 10 years and should be turned every 3 or 4 months. Signs that your mattress needs replacing are waking up with stiffness, numbness, aches and pains, having a better night's sleep in other beds (such as a hotel), visible signs of wear, feeling the springs when laying on it, feeling tired after a full night's sleep and of course if the mattress is more than 10 years old.

✓ You also need to ensure that your pillow provides proper support for neck (cervical spine) while you sleep so that you avoid sleep disturbance and neck pain.

Waking Up

It may sound a bit strange to be talking about how to wake up, but there is a right and a wrong way!

In a perfect world, your body would go to sleep when levels of natural light fades and wake up when light stimulates the release of hormones such as serotonin. If we were to attune ourselves to light levels as nature intended, we would get better quality sleep and a greater amount of it.

However, modern society does not make this practical as we simply cannot go to bed at 5pm in midwinter and get up when it gets light! So, we have artificial light that allows us to stay up as long as we want and alarm clocks to wake us up when we choose.

Of course, waking up suddenly, when it is still dark, shocking the body out of its natural sleep cycle is why we feel so tired, groggy, unrefreshed and take a long time to wake up and feel alert, commonly with the help of caffeine.

How then, can you wake up more naturally, when it is still dark outside? The answer is to get a light alarm, also known as a natural or sunrise alarm clock. When my wife bought ours over 20 years ago there were only a few specialist companies that made them. Now they are widely available.

Unlike the sudden shock of an audible alarm, a light alarm is designed to mimic the rising levels of light in the morning. For example, if I want to be awake by 6 a.m. I set the alarm for this time and half an hour before, a dim white light starts to come on and slowly gets brighter in the next 30 minutes. By waking you up gradually in the same way as normal sunlight would, your hormones change from sleep state to waking state as they should and you feel refreshed when you awaken rather than frazzled!

You may be thinking do these really work? Can this white light really wake you up in the same way as daylight? Well, yes it can; I was sceptical at first but would not be without it now. I have used one for over twenty years and would never go back to an old fashioned audible alarm. I really recommend trying one.

Napping

Some of the healthiest populations in the world are renowned for taking a nap during the day. Mediterranean countries are famous for taking siestas mid-afternoon and it is widely recognised to promote health benefits:

- ☺ In 2007 an extensive study was carried out over six years on 23,681 people in Greece. None of the study group suffered from coronary heart disease, stroke or any other serious disease. Those who napped for an average of 30 minutes a day at least three times a week were found to have a 37% lower chance of dying from a heart related disease.
- ☺ A power nap may help you to relax, decrease fatigue, increase your alertness, improve your mood, improve performance both mentally and physically (including your reaction time), improve memory and may also help lower blood pressure.

What's the best way to take a power nap?

- ✓ Keep naps short, between 10 and 30 minutes, any longer can make you feel groggy when you wake up.
- ✓ The best time is mid-afternoon around 2 or 3 p.m. You can nap any time, to fit around your work or other commitments but of course try to avoid napping too close to bed time to avoid interfering with your natural sleep cycle.
- ✓ Create a quiet and restful environment away from interruptions.

2. DRINK ENOUGH QUALITY WATER

Water is incorporated into every part of your body. You've probably familiar with the statistic that you're approximately two thirds water. Your blood is 82% water, your brain is 85%, and even your bones are 25% water, you simply cannot function optimally without it.

In extreme circumstances, you can go weeks without food but if you are deprived of water for 3 to 4 days you would be in serious trouble and a week without water would almost certainly kill you.

Water is without question, **THE** most important nutrient that you put into your body. It is the major component of the trillions of cells that make up the human body and it is those cells that make up everything from your muscles, connective tissue, skin and brain to your organs; they effectively make you!

Consequently, the quality of every tissue and organ in your body and their resistance to injury and disease, and ultimately your longevity are absolutely dependant on the purity and the amount of water that you consume, whether it's from the foods you eat or the water you drink.

What are the health consequences of dehydration?

Nothing in your body can function properly without adequate water.

☹ One of the first things to suffer is digestion because without proper hydration the digestive system cannot produce the amount of digestive juices required for breaking down food, absorbing the nutrients from it and expelling the toxins and waste products. So, if you're lacking water you're also lacking nutrients.

☹ Without sufficient water, the kidneys cannot cleanse the body of toxins or provide the right water, sodium and potassium balance for the body.

☹ The immune function is impaired.

☹ If you remain dehydrated over months or even years, as many people do without realising it, you are laying the foundation for illness and sub optimal health in the future. This can have a dramatic effect on, not only your longevity, but also the quality of your life.

☹ Long term health problems linked to chronic water depletion include:

gallstones, kidney stones, some cancers, ulcerative colitis (chronic inflammation of the large intestine), allergies, asthma, high blood pressure, depression and a decline in mental ability.

Are you de-hydrated?

Whilst most of us think we drink enough water, it's easy to be dehydrated without knowing it. As you probably know by the time you feel thirsty, you are already suffering from a moderate degree of dehydration. There are many signs that your body will give you that it is crying out for water yet many of us don't necessarily associate these signs with lack of water.

Signs and symptoms of dehydration

Some of these are obvious and some less so. If you have multiple signs and symptoms, I'd really recommend reviewing how many of your drinks each day include pure water.

Of course, some of the symptoms here are not solely caused by lack of water. However, it never ceases to amaze me how many symptoms can disappear once people start to drink more water.

☹ Dry skin and cracked lips

☹ Aching or painful joints

☹ Frequent headaches or migraines

☹ Decreased mental performance / ability to concentrate

☹ Constipation

☹ Lack of energy / fatigue

☹ Dark coloured/ strong smelling urine

☹ Reduced physical performance

☹ Dry membrane surfaces (mouth, eyes, skin)

☹ Dizziness

☹ Hunger

☹ Increased body temperature (inability to sweat)

☹ Bad breath

☹ Muscle cramps

Hydration Check

The following questions used in conjunction with the signs and symptoms will help you to assess whether you are getting adequate hydration.

❒ Do you ever go more than a couple of hours without drinking?

❒ Do you usually only drink when you are thirsty?

❒ Do you have on average, less than one bowel movement a day on a consistent basis?

❒ Are you ever constipated for more than one day?

❒ Do you take a long time to have a bowel movement or need to strain? (When I see magazines in a toilet it is a good indication that someone is constipated and probably dehydrated. You should never be in the toilet long enough to start reading!)

❒ Do you ever feel lethargic, have low energy levels or have trouble getting up in the morning?

❒ Do you add salt to your cooking or eat salty foods most days?

❒ Do you have more than two alcoholic drinks or units of alcohol a day?

❒ Do you eat fewer than five servings of fresh fruit and vegetables a day?

❒ Do you on average drink less than two glasses of water per day?

❒ Do you have fewer than five of any drink a day, excluding alcohol?

If you are experiencing any of the signs or symptoms of dehydration and answered yes to more than four of the above questions, then there is a good chance that you are suffering from dehydration.

Follow the recommendations below to ensure that you give your body all the water that it needs to function effectively.

How to stay hydrated

There are varying guidelines for how much water we need to drink every day. There are of course many factors which affect the amount required such as, how active you are, the temperature of your climate and your physical size. Every person is unique and requirements will differ from one person to the next. As with everything in health it's about balance – over-hydration is equally as life threatening though this tends to be far rarer.

As a ball park figure, men should drink between 1 and 3 litres per day and women between 1 and 2 litres. However, these figures are estimates and it is best to monitor yourself and be aware of the signs and symptoms that indicate you may need more water. Even if you have none of the typical signs and symptoms of water depletion, it may still be worth viewing the tips below to ensure you provide your body with the vital water quality and quantity it needs to reach optimal health.

The following tips will help ensure that you never get dehydrated:

- ✓ Drink a glass of water when you first get up in the morning, preferably warm as this is a wonderful way to flush out the kidneys.
- ✓ Try to make sure that you eat five portions of fruit and vegetables per day as these will contribute significantly to your daily water needs.
- ✓ Be aware that the more processed, sugary, salty and dry food you eat (e.g. crisps, grains, and confectionary) the more water your body will need.
- ✓ Try to get into the habit of having water with you throughout the day and sipping it at regular intervals. You will be surprised at how much you get through.
- ✓ When you are out and about, carry a bottle of mineral or filtered water with you.
- ✓ On a normal day drink about 2 litres spread evenly throughout the day.
- ✓ If you really don't like drinking plain water you can flavour it. Ginger or lemon are good in warm or hot water and have additional health benefits.
- ✓ If you are not used to drinking water you can replace some of your usual drinks with water or have a glass of water in conjunction with your usual beverage.

✓ Sip a glass of water with each meal, although avoid drinking a whole glass in one go as this tends to dilute the digestive juices.

✓ Try some herbal or fruit teas. When they first came out they had a reputation for being a bit bland and not tasting that good but they have really improved over recent years.

✓ Drink before during and after exercise; but sip and avoid drinking large amounts in one go.

✓ Always check your urine; you should be producing copious amounts of pale odourless urine throughout the day. In the summer months, urine may tend to be more yellow and smell stronger as we lose water via sweating so it's a good sign we need to drink more.

✓ When eating out, sip water with your meal and make sure you balance alcohol intake with water – you will definitely thank yourself the next day, particularly if you've really been celebrating.

Should I drink tap water?

The water in the UK is some of the safest in the world but it is not completely pure. The Drinking Water Inspectorate (DKI) is the body that has the task of monitoring the UK's water and keeping contaminants below certain levels which are set for consumer safety.

Amongst the substances monitored are trihalomethanes (environmental pollutants, many of which are considered carcinogenic), nitrates, lead and aluminium. While these are not considered a hazard as long as their amount in drinking water is kept within DKI guidelines, these amounts have occasionally been exceeded in the UK. Even if they are not exceeded, the above substances interfere with your body's ability to assimilate the essential nutrients it requires.

They are also more environmental pollutants that your body has to deal with and excrete, so it is better to drink water that has been additionally filtered to ensure your body gets the purity of water it deserves.

However, there will be times when it is not practical to source filtered water so in these circumstances it is better to drink tap water than to be dehydrated. I want to state at this point, that I am not saying that tap water is dangerous and should not be drunk and if that is what you choose to drink that is fine. I am simply stating that if you want to give yourself the best chance of optimal health then making sure that the water you drink is as pure as possible for as much of the time as possible is a significant step towards this goal.

Water Filters

The best and most cost-effective way of making sure that most of the water you drink and cook with is pure is to fit a water filter at home; an added benefit is that it will improve the taste of your water.

There are several different types and the best are the ones that are plumbed in. They can be installed under the sink and feed a separate tap that you can then use solely for drinking and cooking. They filter out contaminants such as chlorine, lead, herbicides, pesticides, bacteria, parasites whilst retaining essential minerals such as calcium and magnesium.

A high-quality carbon filter system is a good system to use and is relatively inexpensive to buy and install. After installation, the only thing that you need to do is to have the cartridge changed at intervals, usually every six months. The cost equates to a few pence a day - an exceptionally worthwhile investment for the long-term health benefits that the water purity will give you.

Of course, the purer the water you drink the better, particularly if you are looking to take your fitness goals to a new level and want to gain that extra edge in your fitness training. If that's the case, then reverse osmosis systems are worth researching. They can remove impurities as small as ions, however, they also filter out naturally occurring minerals so you need to make sure your diet is healthy to obtain all the minerals you need.

Bottled water

Bottled water is a huge market and the purity of the water offered is wide ranging. At a lecture on water purity from a professor from Surrey University I was fascinated to hear the results of the studies that had been carried out on different brands that were available in the UK. Some were little more than tap water passed through a basic filter to improve the flavour whilst others showed good levels of purity. The best tended to be mineral waters as these come from deep within the earth and are filtered through the underground rocks. Spring waters featured less well as they come from springs that can be affected by pollutants in the water table.

Therefore, if you drink bottled water:

- ✓ Choose mineral rather than spring due to its greater purity
- ✓ Choose glass bottles rather than plastic if possible
- ✓ If you reuse the bottle, make sure you sterilise it before refilling to reduce risk of bacteria
- ✓ Avoid carbonated water as the carbon can bind to and remove minerals from the body
- ✓ Avoid leaving plastic bottles in warm places such as in the car as toxic substances can leach from the bottle into the water

Whilst bottled water is a convenient way of keeping hydrated when you're out and about, it is a far more expensive option for everyday use. I would therefore recommend investing in a good quality fitted water filter. It's not just the purity of the water you are benefitting from, tea and coffee made from filtered water tastes better too!

3. SKIN BRUSH

Your skin is amazing and performs many roles important to your long-term health and wellbeing. It is in fact your largest organ and provides protection to the rest of your body from extremes of temperature and environmental pollutants.

It plays a major role in how we react to the outside world by providing feedback to the brain from numerous nerve endings. For example, the skin helps control body temperature through the evaporation of sweat from its surface.

It also makes vitamin D from sunlight, produces antibacterial substances that help protect you from infection as well as help your body get rid of toxins through sweating.

It is therefore a good idea to keep your skin in top condition so that we can get the full benefit of the many functions it provides.

One of the easiest ways to do this is by dry skin brushing. This can be carried out every day, takes only a few minutes and provides many health benefits that not only improve the condition and function of your skin but also your whole body.

The health benefits of dry skin brushing

☺ Stimulates your lymphatic system

The lymphatic system is probably one of the most overlooked systems in the body. Most people are quite knowledgeable about the cardiovascular system, but only hear about the lymphatic system through phrases like 'enlarged lymph nodes' and may not even be aware that those nodes are part of an incredible system.

Your lymphatic system consists of vast networks of tubes that act as a drainage system for your body. The fluid that the lymphatic system drains is called intercellular fluid or tissue fluid which surrounds your cells. All the nutrients and other components of biochemistry that are essential for your cells to function pass through this fluid from the blood.

By draining your tissues, the lymphatic system removes waste products from your cells, toxins and other debris and feeds it back into your vascular system underneath your collar bone so that it can be excreted from the body if necessary.

The system is also a vital part of your immunity. The largest organ of the lymphatic system is the spleen which lies behind the stomach and fights infection and destroys worn out red blood cells. There are also small fibrous capsules in the lymph system in different parts of the body called lymph nodes (armpits, groin, neck, heart and lungs) which trap dangerous microbes and pathogens and destroy them. When they do this, they swell up and it is these that GPs check to see if they are swelling when you visit them feeling unwell.

So, by supporting your lymphatic system you are benefiting every organ and system in your body by helping to keep tissues surrounding them detoxified. You also make your immune system more effective and improve the function of every cell in your body.

One of the ways that the lymphatic system can be kept active and efficient is through regular exercise as muscle movement encourages pumping of lymph around the body.

Another way is through massage, but the advantage of dry skin brushing over the other ways is that it can be done easily and quickly every day.

☺ Exfoliates the skin

Dry skin brushing removes dead skin cells which improves appearance/texture. It has been shown to prevent and eliminate cellulite and even helps to clear clogged pores thus helping your skin to breathe.

☺ Increases circulation

Dry skin brushing increases circulation to your skin which encourages elimination of metabolic waste.

☺ Relieves Stress

Many people find dry skin brushing very relaxing and meditative. This can reduce muscle tension, calm your mind and relieve stress and it has been compared by some, to a light whole-body massage.

☺ It's invigorating

One reason why people regularly dry skin brush is that it just feels so good! Along with glowing and better feeling skin, many people find that it invigorates them too.

How do I dry skin brush?

Firstly, you will need to buy a high quality dry brush; unfortunately, you can't use any old brush! These are widely available and can be bought from health food shops, chemists and online. You should get one that has bristles made from natural materials and they should feel reasonably stiff but not too hard. The ideal sort has a long detachable handle which allows you to reach all the areas of your back.

Incorporate brushing into your daily routine, maybe before your shower in the morning or a bath in the evening. You can brush twice a day if you wish.

When brushing always start at the extremities and brush towards the heart which is best for the circulation and the lymphatic system. Start at your feet (you can also brush the soles) and brush with long smooth strokes working up your legs and arms to cover each part of the body and finishing with the torso. Personally, I do three brush strokes to each part of the body. Apply a reasonable amount of pressure, this should feel firm but not painful (avoid scrubbing). Your skin should be pink after a session (not red or irritated).

Avoid brushing your face unless you have a special brush designed for delicate skin. Also, avoid genitals and any areas of irritations or abrasions (including varicose veins) as the bristles will be a bit rough on these areas.

To get the most from skin brushing aim for 2 to 3 minutes to begin with and work up to 5 minutes when time allows.

4. PRACTISE DEEP BREATHING

Breathing is so natural and automatic that we forget we are doing it most of the time. It is just something we do to survive, and we only really become aware of it if we are having difficulty in breathing or when we are working hard during exercise or some other physical activity.

Most of the time in modern life we do not breathe in a way that is optimum for our health; in our world, full of labour saving devices we very rarely get out of breath. We therefore spend a lot more time shallow breathing than our ancestors did; breathing with the top of our lungs and not really making use of our full lung capacity. As a result of this our tissues and organs are not as oxygenated as they could be and over time this can lead to excess acidity in the body. This can create the conditions for inflammation and disease.

Taking time to spend a few minutes throughout the day to practice deep breathing can be of great benefit to your current and long-term health and it costs you nothing, just a bit of time.

What are the health benefits of deep breathing?

- ☺ It can help relax you in a stressful situation and relieve ongoing stress by slowing the heart rate and calming the mind.
- ☺ It expels a greater amount of carbon dioxide which can cause toxic build up in the body if it is not expelled efficiently.
- ☺ It replenishes the body with oxygen.
- ☺ It massages the internal organs.
- ☺ It helps the circulation of the lymphatic system.
- ☺ It will help with your energy levels.

Deep breathing technique

If you watch babies breathe, you will see that their abdomen rises and falls because they use their diaphragm to breathe. The diaphragm is a flat sheet of muscle that separates the chest cavity from the abdominal cavity. The base of your lungs is attached to it and when you breathe deeply the diaphragm bows downwards into your abdominal cavity, stretching your lungs and drawing in more air. When you breathe out it returns to its original position, allowing the lungs to contract and expel the air.

This is why you see a baby's belly rise up because the diaphragm is pushing the organs in the abdominal cavity out of the way. Hence a common name for deep breathing is belly breathing.

To practise deep breathing:

- ✓ Find a quiet place if possible and sit comfortably in an upright position with your spine supported.
- ✓ Place one hand on your chest and the other on your abdomen and slowly take a deep breath.
- ✓ Try to feel your diaphragm moving downwards, this may take a bit of practice.
- ✓ You should feel the hand on your abdomen move outwards while the hand on your chest remains still.
- ✓ Hold the breath for at least a couple of seconds. You can hold it longer if you like, between five and ten seconds is long enough.
- ✓ Now slowly release a steady stream of air until your lungs are completely empty whilst feeling your abdomen go back to its normal position.
- ✓ Repeat this technique and try to build up to at least five minutes one or two times a day.
- ✓ Good times to practise deep breathing are first thing in the morning or before you go to bed.

5. AVOID POLLUTION

We live in a world that is awash with man-made chemicals. We use them everywhere; in fuels for our transport, home cleaning products, personal hygiene products, in agriculture, animal farming, every kind of manufacturing and in our food and drink. There are millions of man-made chemicals that have been introduced into the modern world, many of which have been added in the last 50 years and more are created every day.

Now, I don't wish to come across as someone with a chemical phobia who wishes he had his own chemical protection suit before he steps out the front door; but, we simply do not know all the effects these chemicals have on our immediate and long-term health. Results from chemicals that have been studied for human health issues make depressing reading.

Whilst small amounts of toxins from the environment can be dealt with by the body, if we are exposed to many different pollutants over time the accumulation in the body or toxic burden reaches a point that exceeds your body's ability to excrete them (detoxify). It is then that they build up to levels in the tissues that harm your health.

An example is heavy metal aluminium, implicated in neurological health problems such as Alzheimer's, Parkinson's disease and Multiple Sclerosis. Over the years, we have used aluminium cooking pots and utensils, aluminium foil and eaten many foods that contain it. Indeed, use of aluminium is more wide-spread than many of us realise.

It is incorporated in food (bread and bakery products contain high levels of aluminium salts, personal care products (e.g. under arm deodorants, toothpaste, cosmetics), some over the counter medications and vaccines. It is even added to water supplies as aluminium sulphate to improve the clarity of drinking water.

The use of aluminium in products has been so widespread that in 2006 The Joint Food and Agriculture Organisation together with the World Health Organisation Expert Committee on Food Additives (JECFA) re-evaluated the safety of aluminium and concluded to lower the provisional tolerable weekly intake (PTWI) from 7mg/kg body weight (bw) to 1mg/kg including additives.

In 2013 the Food Standards Agency was forced to produce a consultation document for food manufacturers after a new European Commission Regulation came into force on May 23rd 2012 introducing restrictions on the use of aluminium containing additives used in certain foods.

This is just one example of over exposure to a substance in our environment which has no place in our bodies but is still allowed to be used, albeit at lower levels despite much evidence that continued exposure over time contributes to ill health, disease, premature ageing and early death.

You need to think about where you exercise

There are so many toxic substances in our environment that it is impractical to avoid them all. However, you can take steps to cut down unnecessary exposure.

One example of this is something that I see virtually every day and it is something that I have a real bee in my bonnet about. It occurs throughout the year but is especially prevalent in the New Year when health kicks are in full flow.

I observe many well-meaning individuals, whom I admire for their determination and discipline in their pursuit of fitness, running, cycling and speed walking along the busiest most polluted roads you could imagine.

If you think about it, doing your daily exercise along busy roads is one of the worst places you could choose. When you are exercising, especially intensely, you are breathing between 12 to 20 times the air of sedentary people and the pollutants that you are drawing in include the following. Carbon monoxide (CO), Sulphur Dioxide (SO2), Nitrogen Oxide (NOx), Volatile Organic Compounds (VOCs), Ozone (O3), Heavy metals and particulates. This is a real chemical soup and the pollutants in it have been shown to have acute and chronic effects on human health.

These can affect a number of different systems and organs and vary from minor upper respiratory irritation to chronic respiratory and heart disease, lung cancer, chronic bronchitis and asthmatic attacks. Short and long-term exposures have also been linked with premature mortality and reduced life expectancy.

In September 2002, the US Environmental Protection Agency (EPA) published the final version of its much-anticipated assessment of the health consequences of diesel engine emissions. This report—redrafted a total of five times—was the culmination of 10 years of study, review, and public hearings. The principal finding of the report highlighted that inhalation of diesel exhaust fumes from large vehicles such as trucks and buses, and other sources, could substantially increase the risk of developing lung cancer.

Further evidence came in 2012 when the World Health Organisation who had previously labelled diesel exhausts as probably carcinogenic (cancer causing) confirmed that they are definitely carcinogenic. They concluded that they were a cause of lung cancer and may also cause tumours in the bladder.

The report recommended that everyone should reduce their exposure to diesel exhaust fumes. Dr Christopher Portier, who led the assessment, is quoted as saying: *"The scientific evidence was compelling and the Working Group's conclusion was unanimous, diesel engine exhaust causes lung cancer in humans."*

It is ironic that those individuals who are taking time and effort to improve their health and wellbeing are counteracting any benefit the exercise may give them by choosing to exercise on busy roads. Dr Michael Colgan, internationally acclaimed research scientist, author and lecturer sums it up rather well in his 2002 book Sports Nutrition Guide. He says: *"There is no way the benefits of nutrition and exercise can overcome the damage caused by sucking in that much chemical soup. They'd be better off spending an extra hour in bed".*

So, if you want to benefit from your exercise and healthy nutrition and protect your long-term health, you must try to avoid exercising in polluted areas.

What can you do to reduce exposure to pollutants and chemicals?

✓ With respect to what we have just talked about, avoid exercising or walking around polluted environments as much as possible. If you live in a busy town or city, try to exercise early in the morning when traffic is light or in a gym. Not always practical I know but do you really want to undo all your good work and effort by exposing yourself to so much pollution?

- ✓ There are many chemicals in the home that you would do well to avoid. Detergents, bleach, surface cleaners, polishes, cosmetics, personal care products, air fresheners. Look on the labels of many and they read like a chemistry lab. Choose products that are as natural as possible. There are increasing numbers of companies selling excellent products that use only natural safe ingredients that will do the job just as well and will not be toxic to you. (See Product Guide in Appendix 1)

- ✓ If your occupation involves working around chemicals, gases or other toxic products make sure that you use all of the protection that should be provided by the company. Also, be aware of places where there can be a build-up of pollutants such as garage workshops which should be properly ventilated.

- ✓ Eat organic food if possible that is certified by the Soil Association to avoid pesticide residues on vegetables and hormone/antibiotic residues in meat. If you can't buy organic, make sure that you thoroughly wash your vegetables or peel them before cooking and source your meat from a local butcher who can verify that the animal has been reared without the use of drugs. Also, avoid buying produce that has sat outside a shop by a busy road.

- ✓ Fit a good water filter to provide pure water for drinking and cooking.

- ✓ You can help to protect yourself against toxins from pollution by making sure that you have a good supply of antioxidants from your diet. I will cover these in the chapter on nutrition, but suffice to say, they will help to provide protection to your cells from these harmful substances together with other healthy substances that can be found in brightly coloured fruit and vegetables. You can also take a good quality antioxidant supplement to top up your antioxidant levels. What to look for can be found in the antioxidant section in the nutrition chapter.

6. MEDITATE

When people think about meditation the classic image of a person sitting in the cross-legged lotus position with their eyes closed, perhaps making a mystical sound may come to mind. This stereotype is perhaps what prevents many from giving it a try.

However, a greater number of people are practising meditation than ever before and finding it improves their health on a physical, mental and emotional level and they are happier as a result.

What are the benefits of regular meditation?

- ☺ It promotes a profound sense of tranquillity and relaxation and helps you to maintain a balanced psychological view on life helping you think more clearly.
- ☺ It reduces stress and anxiety levels and helps reduce the negative effects of the fight or flight response by decreasing the production of stress hormones such as cortisol and adrenaline.
- ☺ It relieves/reduces fatigue.
- ☺ It has been shown to help lower blood pressure and hypertension.
- ☺ It can aid restful sleep.
- ☺ It can help in reducing unhealthy types of cholesterol.
- ☺ It can promote more efficient oxygen use in the body.
- ☺ It increases production of the anti-ageing hormone DHEA.
- ☺ Concentration improves.

How can I learn to meditate?

There are a huge number of different techniques and many ways of learning them; from books, DVDs, CDs and online. These can be beneficial and it depends on your time and personal circumstances which one you choose. One of the best ways is to get instruction and it should be easy to locate a qualified teacher near you.

The key principles of meditation

- ✓ Meditation is usually done in a comfortable seated position although you can practice it lying down if you wish. Don't worry if you fall asleep when you first start, this is natural and very common.
- ✓ Your eyes should be closed and you focus on your breathing; you can use the technique described in the section on deep breathing.
- ✓ Use your breathing as your main focus but if you find that other thoughts come into your mind, try to relax and let them come and go.
- ✓ To begin with, you may only want to do a couple of minutes a day, you can gradually increase the time as you become more used to meditating.
- ✓ For best results, it is recommended that you aim to practice meditation for 20 minutes twice a day. However, it is entirely up to you how long you want to meditate for, do what feels right for you.
- ✓ The best times being upon awakening and before bed.

Personal experience of meditation

Apart from the health benefits of regular meditation, I have found it to be a wonderful way to start and end the day. It helps to relax me before sleep and to start a new day with a sense of calmness and clear focus which helps make the day go well. You have probably found that if you start your day in a bad mood, things usually go from bad to worse, well, taking a little time to start the day with yoga or meditation can help ensure that this type of day is very infrequent!

I believe it is one of the best practices you can adopt for improving your health and wellbeing, do give it a try.

7. HAVE A PASSION

Have you ever known people who never really seemed to be enthusiastic about anything in life? Who don't appear to have any interests or passions? I have certainly known quite a few people like this, who just gave the impression of existing from day to day but did not have any zest for living. Life was just something you got on with the best you could.

I have always thought that it is so tragic to see people in these situations, lacking a real direction or goal in their lives. It is often seen in people who retire from a long-term career. Perhaps their career has been all encompassing and provided their stability and direction in life. When they retire, they soon find that after enjoying the initial new found sense of freedom, without their old job they are rudderless and lacking in any new meaningful direction. Many people then start to age prematurely and do not enjoy a long and happy retirement.

However, this situation can just as easily apply to a person of any age who lacks a passionate interest.

Those people who are lucky enough to have a job which indulges their passion are those who tend to live longest and avoid serious illness. There are countless examples of this and you probably know retired people, I know I do, who despite their age have an energy and joy about them because they love their life and their passions. These passions give their life direction and meaning which in turn seems to help them stay young mentally and physically, they have a passion for life.

These passions can be literally anything; one of my passions, apart from health and fitness is aviation and there are a couple of examples of people that I would like to mention which demonstrate the power of a passion.

The first is a man called Eric "Winkle" Brown. Eric was called by some, the greatest pilot that Britain ever produced. He started his flying career just before World War 2 and soon proved to be an exceptional pilot. He became a test pilot and holds a world record that will probably never be broken; he flew in his career, more different types of aircraft than any other pilot, 487 to be precise. Eric sadly passed away in 2016 at the age of 97 but shortly before his short illness and death was still in demand to give lectures and talks, which he did with great zeal and enthusiasm. A life truly lived through a passion.

The second example is Wing Commander Kenneth Wallis who served as a pilot in bomber command in World War 2 and flew 28 missions over Germany. He later became an expert builder and flyer of autogyros (if you have ever seen the James Bond film “You Only Live Twice”, the little helicopter is an autogyro and Ken Wallis flew it in filming) and took 34 world records in them of which he still held eight of them at the time of his death aged 97. He flew his beloved autogyros right up until shortly before he died.

These two examples demonstrate perfectly the power of having a passion. Look up either on You Tube and you will see exactly what I mean.

Get yourself a passion in life

You may already have a passion and if you have, that’s fabulous; you will understand all about the positive aspects on psychological wellbeing which in turn contribute to long term physical health.

Today, it has never been easier to find out about clubs or societies or information on anything that you fancy having a go at. The internet is an amazing resource. The bottom line is this, a passion or passions create joy and excitement in your life which benefits you and often others around you as well. I highly recommend it.

8. REDUCE THE AMOUNT OF TIME YOU SPEND SITTING DOWN

The above statement may seem to be an obvious one. We can all appreciate that we need to be more active in our lives to promote optimal health.

When I first came across the research on health problems caused by sitting down for prolonged periods, I had not realised the true extent of the damaging effects that it can have on our long-term health. Now that I am aware of those effects I have taken simple steps to reduce the amount of time I spend seated and I am typing this standing up with key board resting on a box on the desk.

Why does it matter?

I must admit that I was a little sceptical about the research at first. I have always been open minded about new health paradigms, but here was research saying that despite everything that I practised to promote optimal health, now I had to stand up for most of my day as well!

The basic premise behind the research is that we are not designed to sit with our body crammed into an unnatural seated position for prolonged periods of time. Our modern lifestyle means that we do not have to physically exert ourselves to find food, shelter or to travel. The conveniences we now enjoy mean that our bodies are no longer used as they are meant to be. We evolved for continuous movement and not for prolonged periods of sitting down.

Consequently, what the research has found is that even if you spend 30 minutes doing moderate exercise every day, this good work can be undone by then sitting at a desk for 7 or 8 hours.

How much time do you spend sitting down?

It is not until you really think about it that you realise just how many hours most of us spend seated. I thought that I was pretty active most of the time but when I actually analysed how many hours I sat down during my day I was really shocked. It turned out to be 6 to 7 hours per day!

Because sitting down is something that we do without thinking about it, we lose track of how long we do it for; it's a habitual behaviour that we don't even notice. If you add together the average day including meals, travelling, work and relaxing in the evening, the total soon mounts up.

How does sitting down for prolonged periods affect your health?

One of the leaders in this field is Dr James Levine who carries out research at the Mayo Clinic in America. He was one of the first people to highlight the problem and his research together with other studies have found that sitting continuously for hours at a time can cause the following health issues:

- ☹ An increase in blood pressure
- ☹ Elevated cholesterol levels (the bad dense type of LDL)
- ☹ Elevated triglycerides (fats in the blood) to unhealthy levels
- ☹ Elevated blood sugar levels
- ☹ A slowing of the metabolism leading to poor circulation and digestion
- ☹ Postural problems such as back ache
- ☹ Energy systems slow right down making you feel sluggish and tired
- ☹ Your body loses the ability to use fats as energy
- ☹ You are more prone to weight gain and obesity

Dr Levine's research has established links with up to 24 chronic diseases associated with an excess amount of time spent sitting such as diabetes and cancer.

All pretty depressing, just through sitting down longer than you should. However, the good news is that as soon as you stand up (within 60-90) seconds, the cascade of metabolic reactions that controls things like blood sugar, cholesterol and triglyceride levels kicks in and starts to work again.

The research has also shown that cutting down on the amount of time that we spend sitting down can reverse many, if not all the degenerative effects and it's never too late to make a start. Although it may seem an exhausting thought to stand or move around for much of the day, this is only because it goes against what we have come to know as the norm. When you spend less time seated you will find that you have more energy, aches and pains will go and you will have a greater sense of well-being.

So, how can we modify our daily routine so that we sit down less?

Tips for helping to reduce the amount of time you spend seated

- ✓ Try getting up from your seat and standing or walking around for at least 10 minutes out of every hour. This has been shown to be the minimum requirement to help reverse the negative health effects. Research has shown that the more times that you can get up from the seated position spread evenly through the day, the more effective the positive health changes are.
- ✓ Look at your established habits and see if there are times when you could stand and move about when you would normally continue sitting, during breaks at work for instance. You could try standing up and walking around when you're on the telephone. When watching television try standing up and moving around every time the adverts come on or when on public transport perhaps spend some of the journey standing up.
- ✓ Enquire about a stand-up desk at work or if you are lucky enough to work from home, make the change. As mentioned above, I rest my key board on a box or you could perhaps use a pile of large books.
- ✓ Make the transition at a pace that suits you. You may find that you can cut out hours of sitting immediately or you may need a little time to adjust your existing daily routine. You will be surprised at how quickly you adjust to sitting less and moving around more, it's just changing habitual behaviour.
- ✓ Get others involved so they can benefit too, either at work or at home. It's always easier to achieve something if you have support from others.
- ✓ The current research suggests that we should try to spend no longer than 3 hours a day seated if we are to get the maximum health benefits. However, for many people this is a problem if their job requires them to be seated (e.g. drivers). Don't get despondent if you have to spend more hours seated; you can still stand if possible for 10 minutes every hour or take regular breaks to move around. The fact that you are aware of the problem and are doing something to reduce the hours you spend seated will prove positive for your health; spending no more than 3 hours seated every day is just the ideal to aim towards.
- ✓ Visit juststand.org/facts/scientificresearch for more details.

9. OIL PULLING

I had not heard of oil pulling until I attended a health seminar early in 2015. Until then I would have probably thought that it was something that went on in an oil refinery.

What exactly is it?

Oil pulling originates in India and the practice comes from Ayurvedic medicine. It is a way of dramatically improving your oral health and at the same time promoting a cleansing of other organs in the body by simply rinsing your mouth with oil for 15 to 20 minutes. It could be thought of as sort of oral detox.

What are the benefits?

There are a lot of benefits to incorporating oil pulling into your health regime. Let's start with the ones that are directly related to the mouth.

- ☺ Improves oral hygiene by helping to remove fungi, toxins and bacteria in your mouth (sounds disgusting!). Oil does this by blending with and dissolving the fatty cell walls of these nasties and absorbing them into the oil you are rinsing around your mouth.
- ☺ It can improve the health of your gums and heal bleeding gums
- ☺ Helps to stop tooth decay and prevent cavities from developing
- ☺ Stops bad breath
- ☺ Heals cracked lips
- ☺ Soothes a dry throat
- ☺ It is even reputed to help whiten your teeth!

From a wider systemic point of view, the health of your mouth is thought in Ayurvedic medicine to reflect your general health. In fact, conditions like gingivitis and periodontal disease are considered to be directly linked to heart disease.

Oil pulling is said to act on different areas of the tongue which have a connection to different organs in the body. This is similar to souls of the feet in reflexology or the iris in iridology. The systemic benefits of oil pulling are that it can help to:

☺ reduce inflammation in the body

☺ boost the immune system

☺ prevent heart disease

☺ improve skin conditions such as acne due to its detoxifying effect.

How do you do oil pulling?

There are several things to bear in mind to get the most benefit from oil pulling.

✓ Do it on an empty stomach first thing in the morning or when you first wake up, ideally before you drink anything or brush your teeth. It can be useful to scrape your tongue first to remove the white coating (bacteria and food debris).

  If you're not familiar with tongue scraping it also originates from Ayurvedic medicine. As well as giving the oil pulling a head start it removes the bacteria that form plaque that in turn cause gum disease and tooth decay. Gently scrape from front to back. Don't be surprised if you gag at first – it can take a little getting used to!

  Rinse the scraper under running water after each scrape and do this up to ten times. Sterilise after each use in boiling water. (Tongue scrapers are normally near the toothbrushes in chemists or supermarkets).

✓ Take a teaspoon of organic raw virgin coconut oil and pop it into your mouth (you can use olive oil or sesame seed oil, just make sure they are organic, raw and virgin). In a couple of seconds, the coconut oil will melt and become liquid. It may feel a bit strange at first, but you will get used to it. I didn't like the taste of coconut before I started using it for oil pulling, but I now quite like the taste (still not sure I would like a Bounty Bar or Coconut ice though!).

  Swish it about in your mouth, pulling it back and forth in between your teeth. Ideally you need to do this for about 20 minutes but when you first start you may find that you can only do it for 5 or 10 minutes. That's fine, you will soon work up to 20. I get on with other jobs whilst I'm oil pulling and find that the 20 minutes soon goes.

- ✓ Try to relax your tongue and jaw muscles otherwise you will find that they soon start to ache.
- ✓ Do not swallow the liquid as it will contain the bacteria that is being flushed from your mouth. Spit it out in some tissue or directly into the bin. Avoid putting it down the loo or sink because the oil will solidify in the colder months and you might find you need the services of a plumber to unblock your pipes!
- ✓ If you have the urge to swallow when you are just starting oil pulling you can spit the oil out and begin again, adding the time you have already done to your total or end the session, it's entirely up to how your feel.
- ✓ You may find when you first start that you feel a little sick; I experienced this the first time I did it. This is not unusual and is a sign that toxins are being drawn from your body. If you feel like this, just stop and leave it a day or so. You will find that the more you practise pulling, these feelings will disappear.
- ✓ When you have finished and spat out the oil, have a glass of salt water ready to flush any residual oil out of your mouth (I like to gargle when I do this) and spit this out as well. The best salt to use is Himalayan crystal salt which has many health benefits of its own.

I know that oil pulling may sound a little strange, but please just give it a go. I think that you will be amazed at the results you get and how it will complement your existing health regime. Just make sure you do it at a time when you are unlikely to be disturbed and won't need to talk for 20 minutes!

10. GET YOUR HOMOCYSTEINE LEVELS TESTED

There are numerous tests available these days that give an indication of your health. Currently the most accurate test for assessing your overall health is the homocysteine test.

What is Homocysteine and why is measuring it so important?

Homocysteine is a toxic and inflammatory amino acid, a by-product of protein metabolism. Measuring your blood levels indicates how efficiently your body is carrying out a process called methylation, which is vital to your long-term health. Methylation is involved in the regulation of pretty much all your body's biochemistry including:

- ✓ Energy production
- ✓ Inflammation response
- ✓ Your stress (fight or flight) response
- ✓ The production and re-cycling of indigenous antioxidant glutathione
- ✓ Neurotransmitters and the balancing of your brain biochemistry
- ✓ The immune response
- ✓ The detoxification of hormones, heavy metals and chemicals
- ✓ The repair of cells damaged by free-radicals
- ✓ How the information in your genes is used in building and repairing you and in the repair of DNA

If you are methylating properly, your homocysteine will be low.

Who needs to get tested?

Pretty much everyone; there are thousands of studies that show that your homocysteine level is an accurate predictor of most of the health problems we suffer from in modern society. In fact, it has been found that a high homocysteine score is a much more accurate predictor of heart attacks and strokes than usual indicators such as cholesterol levels and high blood pressure. As we get older we can become less efficient at methylation

Factors that can increase homocysteine levels include:

- Prolonged stress
- Not regularly exercising
- Smoking daily
- Drinking too much coffee every day
- Drinking more than 2 alcoholic beverages on average per day
- Being vegan

Symptoms that could indicate increased homocysteine levels include:

- Constantly feeling tired
- Lack of stamina
- Muscle aches and pains
- Migraines
- Having difficulty in concentrating and thinking clearly
- Having memory problems
- Often feeling depressed
- Not sleeping well
- Cardio vascular problems
- High blood pressure
- Losing your temper easily

How can I get tested?

You can get tested by using a simple blood spot test which you receive through the post. (Please see Additional Resources) The test is not cheap but it could just turn out to be the best money you ever spend.

Interpreting the results

Results will be given in micrograms per mol/L

6 or below	is great, you are getting it right. Continue what you are already doing and take a high strength multi vitamin supplement to help to maintain this level.
6 to 9	is still good but you may want to consider ways of bringing your score down.
9 to 12	is high and you should take action to bring down your score.
12 to 15	is getting into the higher risk area and you should use all the means at your disposal to bring down your score.
15+	This is the very high-risk category with a significant chance of developing a major disease.

Please don't worry if you find your score is high. Even in cases of people with very high scores, by taking positive steps they were able to reduce their scores to the healthy range in a few months.

What you can do to bring down your score

Whatever your score is, the good news is that there is a lot that you can to bring down your score quite quickly and then re-test after 3 months to see your progress.

- ✓ Take a specialist homocysteine supplement which will help you reduce your levels. This should include vitamin B2, B6, B12, Folic acid, zinc and magnesium. The B vitamins should be in methylated form (e.g. methyl folate, methyl B12)
- ✓ Take a high potency B vitamin complex
- ✓ Use coconut fat in your diet (you can take 1 to 2 teaspoons per day)
- ✓ Don't smoke

- ✓ Avoid drinking excessive alcohol. However, the good news is that one glass of beer per day can help reduce homocysteine. Avoid spirits as they raise levels and wine has a neutral effect.
- ✓ Try to limit the stress in your life as much as possible. See chapter 6
- ✓ Avoid coffee or limit consumption to one per day if possible.
- ✓ Do some exercise daily, See chapter 4. Always support exercise with supplementation, especially intense exercise as this can use B vitamins that are so vital for methylation.
- ✓ Have two servings of green vegetables every day.
- ✓ Eat foods that are rich in nutrients required to support methylation. B2 (wild rice (cooked), salmon, mackerel) B6 (sunflower seeds, lentils (cooked), white fish (cooked)). B12 (mackerel, pilchards, sardines, crab). Folate (spinach (chopped raw), chickpeas, lentils), Zinc (sesame seeds, oysters, walnuts), Magnesium (pumpkin seeds, Brazil nuts, Lima beans (cooked)).
- ✓ Support your beneficial bacteria in your gut as they help to produce and absorb B vitamins and folate. See chapter 3
- ✓ Follow the advice in this book. A simple rule of thumb is that anything that is good for health reduces your homocysteine score and anything that is bad is more likely to increase it.

INCORPORATING THESE 10 SUGGESTIONS INTO YOUR LIFE

When we're keen to make improvements in our health it can be easy to try to do too much at once and then get disheartened when it's difficult to keep the momentum. I'd therefore recommend focusing on a few areas at a time that are most important to you and setting yourself some practical targets to implement the changes you wish to make.

Whilst you may wish to focus on the areas that are most important to you, you may also like to consider areas that are less of a priority for you and may be easier to implement. Achieving some quick wins can be a great way to get started and create some momentum for your longer term plans.

Chapter 2 Review & Ideas For Your Action Plan

To help target your action plan and address the areas you would like to focus on, circle the score that best reflects the degree to which it is a priority.

Date: ______________	Low Priority									High Priority
1. Get enough quality sleep	1	2	3	4	5	6	7	8	9	10
2. Drink enough quality water	1	2	3	4	5	6	7	8	9	10
3. Skin brush	1	2	3	4	5	6	7	8	9	10
4. Practise deep breathing	1	2	3	4	5	6	7	8	9	10
5. Avoid pollution	1	2	3	4	5	6	7	8	9	10
6. Meditate	1	2	3	4	5	6	7	8	9	10
7. Have a passion	1	2	3	4	5	6	7	8	9	10
8. Reduce time sitting down	1	2	3	4	5	6	7	8	9	10
9. Oil pull	1	2	3	4	5	6	7	8	9	10
10. Homocysteine test	1	2	3	4	5	6	7	8	9	10

Note down some action points to help move you forward with your goals.

As mentioned earlier there may be areas that are less of a priority but could be a quick win so, for example:

1. Quality Sleep – Priority Low.

Happy with quality and quantity of sleep I'm getting though would like to investigate getting a light alarm.

2. Reduce Time Sitting Down – Priority Medium.

On days I work from home put lap top on pile of large books. When in the office stand up during coffee breaks and when on conference calls. Suggest 'stand up' team meetings.

3. Homocysteine Test – Priority High.

Cut down on coffee to 1 cup a day. Give up smoking and supplement with B vitamins for 6 months then arrange homocysteine test.

4. Review Date - Put date in diary for 3 months' time to review this chapter and collate new action points.

Chapter 3

Transform Your Health by Looking After Your Digestive System

Transform your health by looking after your digestive system

The ubiquitous phrase "you are what you eat" is useful for reminding us that our vitality is intrinsically linked to the food we choose. It makes perfect sense that the more nutritious the food the more chance we have of being healthy. But that's not the whole story as so many of us have inefficient digestive systems so we are not actually utilising all the nutrients we consume.

You can eat the healthiest foods available, but if your digestion is not breaking them down and absorbing them efficiently, many of the nutrients will be wasted and your cells will in time become malnourished. Consequently, as every organ and structure in our body is dependent on the quality of our cells, they will not be able to function optimally. So, it's more accurate to say "you are what you eat and absorb"

THE EFFICIENCY OF YOUR DIGESTION IS CRUCIAL TO LONG-TERM HEALTH

Look upon optimal digestive function as the corner stone of your health. It provides the foundation upon which the rest of your body depends. In fact, most ill health and disease starts with an under-functioning digestive system.

So, in this chapter we'll look at the factors that can undermine its efficiency, the signs and symptoms that tell you all is not well and what the consequences could be for you. We will then explore the best ways of looking after it and nurturing it.

YOUR DIGESTIVE SYSTEM IS AMAZING!

If we think of the digestive system in the simplest way, it is basically just a muscular tube that runs through your body which can open at both ends! This tube is approximately thirty feet in length and over a lifetime it has been estimated that as much as a hundred tons of food may pass through it.

This is of course a very simplistic explanation of a truly incredible, intricate system, which, after you have swallowed food or drink, processes and extracts the nutrients your body needs to survive and safely excretes bodily waste. It completes this remarkable feat automatically with no further thought or action from you; it is self-running and self-healing.

We tend to think that the only part of our body that is exposed to the outside world is our skin and our respiratory system. However, the entire length of our digestive system is also exposed because it comes into contact with the food and drink that we consume. So, it not only has to break down food and absorb the nutrients that our cells require, it also needs to prevent ingested pathogens (anything that causes disease) and antigens (foreign substances, bacterial products and large undigested molecules) from passing through the intestinal lining and into the bloodstream. It provides you with what you do need whilst protecting you from what you don't; a very fine balancing act!

To do this, the intestinal lining acts as a barrier that protects your body and it also forms part of your immune system with immune cells in your digestive tract and trillions of beneficial bacteria that work together to protect us from the outside world like body guards.

The lining that does this is not very thick at all, approximately three millimetres, and the billions of cells that line it are renewed by the body approximately every 4 days! The small intestine which forms a large percentage of the thirty-foot tube is where most nutrients are absorbed and has an enormous surface area for better absorption. Its surface area is the subject of one of the best known anatomical facts, being roughly the equivalent of the area of a tennis court if it was spread out; some say even two! It achieves this incredible feat by an amazing biological design; it has millions of finger-like projections covering its lining called villi which are 0.5 to 1.5 mm in length and on each of these are yet more microscopic finger shaped projections called microvilli which enable it to have that immense surface area packed into such a small space.

This example represents only a part of your digestive system that works incredibly hard for you every single day. Even if you have no cause for concern about your digestion at present it is well worth checking to see if you can make some improvements to support it and optimise its efficiency. As we get older our digestive system can become less efficient, so it is important that we support it as much as possible. It will prove a worthwhile investment for your long-term health.

HOW IS YOUR DIGESTION?

Like all the functions of our body, it is very easy to take digestion for granted until it is not working as it should. Throughout this book, I will be continually encouraging you to tune into what your body is trying to tell you.

What do I mean by this? Well, there are many ways in which the human body tells us that all is not well. These can range from what are perceived as everyday aches and pains, headaches, rashes and inflammation to more debilitating illnesses. To keep your body in optimal health it's important to learn to take notice of even the simplest symptom and ask yourself what does that mean? Learning to do this can help you identify problems early on and contribute significantly to your long-term wellbeing.

I am not suggesting that you turn into a hypochondriac, just that you don't ignore what could be warning signs and put them down to, for example, age, which, as we've already established, seems to be a favourite default explanation.

As symptoms are an inconvenience and stop us from getting on with our lives, it is all too easy to suppress them with pain killers, anti-inflammatory drugs or other 'magic bullets'. This can be even worse than ignoring the symptoms, particularly in the long-term, because if you suppress something by, for example, taking away the pain, you are not dealing with the root cause, which will still be there and could manifest itself in the future with far more serious consequences.

What we are effectively doing when we suppress symptoms is telling our body to "shut up". Of course, sometimes painkillers are necessary in an emergency. However, remember that they do not solve the problem, only the discomfort caused by it. So, we need to take action by finding out about any symptoms and what your body is trying to tell you.

Let's put this into practice and look at symptoms which point towards an under functioning digestive system.

Do you do any of the following?

- ❐ Eat too quickly without chewing thoroughly
- ❐ Burp after meals
- ❐ Eat wheat products (such as bread, pasta, cereal, pastry) at least twice a day
- ❐ Use indigestion or antacid tablets regularly
- ❐ Have less than one bowel movement a day
- ❐ Have a history of using antibiotics (especially in the last six months)

Do you have or have you had any of the following?

❐ Abdominal bloating

❐ A feeling of fullness for an extended time after meals

❐ A feeling of nausea for an extended time after eating

❐ Bad breath

❐ Poor appetite

❐ Excessive or foul-smelling gas

❐ Food poisoning or gastric infection in the last six months

❐ Foul smelling stools

Do you suffer from any of the following?

❐ Regular stomach ache/upsets

❐ A history of constipation (less than one bowel movement a day)

❐ Food allergies

❐ Abdominal cramps

❐ Fatigue after eating

❐ Alternating constipation and diarrhoea

❐ Very loose stools or diarrhoea

❐ Heartburn (acid reflux), or get a burning sensation in your stomach

❐ Frequent infections (e.g. colds)

❐ Eczema or rashes

These are some of the ways our body is telling us that it needs help; and these are just the more common ones, there are many more!

Firstly, don't be overly concerned if you ticked lots of the boxes! You won't be alone – so many of us in the 21st century have digestive systems that aren't working as well as they could be. Use this exercise as simply a chance to review where you are now. The tips in this chapter will help you make the necessary tweaks and changes.

If you highlighted **no more than 2** of the above you have nothing to be concerned about and your digestive system is likely to be in good order, well done! However, we can all benefit from a bit of a tune up so you can still benefit from following the tips in this chapter.

If you highlighted **between 3 and 5**, I would recommend that you follow the dietary advice for improving digestive function and tips for improving the condition of your digestive system.

If you highlighted **between 6 and 8**, there is a strong possibility that you have a degree of under function in your digestive system. You should consider testing for food intolerances or pathogens and start implementing the advice in this chapter.

If you **highlighted 8 or more**, it is extremely likely that you need to give your digestive system some support. As mentioned above, it could be useful to consider tests for food intolerance or pathogens. Follow the advice in this chapter on diet (and the chapter on nutrition) and ways that you can improve the overall function of your digestive system. There are also tips on how to repair any damage that may be compromising your ability to digest efficiently.

THE IMPORTANCE OF BACTERIA IN YOUR DIGESTIVE SYSTEM

It is estimated that there are approximately 100 trillion bacteria in the gut, a number about 10 times greater than the cells in the average human. Although that may sound a bit disgusting to some, you simply could not survive without them. They are intrinsically involved in many aspects of your well-being including your immune system, the manufacture of certain vitamins, assisting in digestion and the control of cholesterol and fat levels in the blood.

However, not all these bacteria are beneficial. There are also bad bacteria which cause health problems when their numbers get too high. When this happens, there is an imbalance in the good and bad bacteria, in favour of the bad; it is called "dysbiosis".

Signs and symptoms include indigestion, bloating, abdominal pain, feeling sleepy after meals, frequent stomach upsets, diarrhoea or constipation. This is opposite to "symbiosis" which means living in harmony. So, the trick is to tip the balance heavily in favour of the beneficial bacteria and keep it there! If you can achieve this, it is a major step towards improving digestive function and consequently your overall health.

HAVE YOU GOT A LEAKY GUT?

There are many conditions that can affect the digestive system but one of the lesser known but more common is called leaky gut syndrome or intestinal permeability. In fact, you may not even realise that you have it; but leaky gut is behind numerous health issues, many of which you would never think to associate with a digestive problem.

With this condition, the wall or lining of your intestines literally develops leaks. Instead of just allowing properly digested and broken-down fats, proteins and carbohydrates to cross the intestinal barrier which provide the essential nutrients your body needs, the increased permeability ceases to provide an effective barrier allowing pathogens and antigens to cross into the bloodstream. Once this happens it can be a contributing factor to many health conditions.

Factors that can be associated with leaky gut

- ☹ Abdominal pain
- ☹ Ageing
- ☹ Aggressive behaviour
- ☹ Alcoholism
- ☹ Ankylosing spondylitis
- ☹ Anxiety
- ☹ Autism
- ☹ Autoimmune diseases such as rheumatoid arthritis or psoriasis
- ☹ Bloating
- ☹ Celiac disease

- ☹ Child hyperactivity
- ☹ Chronic fatigue or tiredness
- ☹ Chronic fatigue syndrome
- ☹ Chronic muscle pain
- ☹ Chronic or frequent inflammations
- ☹ Confusion
- ☹ Constipation
- ☹ Crohn's disease
- ☹ Depression
- ☹ Diarrhoea
- ☹ Dysbiosis
- ☹ Food allergies, food sensitivities or food intolerance
- ☹ Fuzzy thinking
- ☹ Hives
- ☹ Indigestion
- ☹ Intestinal infections
- ☹ Irritable bowel syndrome (IBS)
- ☹ Joint pain or swelling
- ☹ Liver dysfunction
- ☹ Mood swings
- ☹ Nervousness
- ☹ PMS (pre-menstrual syndrome)
- ☹ Poor exercise tolerance
- ☹ Poor memory

☹ Recurrent bladder infections

☹ Recurrent vaginal infections

☹ Rheumatoid arthritis

☹ Schizophrenia

☹ Seasonal allergies or asthma

☹ Sinus or nasal congestion

☹ Skin conditions such as eczema, rashes, acne, psoriasis

☹ Ulcerative colitis

☹ Wind/gas

Phew! As you can see by the length of the list, leaky gut is prevalent in modern society and can cause a diverse range of unappealing symptoms. Of course, just because you suffer from anxiety, for example, does not necessarily mean you have a leaky gut! The above list of conditions or symptoms are simply useful clues.

What causes leaky gut?

As with anything in health, nothing is caused by a single factor and intestinal permeability is no exception. There are many contributing factors. The five main ones are:

1. <u>Chronic stress</u>

Prolonged stress has a detrimental effect by slowing down digestion peristalsis (movement of digested food through the gut) and reducing blood flow to the digestive organs. It also increases the time that food takes to travel through the digestive tract (intestinal transit time) which can cause dysbiosis and inflammation of the gut wall. All of which impairs the ability of the gut lining to replace cells and stay in optimal condition.

2. <u>Dysbiosis</u>

As mentioned above dysbiosis is an imbalance in the intestinal bacteria in favour of unhealthy bacteria or fungi. An example of this is an overgrowth of a naturally occurring yeast-fungal organism in the gut called Candida. This little blighter can cause havoc because it grows a bit like a plant and puts roots down which penetrate and grow through the gut wall.

3. Contaminated foods

Contaminated foods can weaken the intestinal lining and lead to leaky gut. These include:

☹ Foods contaminated with harmful bacteria or parasites.

☹ Animal products containing antibiotic and hormonal residues such as over consumption of farmed fish or meat that it is not reared organically.

☹ Chemicals such as additives and preservatives found in processed foods.

4. Poor diet choices

A poor diet alters the pH of the body, making it too acid which in turn leads to dysbiosis and slow intestinal transit time (see chapter 5 for more information). Whilst our digestive systems can cope with a great deal, it is worthwhile not over consuming the following that can damage and encourage inflammation of the intestines:

- dairy products
- grains
- animal protein
- processed foods
- sugary processed drinks
- coffee or caffeinated drinks.

5. Frequent use of orthodox pharmaceutical medications

Frequent courses of antibiotics, non-steroidal anti-inflammatory drugs (NSAIDs) can cause dysbiosis and damage the intestinal lining. Birth control pills can also create conditions for fungal over growth, such as Candida, which as mentioned above, damages the lining.

In modern day living it can be difficult to steer clear of these 5 main factors. It follows that the more your digestive system is exposed to, the higher the likelihood of developing higher permeability in the gut lining. It's becoming increasingly common so please don't feel alone if you feel you may be at risk.

There are tips further on in this chapter to help heal the gut lining and protect its permeability. If you wish to find out if you have a leaky gut, there are several tests to choose from. Here are a few examples:

1. Stool Test

   This test looks for a specific enzyme (Alpha-1-antitrypsine) that is not broken down where there is increased gut permeability and therefore it can be detected in a stool sample that is sent for laboratory analysis. Stool tests can also give a good indication of the overall health of the gut (levels of good/bad bacteria, inflammation in the gut etc.)

2. Microbial Organic Acid Test

   This test uses a sample of the first urine you pass in the morning. The laboratory then tests for a range of biological markers that are strongly indicative of leaky gut. These include balance of good/bad bacteria, nutrient deficiencies, yeast overgrowth (such as candida) and other indicators of dysbiosis.

3. Zonulin Test

   Zonulin is a protein that regulates the size of the tight gaps between the cells in the gut wall. The higher the level of zonulin the larger the gaps. Zonulin can be triggered by harmful bacteria and by some of the foods we eat, such as gliadin in wheat. Measuring the amount of zonulin in a blood sample can therefore be a useful indicator of intestinal permeability.

4. Lactulose Test

   Another valuable way to assess the gut's permeability is via a urine test that measures the ratio of two sugar molecules, lactulose and mannitol. Mannitol passes through the intestinal wall easily whilst lactulose is larger so should not be absorbed into the bloodstream if the intestinal wall is healthy.

All these tests are useful, but it is best to consult a health professional to advise you which, if any, would be best for you.

How can I heal a leaky gut?

The following tips help to heal as well as prevent a leaky gut:

✓ Take a supplement called glutamine. It is an amino acid; which as I'm sure you are aware are the building blocks that your body uses to build the physical you. Glutamine also happens to be vital to the correct functioning of the intestinal lining. The cells that line the gut use glutamine as fuel and use it for repair when they become damaged as in leaky gut.

Supplementing with glutamine can therefore help hugely in repairing the intestinal lining and can be taken continuously to help maintain optimum function. It is also highly beneficial to your immune system and brain.

TIP: Don't take glutamine in conjunction with a hot drink as heat destroys it. It is best taken on an empty stomach last thing at night or first thing in the morning.

✓ Find out if you are eating or drinking anything that you are allergic to and eliminate from your diet. (See the following section on Allergies and Food Intolerances).

✓ Follow the advice in chapter 5 on Nutrition to ensure your diet provides the maximum benefit and support for your digestive system.

✓ Re-balance the bacteria in your gut in favour of beneficial bacteria to help prevent dysbiosis. You can do this by taking a quality probiotic supplement every day which will help to re-populate the digestive system with beneficial bacteria. You can also help these bacteria to proliferate by feeding them with pre-biotics. (See tips in the Digestive Tune Up section of this chapter)

✓ Take digestive enzymes for 30 days with main meals to support your body in breaking food into its component nutrients. As well as helping the body to absorb nutrients easily they also assist in healing the gut wall.

- ✓ You can take the glutamine, probiotic and digestive enzymes separately if you wish or there are supplements that combine all three that could be used for 30 days. After this time, if you are eating a healthy diet, you should be able to discontinue taking the digestive enzymes and take separate glutamine and probiotic supplements. It may be worth working with a nutritionist who can advise you on the best course of action.
- ✓ Work on reducing your stress levels. (see chapter 6)
- ✓ Avoid using non-prescription pharmaceutical medications if possible.
- ✓ Eat organic food whenever possible and be mindful of where your food is sourced. This will help you to avoid pesticides, hormones and antibiotic residues.
- ✓ Make sure that the food you eat is prepared and cooked properly to avoid contamination by parasites or bacteria such as E-coli.

ALLERGIES AND FOOD INTOLERANCES

What is the difference between an allergy and food intolerance? Well, it is essentially a case of how your immune system reacts to certain foods or drinks. Both are caused by the immune system responding to incompletely digested food particles or molecules that have passed through the gut wall and that are too big for the body to deal with. It therefore sees them as an invader and initiates an immune response. In time the immune response becomes trigger happy and any contact with the offending food group, for example, gliadin in wheat will cause a number of symptoms.

The difference between an allergy and food intolerance

With an allergy the immune response tends to be more immediate and obvious, usually varying from a few minutes up to one hour and can be very aggressive due to the type of antibody produced by the immune system, with reactions such as vomiting, closing of the airways (asthma), rashes appearing on the skin and in extreme cases can be life threatening. The response is not always so dramatic but with this type of immune reaction people may suffer for life, especially if the reaction is immediate and aggressive, as in peanut allergies. This is not always the case and some allergies do disappear over time with the right treatment and lifestyle changes.

In contrast, food intolerances result from a different type of antibody being produced by the immune system. They are usually less dramatic and may not appear for hours or even up to three or four days. Because of this, they are sometimes known as delayed or hidden intolerances. Food intolerance can be behind a range of digestive problems including irritable bowel syndrome (IBS). There are also many conditions that you would not necessarily associate with food intolerance. These include: fatigue, migraines, asthma, arthritis, chronic fatigue, and skin problems such as eczema.

Like many people who become nutritionists, I decided to study nutrition because it transformed my own health. I was suffering from food intolerance to wheat and by excluding it from my diet for a while all my symptoms and conditions disappeared over time. I am now able to tolerate wheat in moderation so the odd cheese sandwich, one of my favourite meals, no longer causes me a problem - it's all a question of balance.

Testing for allergies

Because allergic reactions are usually more rapid it is often quite obvious to pin point the culprit; especially if it is a food. However, sometimes this is not always the case and you may want to get yourself tested.

<u>Skin Test</u>

This can be done in a doctor's surgery. A drop of a suspected allergen is pricked on the surface of the skin (usually on the forearm) and if you are allergic to a raised inflamed red spot or wheal will quickly come up on the skin within 15 minutes.

<u>Blood test</u>

This alternative to the skin test is where a small blood sample is sent to a laboratory and the reaction of specific antibodies in the blood to types of food are recorded.

Both of these tests have a reasonable accuracy rate but are far from full proof.

Oral Food Challenge ORC

This is the most accurate test because it introduces a suspected food allergen to be eaten slowly and in increasing amounts and relies on good old fashioned "how do you feel". The disadvantages of this are that it should be done in the presence of a doctor in case there is a sudden and aggressive reaction and medical intervention is required. It is also time consuming, testing one suspected food at a time.

Testing for food intolerance

Exclusion method

It is worth noting that the foods we crave are often the ones that can be causing the problems. Excluding those foods or drinks can be a very effective starting point. Do this for one week and then introduce them one at a time allowing up to four days for a reaction. If there is no discernible reaction, move onto the next one. This can be a useful method, but it can be difficult to fit into daily life as some of the products you are excluding may be hidden in other foods, so you need to read labels carefully.

Also, if you are eating out you need to find out if those foods are a hidden ingredient in items on the menu. If you are strict in what you eat during this test it can help in identifying food and drinks to avoid very effectively.

Laboratory testing

An accurate and more straightforward method is to get a sample of your blood tested at a laboratory. This will identify which foods you should avoid and will also provide advice on how to do this. All you do is provide a blood sample from a pin prick and return it to the lab for analysis. It could prove a worthwhile investment by providing a crucial component to transforming your health and well-being.

It is important to bear in mind that most food intolerances and less aggressive allergies are not necessarily for life. Once identified, if they are removed from the diet, your immune system will become desensitised to them and you should be able to introduce them in a limited way, should you wish to do so. The amount of time for this to take place will vary from person to person but usually takes between 4 to 6 months.

Signs and symptoms of food intolerance

Many of the signs and symptoms are common to the general digestive problems listed previously, but specifically, the main ones to look for are listed below. Review the list and tick those that apply to you.

- ❐ Chronic headaches, migraines, difficulty in sleeping
- ❐ Asthma, shortness of breath.
- ❐ Rashes, itches, eczema, dermatitis, psoriasis, dry skin, acne.
- ❐ Mood swings, sometimes depressed, confusion, anxiety, tension, short temper, food cravings, poor concentration
- ❐ Hay fever, sinus problems, excess mucus, runny or stuffy nose
- ❐ Feeling excessively sleepy or tired after eating
- ❐ Stomach pains or bloating after eating
- ❐ Fluid retention
- ❐ Allergies
- ❐ Intermittent muscle and joint aches, pains, swelling, stiffness and or arthritis
- ❐ General aches and pains that come and go
- ❐ Regular use of painkillers
- ❐ Disease conditions of the digestive system (colitis, crohn's disease or diverticulitis)
- ❐ Improvement in condition when diet is changed (e.g. on holiday)

If you ticked **more than 5** it would be a good idea to look at the possibility of a food intolerance using one or both of the methods described.

Bear in mind that although the symptoms listed in this chapter are indicative of digestive problems they can of course be a result of other factors as well.

In conclusion, testing and verifying that you have an allergy or food intolerance is not about permanently banning an ever-growing list of foods from your diet. It is about identifying a symptom of a deeper problem that needs to be solved.

TOP DIGESTION FRIENDLY HABITS

Outlined below are some tips to help you nurture and support your digestive system to enable it to work efficiently for you throughout your life. People I have worked with have been amazed at the results they have achieved in either regaining their health or achieving levels of energy they did not think possible.

The tips are divided into 3 sections:

Section 1:	Top 12 things to do
Section 2:	7 things to avoid
Section 3:	4 supplements key to digestive health

SECTION 1 Top 12 things to do

1. Chew your food properly

I remember being told off by my mother when I was growing up, for gulping down my food too quickly and not chewing properly. She was right; the digestive process starts in the mouth where saliva helps soften your food and liquefy it so that your stomach does not receive large chunks of food that are difficult to break down.

The saliva also contains enzymes which start to break down carbohydrates. The more you chew the better your absorption will be. Also, if we fail to chew properly, undigested food particles can feed undesirable bacteria in the intestine.

2. Try to make sure that you are relaxed when eating

Stress interferes with digestion, slowing it down and diverting blood away from the digestive organs. This can cause all sorts of digestive problems such as constipation, diarrhoea, inflammation of the gastrointestinal system and make you more susceptible to infection. It can also give you indigestion by causing an increase in the acid in your stomach or stop the stomach functioning altogether which can make you feel nauseous. Stress causes incomplete digestion of food and can ultimately result in damage to the digestive system.

✓ If you notice you are feeling stressed when you're about to eat focus your attention on calming down and use whatever techniques you find help you to de-stress (for tips on this see chapter 6).

✓ Give attention to what you are eating, notice the different smells, flavours and textures.

✓ Whenever possible, use meal times as a time to switch off.

Sounds simple, but you will notice a positive difference.

3. Stay hydrated

Although it's wise not drink too much during a meal; you need to stay hydrated as de-hydration is one of the most common causes of poor digestive function and constipation. Drink at least 1 to 2 litres of water spread evenly throughout the day. (See Chapter 2 for more information on keeping hydrated)

4. Feed your good bacteria with prebiotics

A prebiotic is a food that encourages the growth and activity of beneficial bacteria (probiotics). One type of prebiotic which has been extensively researched is a group called fructo-oligosaccharides shortened to FOS, which has been proven to be highly effective for beneficial bacteria. These are commonly found in foods such as bananas, onions, chicory root, garlic and asparagus. A convenient way to feed your healthy bacteria is via a FOS prebiotic supplement which will provide FOS in a concentrated dose. You can also buy supplements combining FOS and probiotics.

Other foods that can assist in the growth of good bacteria are those rich in fibre such as fresh fruit, vegetable, pulses (lentils, beans, chickpeas), seeds, chicory and Jerusalem artichokes.

Fermented foods are excellent at promoting growth of beneficial bacteria. They also help your body get rid of toxins and pollutants such as heavy metals and pesticides. As they have already been partly broken down by bacteria they have the added benefit of being easier to digest.

The following are examples of healthy fermented foods. In addition to their capacity to support the digestive system their other health benefits are outlined below:

- ✓ **Sauerkraut** - Made from fermented cabbage, it's high in dietary fibre and vitamins including A, the B vitamins, C and K. It's a great source of minerals such as calcium, copper, iron, magnesium, manganese and sodium. It also can aid circulation, fight inflammation, strengthen bones and reduce cholesterol levels.

- ✓ **Pickles** – These contain high levels of vitamins and minerals, plus antioxidants and beneficial bacteria. They are a great source of vitamin K that is important for bone and heart health and which many people are deficient in.

- ✓ **Kefir** - The word kefir means 'feel good' in Turkish. It is like a thin yoghurt drink and is made from either fermented cow's, goat's or sheep's milk. It has high levels of biotin, vitamin B12, calcium, folate, enzymes, vitamin K2, magnesium and billions of gut friendly probiotic bacteria. It can help with allergies, boost immunity, help heal IBS, increase bone density as well as kill candida.

  You can buy kits to make your own kefir which greatly reduces the cost. I make my own by buying freeze dried kefir starter cultures which contain individual sachets. Each sachet makes 1 litre. It can be made using cow's, goat's, sheep's milk or alternatives such as rice or almond milk. I use rice milk which I find makes delicious kefir.

- ✓ **Tempeh** - This is a soybean product that is cake-like in consistency. Tempeh helps control cholesterol levels, can improve bone density, reduces menopausal symptoms, promotes muscle recovery and has the same protein quality as meat. It contains high levels of vitamins B2, B3, B5 and B6.

- ✓ **Miso** - Miso comes as a paste and can be added to flavour savoury foods. It is made by combining a fungus called koji with fermented barley, brown rice or soya beans. It boosts the immune system, lowers the risk of cancer, improves bone health, promotes a healthy nervous system, helps to maintain healthy skin and even has anti-ageing properties.

- ✓ **Natto** - Consists of fermented soybeans. It contains the extremely powerful probiotic bacillus subtilis, which may help to support the immune system and cardiovascular health; it also enhances the digestion of vitamin K2 and contains a powerful anti-inflammatory enzyme called Nattokinase, which is useful for reducing the inflammatory effects of eating meat. However, it resembles stringy frogs spawn so not the most appealing food to look at. The enzyme Nattokinase is available as a supplement (it may also be marketed as Nattozymes)

✓ **Yoghurt -** Yogurt is perhaps one of the best known and most commonly consumed fermented foods. It's high in calcium, a good source of protein and is one of the top probiotic foods. Buy organic, from grass fed animals if possible and try sheep or goat's yoghurt as an alternative to cow's.

✓ **Olives -** Olives are a great fermented food and one of the most nutrient-dense fruits around. Although they are mostly fat, the fat is a healthy monounsaturated kind which translates into benefits to the heart and brain.

✓ **Kombucha** – A fermented drink which can not only help increase the number of healthy bacteria in your gut but also assists in weight loss, supports the immune system and reduces inflammation.

To get the best results, try to combine as many of these foods in your diet as possible.

5. Eat plenty of enzyme rich whole foods

Enzymes are substances that are vital to digestion and are produced by specialist cells in your body. They initiate the breakdown of macronutrients such as proteins, carbohydrates and fats so that they can be absorbed. As we get older our capacity to create these enzymes can diminish so it is worthwhile choosing foods that include these enzymes. Foods that are high in enzymes include:

✓ Papaya, pineapple, mango, kiwi, and grapes

✓ Avocado

✓ Raw honey

- ✓ Bee pollen
- ✓ Extra virgin olive oil and coconut oil
- ✓ Raw dairy
- ✓ Fermented Foods (see previous section)
- ✓ Raw vegetables
- ✓ Sprouting seeds and legumes

6. Eat fruit, especially soft fruits away from main meals (see section on food combining in chapter 5)

Although fruit is a great part of a healthy diet, eating it with a main meal can cause problems with digestion and adversely affect the conditions in your intestines. It is therefore best to eat fruit away from main meals as a snack.

7. Include good levels of fibre in your diet (see also chapter 5)

This will seem blindingly obvious advice to some, but it is still remarkable, despite it being one of the most common health tips, how many of us still do not achieve our daily quota of fibre. When fibre is in the digestive tract it absorbs water and swells which has a number of positive effects.

It helps your food matter travel through your digestive system, especially the colon where it keeps stools soft and bulked so that they travel through your large intestine smoothly. This decreases the amount of time faeces spend in the colon preventing constipation and the development of disease conditions such as diverticulitis and bowel cancer that can be caused by long term constipation. Fibre also helps give you a feeling of being full and helps curb your appetite.

Eating a whole food diet should naturally give you all the fibre you require. Fruit and vegetables, particularly vegetables, have great fibre and water content. Be aware that foods containing no fibre such as meat, eggs and cheese can slow intestinal transit time if eaten on their own, so reduce the proportion of these in your meals in favour of fibrous vegetables or make sure that you always include fibrous foods in these meals. Replace wheat, whenever possible, with ancient grains such as spelt, amaranth and kamut.

(See section on fibre in chapter 5)

8. Use ginger daily

Ginger has many beneficial properties which can help to improve the condition and function of the digestive system.

☺ It has an anti-inflammatory effect

☺ It is soothing to the digestive tract

☺ It can help relieve indigestion.

☺ It has been shown to reduce flatulence

☺ It is very effective at alleviating nausea

☺ Stimulates gastric contractions and gastric emptying improving movement of food and waste through the digestive tract.

The root can be used in cooking or as an ingredient in a juice. I personally like to pop a few slices of fresh ginger root into boiling water and leave it to infuse for about 10 minutes, which incidentally, is very effective on a sore throat.

9. Drink Peppermint tea everyday

Peppermint can calm and help to alleviate cramps and spasms in the intestine.

10. Eat garlic regularly (everyday if possible)

Garlic has anti-fungal properties and can help get rid of fungal overgrowths in the colon or small intestine. It is also effective against yeast overgrowths such as Candida Albicans.

11. Check your faeces and your transit time

Check your faeces

I have had some strange looks from clients over the years when I have told them to check their stools. It sounds rather disgusting but checking your stool tells you a lot about the condition of your digestive system. The ideal healthy stools should be light brown in colour, be soft and the shape of a banana or it may have cracks in the surface.

If they are hard to pass, lumpy and look like small pieces pressed together or small balls, it is an indication of constipation.

If they are too loose and it frequently looks like a cow has used your toilet, then food may be travelling through too fast. This could be due to your body having a reaction to a specific food and getting rid of it as soon as possible or you may have picked up a stomach bug. It could also be caused by stress.

With respect to the ideal shape of faeces, The Bristol Stool Chart was developed at a hospital in Bristol England as a diagnostic and research tool. It classifies faeces into 7 groups and gives a picture, short description and says what each type of faeces tells you about your digestive system. The Bristol Stool Chart is easily accessible on-line and a useful resource.

You should also check for blood in stools. Bright red blood is an indication that it comes from the rectum or anus and may be from haemorrhoids. Darker blood is likely to have come from further up in the digestive tract. Either way, if you find blood in your stools, especially darker blood it is worth seeking medical advice. Foul smelling stools are an indication of dysbiosis in your colon which needs to be remedied by following the advice in this chapter.

The simple message is, keep an eye on what comes out!

Check your intestinal transit time

Transit time is very important because you want food to stay in the digestive system long enough so that you can extract the maximum amount of nutrients from it. But if it stays there too long it has an adverse effect on health.

The optimal time for food to pass from one end of the digestive system to the other will vary according form person to person as we are all unique and the way that we react to factors in our environment is unique as well.

There are a number of factors that affect transit time:

- Age
- Gender
- Levels of stress (can speed up transit time of slow it down depending on the individual)
- The amount of exercise you do
- Types of foods you are eating
- Hydration (makes up about 75% of faeces)
- Diabetes have slower transit times
- An under active thyroid can also slow transit time
- Regularly suppressing the urge to go can result in your bowel adapting to holding stools for longer than it should

When a healthy bowel is working well, total transit time should be approximately 12 to 48 hours.

You can easily check your bowel transit time by eating two of three beetroots which will turn stools a deep red colour. By noting the number of hours in between you can get a good idea of transit time. But make sure that you check whether more than one bowel movement is deep red. The first could be in a healthy 18 hours but if the second appears after 48 hours your bowels could be sluggish. If you can't stand beetroot, you can do the same with sweetcorn (which seems to be pretty much indestructible to the digestive process).

☹ Less than 12 hours means you are unlikely to be absorbing your nutrients properly.

☹ More than 48 hours indicates that waste is sitting inside your colon too long.

Your large intestines (colon) are where waste collects after the main nutrient absorption has taken place in the small intestine. Water is extracted from this waste and various minerals such as potassium and sodium are either re-absorbed or secreted into the colon depending on the body's need for them. Vitamin K is also manufactured here and absorbed into the body. The remaining matter is then excreted from the body.

A poor transit time greatly increases the risk of inflammation and damage to the mucosal lining of the gut and serious diseases of the colon. Substances that are supposed to be excreted are absorbed back into the blood stream and can put your liver under stress. Follow the advice given in this chapter and chapter 5 to help prevent this.

NOTE: It is important to pass all the waste from your body; no point in having a great transit time if you can't get rid of it all properly! However, if you sit on the toilet in the traditional way this can be difficult.

The problem is that there is a muscle called the puborectalis which effectively lassos the rectum and effectively chokes it so that we can remain continent. So, when we sit in the normal position on the toilet we are not in a full squat, which means that this muscle does not completely release the anal canal, preventing or making it very hard to pass all waste.

By raising your legs up with a stool or box, simulating the squat position, the puborectalis completely releases and allows the anal canal to fully open, happy days! Check out **squattypotty.com** for more information.

Finally, the advice in this section is intended to give you a general feel of what you should be aiming for. However, everyone is different, and no one is perfect. We all fall outside the ideal for faeces or transit time sometimes but as long as you follow the advice in this book you should achieve it most of the time. However, if you are in any doubt about the health of your digestive system always consult a health professional.

12. Exercise

Regular daily structured exercise or physical activity helps prevent constipation through indirect muscular massage and movement. It also increases blood flow and circulation and consequently, your colon (and entire gastrointestinal system) gets more oxygen helping to keep evacuations regular.

SECTION 2: 7 key things to avoid

1. Try not to drink too much when eating

It is fine to have a drink during a meal, in fact it can help soften the food, but it is better to sip the drink during the meal rather than drink large quantities at once (such as whole glasses of water). We tend to like to do this to "wash our food down" but too much liquid can disrupt the function of the stomach.

Once you have chewed your food properly and swallowed it, your stomach churns it up (it does this by rhythmically squeezing the food as it is essentially a muscular bag, the body's blender if you like) to prepare it for entry into your small intestine where further digestion and most of the absorption into your body takes place.

The stomach is also where the protein in your meal is broken down by enzymes which rely on concentrated hydrochloric acid produced by millions of cells in the stomach lining. If you drink too much (e.g. several pints of fluid) during the meal this tends to dilute the hydrochloric acid which leads to incomplete protein digestion.

TIPs:

✓ Try not to drink glasses of water less than ½ hour before a meal.

✓ It is okay to sip water during a meal.

✓ Putting a squeeze of lemon or apple cider vinegar in the water can help in the digestive process.

✓ Sip water at room temperature. Avoid drinking cold water during a meal, especially iced, as it can interfere with digestion.

✓ After your meal, try not to consume too much water for at least 1 to 2 hours.

2. Avoid/cut down on foods that irritate and damage the gut lining

Certain foods create conditions that can cause inflammation and possible damage to the lining of the gut. They do this by causing dysbiosis which allows toxic by-products of digestion to build up in the gut and tips the balance away from friendly beneficial bacteria in favour of pathogenic bacteria.

The most common culprits that can irritate and damage the gut lining are:

☹ Wheat and any processed products that contain it, for example pizza, pasta, pastry, cereals, soups (carefully check the labels).

☹ Any modern grain that has been refined into a processed product such as commercial cereals

☹ Processed foods in general as they tend to be high in sugar and other chemicals such as preservatives.

☹ Caffeinated drinks

☹ Sugary drinks

☹ Alcoholic drinks

☹ Refined dairy products

Even if you can tolerate these foods it is best to at least reduce the frequency you eat them to, ideally, occasional treats.

3. Avoid frying or burning your food

Although fried food may taste good, it creates harmful by-products in the food. These are called oxidants and can cause inflammation and create conditions that damage the digestive tract.

4. Avoid or limit use of painkillers and antibiotics whenever possible

Unfortunately, our society has become reliant on pharmaceutical drugs as a quick fix to anything that gets in the way of us getting on with our lives. Two of the most popular are antibiotics and over counter painkillers. Painkillers can cause ulceration to the digestive tract and antibiotics decimate friendly intestinal bowel flora which leads to dysbiosis. Both types of drug also put a strain on the liver which plays a pivotal role in the digestive process.

5. Avoid or limit your alcohol intake

Many of us like a drink, perhaps to celebrate with friends or simply to relax and I am certainly one of them. However, as I'm sure you're aware, excessive alcohol intake puts a strain on liver function which in turn adversely affects digestion. It can also damage the gut lining and has been linked to diseases of the intestinal tract and stomach cancer.

As with anything in life it's about balance – so avoid binge drinking as this puts excessive pressure on the liver, and if alcohol is a daily habit then perhaps consider having alcohol free days.

6. Try to limit your intake of red meat and dairy produce

Too much meat and dairy produce can be pro inflammatory and puts a strain on your digestive system. Many of us really enjoy eating meat and dairy and it's really challenging to give them up completely.

As ever, balance is key and over doing it can be detrimental to your long-term health. So at least try to restrict your intake to a treat once or twice a week, preferably organic.

7. Cut down on foods that may be hard to digest

There are foods that may give you symptoms such as indigestion, heartburn or bloating. Cutting down and eliminating common allergens such as dairy and wheat can help to prevent this. Lentils, beans and soya products are often heralded as healthy choices. Whilst rinsing them first and cooking them thoroughly will make them much more digestible, some people find they simply don't suit their digestive system.

We are all different so it's worthwhile tuning into your body and spotting subtle differences. For example, whenever you feel bloated, jot down the foods you've been eating. You will probably notice a pattern over time which can help to pinpoint foods that don't agree with you. It's amazing what our body can tell us if we take the time to listen and if you find it difficult to identify potential culprits then you may wish to test for food intolerances.

SECTION 3: 4 digestive supplements

1. Digestive enzymes

If you suffer from symptoms such as constipation, bloating, cramps, flatulence, belching and heartburn (acid reflux) you may be lacking certain digestive enzymes which enable foods to be broken down and you can test this by taking a digestive enzyme supplement with your meal. If this eliminates the symptoms then a lack of enzymes is the cause.

Good supplements have all the digestive enzymes you need and you can take them for a month as a digestive tune up or after eliminating a food allergy if you wish to re-introduce the food on a limited basis.

2. Take a probiotic supplement everyday

Taking a good quality mixed strain (multiple bacteria) probiotic supplement every day will help to make sure you have healthy amounts of good bacteria in your gut.

3. Take glutamine daily

In the section "How can I heal a leaky gut?" I mentioned the invaluable role glutamine plays in the health our digestive system. To protect our intestines and maintain the efficiency of our digestive system I would thoroughly recommend taking glutamine every day. If you want to nurture your digestive system and give it a kick start for a month, it may be useful to choose a product that combines glutamine with probiotics and digestive enzymes.

4. Take aloe vera juice daily

Aloe Vera juice has many health benefits and is very beneficial to the digestive system. Taking Aloe Vera juice daily has been shown to improve the production of digestive enzymes, help relieve constipation, improve the population of healthy bacteria in the gut, inhibit excess stomach acidity (which is commonly treated with antacids) and help heal damage to the lining of the gut. It has been found that taking Aloe Vera everyday improves the conditions throughout the digestive tract and can be regarded as a very effective tonic for the whole digestive system.

This is one of my favourite supplements and I take it daily. I was introduced to it by biochemist and naturopath Dr Lawrence Plaskett who designed and taught the nutrition course that I studied. He was a keen advocate of the health benefits of Aloe Vera and was a health industry expert on it, publishing numerous research papers.

To ensure that you get premium quality juice you should check that the product is endorsed on the pack by the Health Food Manufacturers Association (HFMA) in the UK and the International Aloe Science Council in the USA.

A FINAL THOUGHT

I hope in reading this chapter you have a feel of how important it is to look after your digestive system. Our health is unquestionably dependent on how efficiently we digest our food and the root cause of most diseases can be traced back to a damaged and/or toxic digestive system.

It is absolutely remarkable and looked after properly it plays a huge role in your ability to live a long, healthy and disease-free life. Get it right and it will improve every part of your body as well as your energy level, state of mind and longevity. Putting a little effort into looking after it (showing it some love and TLC) is one of the best investments in your health that you will ever make.

Chapter 3 Review & Ideas For Your Action Plan

How is my digestion?

Review the tick list exercise at the beginning of this chapter. Which boxes did you tick? Collate any symptoms you have that you want to heal:

Twelve Digestion Friendly Habits

Which of the following would you benefit from trying or focusing on?

❐ 1. Chew my food thoroughly

❐ 2. Relax more when eating

❐ 3. Stay hydrated

❐ 4. Take prebiotics and/or eat more foods that promote good bacteria

❐ 5. Eat more enzyme rich foods

❐ 6. Eat fruit away from meals

❐ 7. Eat a fibre rich diet

❐ 8. Use ginger daily

❐ 9. Drink Peppermint tea everyday

❐ 10. Eat garlic regularly

❐ 11. Check faeces and intestinal transit time

❐ 12. Exercise

Seven Things to Avoid or Limit

Which of the following would you benefit from addressing?

❒ 1. Drinking too much with meals

❒ 2. Foods that irritate the gut lining

❒ 3. Frying or burning food

❒ 4. Painkillers and antibiotics

❒ 5. Alcohol intake

❒ 6. Red meat and dairy produce

❒ 7. Foods difficult to digest

Four digestion supplements to consider

(See Useful Websites for suppliers)

❒ Digestive enzymes

❒ Probiotics

❒ Glutamine

❒ Aloe Vera juice

Action Points **Date:**____________ **Review Date:** ____________

Chapter 4

Exercise – Unlock the Amazing Potential of Your Body

Why exercise?

"Form follows function. If you sit like a slug – You grow like a slug"

Michael Colgan – Sports Lecture Series, 2002

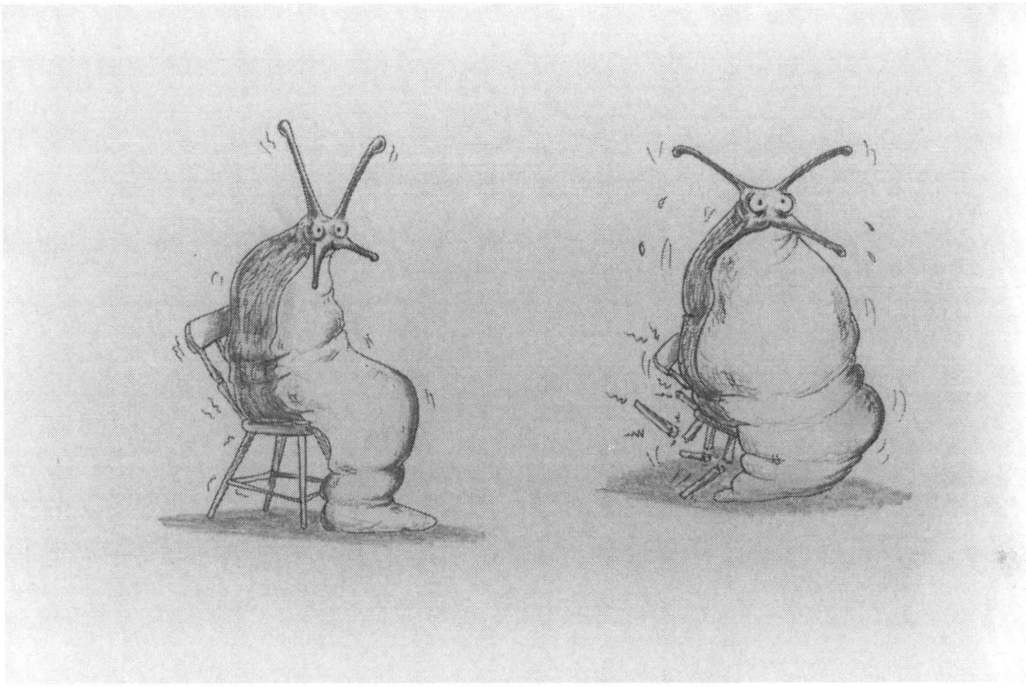

We all know that we should exercise, but I think that it is important to consider why, in modern society, it is more important than ever.

The human body has evolved over millennia to be active because we needed to be able to find our food, protect ourselves, reproduce, find shelter etc.; all the basics required to enable our species to survive. Since the industrial revolution our lives have continued to be transformed by new labour-saving devices. Whilst this has provided us with a great deal of freedom, it has also meant that for many of us our daily lives do not incorporate the amount and correct type of physical activity that is required for our bodies to function well.

Our bodies are adaptive organisms, changing according to their physical environment. This is great if we exercise regularly and are physically active but unfortunately it also works the other way. Obviously, our bodies don't respond well to prolonged inactivity and if you have a sedentary job and do little or no regular exercise, your body will inevitably start to degenerate over time:

☹ Muscles will shorten

☹ Flexibility will be lost

☹ Cardiovascular fitness will decline

☹ You may well put on weight

☹ Physical strength and endurance will decline.

☹ Mental health may also suffer as lack of exercise can often result in us being less able to deal with stress.

Essentially, you will age faster and be more prone to developing a host of degenerative diseases.

Inspired by a 66 year old

We all meet people in our lives who inspire us and whilst I have admired many people over the years. One man stands out when it comes to exercise; his name is Dr Michael Colgan. I first became aware of his work whilst studying nutrition and reading his books on sports nutrition. Dr Colgan is an internationally acclaimed research scientist, author and lecturer who advised on nutrition and training to everyone from amateurs to world champions in numerous sports.

In 2004 and 2005 I had the opportunity to go to Canada and train with Dr Colgan to become one of his Certified Trainers. Together with lectures we were taught an exercise program that he had developed to improve the muscular speed and strength of athletes, but which could be applied to anyone. I can remember practising and struggling to perform a particular exercise and Dr Colgan calmly walked over and demonstrated the exercise to me. He made it look so easy, which was even more remarkable as he was 66 at the time and I was 42!

So here was this guy, at an age where many would expect him to be in physical decline and having to take it easy, kicking my butt (an operational fire-fighter, who considered himself to be pretty fit) and performing strength exercises that most people 40 years younger than him would have trouble doing. It was this amazing personal demonstration that really excited me. I too wanted this level of fitness and to be able to maintain it as I got older as he had done.

In a nutshell, this is the crux of what he taught - if you look after yourself and exercise correctly by mimicking natural movement you can achieve the most amazing fitness and maintain it into old age. This could be achieved simply by following very basic principles, working with nature, not against it.

A major part of his philosophy was that we greatly underestimate what the human body is capable of and that we need to ignore the negative messages we are surrounded by in western society about the perils of ageing.

He believed in the concept of synergy, enhancing health by focusing on each area of your fitness and lifestyle to achieve optimum fitness. He taught that if you optimised your nutrition, exercised and nurtured yourself, then you could unlock the amazing physical potential of your body. It proved to me what was possible and inspired me to want to master his exercise program and pass this inspiration on so that others could see what was possible and reap the benefits.

Exercise and My Five Health and Fitness Principles

In the years since completing Dr Colgan's course I have built on the philosophy he taught. Together with the invaluable experience I have gained in helping people with their fitness, I was able to develop five principles which have evolved and can be applied to all areas of health and fitness. As mentioned in the introductory chapter these principles form the underlying philosophy of this book.

As far as exercise is concerned, I have been using and teaching these principles since 2005. They have enabled me to transform my own fitness and help others to transform theirs. For me, there is nothing more rewarding than to help people recognise their own potential, no matter what their age, and then achieve results they never thought possible.

Principle 1: Don't underestimate what your body is capable of

Principle 2: Synergy & Balance

Principle 3: Do what you love .....consistently

Principle 4: Listen to your body – be in tune with it

Principle 5: Less is more – smart training

In this chapter we will be looking at how each of these principles can be applied so that you have the **best** opportunity to reach and maintain your optimal level of fitness.

I will talk about the specific training techniques that I favour, how to use them and how they can be incorporated into new or existing fitness regimes to enhance your results and overcome those inevitable plateaus. So, for example, if you love cycling you may want to consider using techniques such as High Intensity Interval Training (HIIT) to take your performance to the next level, whether you cycle for fun or competitively. It's amazing how much more enjoyable those steeper hills will feel integrating HIIT into your fitness programme!

We will also look at the pros and cons of common forms of exercise to help you decide what would be best for you in terms of enjoyment and results whether you are new to exercise, returning to it after a break or looking for new options to add some variety to your fitness.

Principle 1: Don't underestimate what your body is capable of

The negative messages that surround us in Western society with respect to the level of fitness we can expect as we age are pretty depressing. Declining physical abilities are expected to include muscle wasting (sarcopenia), declining strength, reduced co-ordination, slower reflexes, poor balance; the list goes on!

I have lost count of the amount of times that I have heard people talk about members of their family or friends who are struggling with some physical problem which is considered to be par for the course for everyone as you get older. Phrases such as "that'll be me in 20 years" or "that's what we've all got to look forward to" are all too common and I expect you have heard something like it at some time or other. You may have even thought it or said it yourself!

The examples given in chapter one however, demonstrate what can be achieved as we get older. These individuals, for many, are exceptions to the rule, the lucky ones. But what they actually show is that most of the time it is our mind-set that holds us back. These people are not super human; the only difference between them and the majority of us is that they believe that they can sustain great levels of fitness as they get older and consistently apply the principles required to do it.

As I'm sure you're aware by now I am passionate about changing the negative message instilled into society that you might as well resign yourself to greatly reduced physical abilities. Be aware of your own mind-set and what you're aiming to achieve. Are there any limiting beliefs that could be holding you back? For example, "I've never been sporty", "I can't expect to be as flexible as I used to be". By believing in what your body is capable of and applying the principles, tips and techniques throughout this book get ready to be amazed at what you can achieve. Those people in the first chapter should be the norm not the exception!

Principle 2: Synergy & Balance

A balanced approach is absolutely vital when it comes to exercise. The cumulative benefits of a properly balanced regime with exercises that complement each other will enable you to attain truly astounding levels of fitness and maintain them for life!

An example of an unbalanced exercise regime can be seen in individuals who weight train in gyms for purely aesthetic purposes, to achieve a certain look. They are interested in looking good, nothing wrong with that, but they are only interested in exercising the so-called mirror muscles, (arms, shoulders, chest, 'six-pack' abdominals), not using a properly balanced program, to the detriment of other muscles. This can lead to:

- ☹ imbalances between opposing muscles or muscle groups
- ☹ unbalanced development of the muscular skeletal system
- ☹ restrictions in the range of movement
- ☹ problems with posture
- ☹ injury by putting uneven loading across joints

I don't think that any single form of exercise will provide you with all of the different components required to give you a balanced regime, it's important to combine several different exercise routines to cover all bases. It comes back to synergy again, using combinations that will give you greater results than just relying on one form of exercise. There are numerous ways of achieving this all-important balance. It will also stop you getting bored as variety makes things more interesting. If you want some ideas of different types of exercise to combine there is a list of popular activities included in **Principle 3: Do what you love ....consistently**. **Benefits of a Balanced Approach**

The good news is that generic benefits of a well-balanced exercise routine include:

☺ Improved cardiovascular health and reduced chance of heart disease.

☺ Improved muscular strength and endurance.

☺ Improved flexibility and posture with less chance of injuries or suffering from postural problems such as a bad back.

☺ Improved motor skills (balance, co-ordination, speed, reaction time, power and agility)

☺ Greater resistance to degenerative diseases, especially in later life, such as osteoarthritis, cancer and diabetes.

☺ A slowing down of the ageing process so that you build more robust health and remain active for longer.

☺ Improved circulation which results in a more efficient vascular system and reduces problems such as cramp.

☺ Better control of weight and all the health benefits that this brings such as less wear and tear on joints and diseases associated with being over-weight (e.g. cardiovascular disease, diabetes)

☺ More energy and a feeling of vitality.

☺ A more positive outlook on life as a result of feeling good

☺ Improved stress tolerance.

☺ Potentially more healthy years on this planet!

Motor Fitness Enhanced by Synergy and Balance

I think that this is an interesting example of synergy at work. Improvements in motor fitness is one of the best but widely unrecognised benefits of a balanced exercise regime.

It refers to your motor neurones which are nerve cells that transmit impulses from the nervous system to glandular and muscle tissue to stimulate activity (e.g. contraction of skeletal muscle tissue). Improving the efficiency of these nerve cells through regular structured exercise will give you the following benefits:

☺ Increased agility

☺ Improved balance

☺ Better co-ordination

☺ More muscular power

☺ Better speed of movement

☺ Improved reaction time

Better motor fitness is a positive boon for everyone, it does not matter what your age is, whether you are inherently sporty or not, whether you play sports or not; having these improvements will enrich your enjoyment of life.

This is especially true as we get older, when the traditional western view is that our performance in these areas will inevitably decline. Whilst we have to accept some reduction in these physical abilities, we can maintain them at levels not thought possible by many in society as per the examples in chapter one.

Building Blocks of a Balanced Approach to Exercise

As I'm sure you're aware, to get the best results you need to incorporate 3 main types of exercise.

1. Cardiovascular (CV) – CV training works by raising the heart rate to levels which cause beneficial metabolic and physiological changes to your heart, vascular system, lungs and muscle cells.

2. Resistance – This type of training incorporates exercises to improve your muscular strength and endurance. If performed in a certain way it can also provide good CV benefits.

3. Flexibility – This is often overlooked yet is an essential part of an effective exercise programme. Cardiovascular and resistance training will not be as effective without working on your flexibility.

Let's look at each of these in turn:

1. CARDIOVASCULAR (CV)

The benefits of regular cardiovascular exercise include:

☺ Improved circulation and blood flow from a stronger and more efficient cardiovascular and pulmonary system, boosting oxygenation of the tissues in your body.

☺ Helping to normalise blood sugar, insulin and leptin levels through enhanced insulin and leptin (a hormone that helps control hunger) receptor sensitivity.

☺ Keeping blood pressure at optimal levels and helping to prevent hypertension as we get older.

☺ Helping to regulate optimal levels of good types of cholesterol and reduce the levels of bad type (see chapter 5).

☺ Reducing the risk of suffering from cardiovascular disease/conditions.

☺ Helping to control weight and increase the amount of lean body tissue.

☺ It can help to improve cognitive function, and neurotransmitter production, which helps lift your mood.

There are two ways to achieve CV fitness.

1. Steady State CV Training or Aerobic Training

This is the traditional way to develop cardiovascular fitness. In this method, you choose some form of aerobic exercise such as running and you perform that activity for a set period of time, say 30 minutes, keeping your heart rate raised to approximately 80% of your maximum theoretical heart rate (220 – your age). Performing this type of exercise 4 or 5 times a week will give you good benefits and if you have an activity that you love doing, such as cycling it's seemingly a win- win solution.

2. High Intensity Interval Training (HIIT)

I've found HIIT training can give equal benefits to steady state and in some circumstances, better results and it takes far less time than steady state training. It's therefore great for people with very busy lives and limited time available to assign to exercise. I would highly recommend that you give it a go. I cover HIIT in more detail and further benefits specific to HIIT in **Principle 5: Less is More – Smart Training**.

2. RESISTANCE

The benefits of regular resistance exercise include:

☺ Improved muscle strength and tone.

☺ Helping to protect your joints from injury

☺ Improved circulation

☺ Weight management – resistance exercise is one of the most effective ways to control your weight.

☺ Improved stamina – as you grow stronger you can continue physical activity for longer without fatigue.

☺ Prevention or control of chronic conditions such as diabetes, heart disease, arthritis, back pain, depression and obesity

☺ Helps to improve posture

☺ Decreased risk of muscular injury

☺ Increased bone density and strength help to reduce risk of osteoporosis

☺ An improved sense of wellbeing – resistance training can boost your self-esteem, improve your body image and your mood

☺ Enhanced performance of everyday tasks thereby helping you to remain independent as you get older.

☺ Better quality sleep (this is just from personal experience – I always have my best night's sleep on days I do my resistance training!)

Balanced Approach to Resistance Training:

- Muscular Endurance
- Muscular Strength
- Core Training

<u>Muscular endurance</u> – This is the ability of a muscle or group of muscles to carry out a physical task repeatedly without becoming fatigued. Examples of this would be the ability to easily cycle 20 miles or carrying a heavy load for a distance without having to stop and put it down.

CV activities such as swimming, cycling and running do help to develop muscular endurance, but to get the best results, you need to include regular resistance training.

<u>Muscular strength</u> – This is the ability of a muscle or group of muscles to apply maximum force for a single movement. Examples of this range from lifting a heavy object to unscrewing the lid of a jar!

There is some cross over benefit between training for muscular strength and muscular endurance. So, if you were only to train for muscular endurance, you would experience some degree of increase in muscular strength and vice- versa. However, this benefit is not sufficient to get the best combination of strength and endurance; to achieve that you must include varied types of resistance training in your fitness regime.

Now, at this point, if you are reading this and thinking, that you don't do sport and are not someone who would need more strength and endurance in your everyday life, think again. Everyone needs good muscular strength and endurance; it makes every day physical activities easier and helps to slow down and even retard the decline in physical abilities as we get older.

This does not mean that you have to go into a gym and push weights if you don't want to; you can obtain the benefits of resistance exercise from a number of different types of exercise. There are numerous classes which use resistance exercises from beginners to advanced. If you don't fancy a resistance class, then you could try Yoga, Pilates or Calisthenics. All of these are excellent forms of exercise that will help to increase your strength and endurance.

Resistance training can also have a CV training effect without the use of CV exercises. One example of how you can achieve this is instead of using a CV exercise such as cycling or rowing to achieve your desired training effect you use a combination of resistance exercises done in quick succession.

This puts a demand on your CV system to shunt blood quickly to different muscle groups (e.g. from an upper body exercise such as a pull up to a lower body exercise such as a squat). Alternating between upper and lower body exercises is one way to provide a very effective CV workout.

Another type of resistance workout that is becoming increasingly popular owing to the impressive benefits that it provides (including amazing CV benefits) is High Intensity Resistance Training (giving the ironic acronym HIRT). This is also known as High Intensity Strength Training (HIST) or Super Slow. I cover this form of exercise in **Principle 5: Less is More – Smart Training** and would highly recommend you incorporate it into your fitness regime.

CORE TRAINING

Core training is an essential part of resistance training and involves strengthening muscles in your spine, abdomen and pelvic floor. There are 29 altogether and they encase your abdomen, back and pelvis, making your whole body more efficient at movement. This is because your core muscles provide a link between your upper and lower body.

If these muscles are weak as is the case in a lot of people you are more susceptible to back injuries and general degeneration (especially the lower back). All the time that the link between your upper and lower body is weak it is impossible to develop your full athletic potential in muscular power and movement.

"

Without a strong and balanced core, powerful, co-ordinated movement cannot occur" Michael Colgan – Colgan Institute, 2004

Any good instructor should incorporate core training in your fitness regime. This is usually done as part of your resistance training. Yoga and Pilates are also excellent ways to develop your core strength.

Advantages of having a strong core include:

☺ Improved posture

Many of the muscles of the core are directly involved in maintaining a good posture. A good posture will help prevent injuries and premature degeneration of the spine.

☺ Protection for the lumber vertebrae

One of the core muscles is called the transverse abdominus which, when properly strengthened, plays a major role in enhancing the stability of the lower back (lumber). The lumber region of your spine takes the greatest loads so is the most susceptible to wear and injury. A strong transverse abdominus acts rather like a muscular corset, helping to protect you lower back.

☺ Enhanced athletic ability

Having a strong core allows you to move your body as one, movements are co-ordinated and fluid; effectively transferring power from your lower body to your upper body or vice versa. This means that you maximise your muscle power and athletic performance.

☺ Enhanced stability

A strong core makes your whole body more stable, thus improving movement, balance and agility.

☺ Increased ability in everyday actions

As well as being better at exercise and sport, a strong core gives you increased abilities in everyday actions such as lifting heavy objects.

A Useful Technique to Improve your Core Strength

When doing any skeletal muscle exercise or when I need to do heavy manual work, I always use a technique known as locking your core. This not only helps to stabilise your body and protect your lower back but also serves to strengthen the core muscles at the same time.

This technique can also be used in isolation pretty much anywhere and will help to develop and strength your core musculature. So, you can perform this technique for example, whilst at your desk, sitting in the car or waiting in the queue at the supermarket; it can literally be done anywhere, and no one knows you are doing it.

<u>How to lock your core</u>

To lock your core, you need to contract certain muscles and hold them for the duration of the concentric phase of a resistance exercise (the muscular contraction phase). You then breathe out slowly during the eccentric phase. This is how it is done:

1. Pull your stomach muscles back towards your spine as much as you can. This is everything from the base of your ribs to your groin. This will activate the deepest core muscle called the transverse abdominus. This is a flat sheet of muscle that runs across the front of your abdominal cavity, passes around your sides and fuses into the tissue each side of the lower spine.

   It acts as a natural weight belt or muscular corset, compressing the abdomen, stabilising the core from your diaphragm to your pelvis. When it is strong, it also helps to support your lower back when physical loads pass through your body (such as when lifting a heavy object) and, also helps to prevent it from injury

2. With the transverse abdominus contracted, next you need to perform what is known as a Kegel exercise. This is an exercise where you strengthen the pelvic floor muscles. These form a muscular hammock that supports the organs of the abdominal cavity and prevents them from dropping through the pelvis.

   These pelvic floor muscles need to be strong as they are part of the musculature that stabilises the abdominal cavity from the bottom. You activate these muscles by pulling up on your pelvic floor. The easiest way to describe this technique is that it is the same movement that you do when you desperately need to use the toilet and are stopping yourself from going until you get there.

3. So now that you are performing the movements from 1 and 2 there is one last thing that you need to do. You need to stabilise the core from the top. To do this, you need to activate the diaphragm (the sheet of muscle that separates your abdominal cavity from your chest cavity and that is attached to the base of your lungs) this is used when you breath in, so to activate it we simply breath in and fill our lungs approximately ⅓.

Once you have initiated all the above steps, your core is now locked. You can now use this technique to improve core strength on its own (by locking your core and holding that position for as long as you can, releasing then repeating) or when you are doing resistance exercises. One point that should be clarified is that although you have filled your lungs by approximately 1/3 you do not hold your breath, you simply maintain this air in your lungs by shallow breathing for the duration of the time that the core is locked.

Note: If you suffer from Hypertension (high blood pressure), you should not do step 3. Also, you can lock your core when doing resistance exercises, except if you are going for maximal effort (e.g. a maximum effort dead lift). Then use only steps 1 and 2.

3. FLEXIBILITY

One of the best feelings in life is the ability to move freely, unencumbered by pain or restricted movements. Truly flowing, fluid movement is a wonderful sensation and one that we all want to have throughout our lives. It allows us to live life to the full and enjoy whatever physical activity we choose.

If, however, your flexibility is poor, you cannot reach your full physical/athletic potential. Even if you have great CV and resistance fitness programs, your ability to use your improved CV health and strength will be restricted and you will be more likely to be prone to injuries.

It's therefore important to make flexibility training an integral part of your exercise regime. It is often the most neglected part of training, owing to factors such as a lack of time, confusion of when to do it, or simply not appreciating its importance.

The benefits of regular stretching include:

☺ Increased range of motion (ROM)

Flexibility can be defined as the range of motion (ROM) of a given joint, that is, a joint's ability to allow the greatest angles (degrees) of movement relative to the body. We see incredible examples of this range of motion in ballerinas and anyone who can do the splits has amazing flexibility in their hips.

If your muscles and tendons (strong, fibrous connective tissue that attaches a muscle to a bone) are tight, they can cause a reduced ROM throughout your body. As well as constraining how effectively we exercise, lack of flexibility can affect everyday movements such as bending down or looking over our shoulders – lots of people suffer from tight necks these days.

Becoming more flexible can make these types of activities, and indeed, any form of exercise you choose to do, easier. It improves the range of motion throughout the body to help the body move more easily making movements more effortless.

☺ More power in your movements

By having a greater ROM, your muscles can transmit power more efficiently. If you take part in sport, this will improve your performance and make you more competitive and successful. It will also, improve your ability to do everyday tasks and help you to remain independent as you get older.

☺ Injury prevention

Muscles, tendons and deep fascia (a layer of dense fibrous connective tissue that surrounds individual muscles and divides groups of muscles into fascial compartments) can shorten over time through inactivity or exercise regimes that include limited flexibility exercises.

Tight muscles restrict your range of motion so it's easier to go beyond the restricted range and injure yourself. Improving your flexibility increases your ROM and thereby reduces the risk of an injury.

☺ Eliminating back pain caused by tight muscles

This is one of the most common health issues that can be directly related to inflexibility. Tight muscles in the back and lower body can pull your spine out of its optimal alignment and result in back pain.

However, it can be prevented by performing regular stretching to improve your flexibility. It can also, in many instances, eliminate chronic back pain caused by tight muscles without the need to resort to long term use of pain killers or even surgery.

☺ Improved circulation

Tension in the muscles affects circulation; when the muscles are more flexible, they relax and circulation improves. This improves oxygenation of tissue, helps to ensure a better supply of nutrients to muscles and joints and facilitates the removal of metabolic waste products such as carbon dioxide, ammonia and uric acid.

☺ Less stress and better posture

Flexibility can improve your posture because tight muscles can affect the alignment of your neck, spine, shoulders, hips and knees. Flexible muscles also have less tension, so it makes sense that you'll feel less stress than you would with a tight and tense body. This has been backed up by studies by the American Council on Exercise.

☺ Helping recovery from intense exercise

Stretching muscle tissue enables you to recover quicker after high intensity exercise helping to reduce post exercise soreness.

Seven Simple Stretching Tips

These tips will help you gain the maximum benefit from your sessions.

1. **Choose a warm environment, warm up and RELAX!** Always make sure that you are thoroughly warmed up so that your tissues can get the maximum benefit. A hot shower can be really useful to warm up though light physical activity provides extra advantages as it warms the muscles up through natural movement. A five minute walk or cycle ride can be a great way to get ready for stretching or doing some squats for one minute as this warms up the large muscle groups.

   A time efficient way to incorporate stretching into your day is to time your routine after day-to-day tasks such as hoovering, gardening or walking to the post box to send a letter. Make sure that the place that you have chosen to stretch is a comfortable temperature. This will help to relax you and make the session more effective.

2. **Stretch daily**. Stretching is very adaptable - a session can be done in as little as 5 to 10 minutes. It's therefore easy to fit into a busy schedule and can have a very calming effect after a hectic day. Try to stretch everyday if you can. The important thing is to establish a habit and routine.

   On days when you don't get chance to complete your stretching routine incorporate incidental stretches into your day-to-day tasks at your desk, while you wait for the kettle to boil or even in the supermarket queue!

3. **When to stretch.** As a rule of thumb, try to do most of your stretching away from other forms of exercise. I find a great time to do stretching exercises is after a warm bath before bed. Relaxing the muscles in this way enables you to stretch very effectively and is a great way to get a refreshing night's sleep.

   Many of us were trained to stretch before and after exercise. However recent research has shown that to achieve best results and to avoid injury we need to be aware of when it's best to stretch when exercising:

<u>Cardiovascular Exercise or HIIT</u>	Warm up first ***then stretch*** before exercising using the dynamic/ active stretching method described below.
<u>Resistance/Strength Training</u>	***Avoid stretching before***, as this can reduce stability and strength during the workout.

Avoid stretching immediately after any training as your muscles are tight and full of the metabolites of fatigue. Give it at least an hour before stretching.

4. **Breathing.** Use the deep breathing technique that is described in chapter 2 as this aids in muscle relaxation. When you perform a stretch, exhale as you go into the stretch position and inhale as you back off.

5. **Listen to your body.** With any form of exercise, you need to listen to your body and this is especially important with stretching; particularly if you are new to it. Work with your body, not against it.

   When we're keen to progress it's easy to go beyond what our bodies are ready for. Only stretch to the point of acceptable (comfortable) tension in the muscle and never bounce. Concentrate and monitor h

6. **Be consistent and patient.** It can take time to improve flexibility, particularly if muscles have been tight for a while. Be consistent and patient. It will be worth it when you experience the amazing benefits.

7. **Skeletal stretch programs**. Your stretching program should incorporate stretches that cover all of the skeletal muscles in the body. Stretching sessions can be divided up so that they fit into a busy schedule.

   So, instead of trying to do a comprehensive stretch of all muscle groups in one go you could divide stretching for the upper and lower body into two separate sessions. This helps to keep sessions shorter and makes it easier to maintain a comprehensive stretching program.

Dynamic/Active Stretching

There are numerous stretching techniques that you can use. One of my favourites is dynamic/active stretching, which involves holding the stretch for a maximum of 3 seconds.

In this example, we are going to stretch the quadriceps, which are the four large muscles at the front of the thigh:

1. Lie on the ground on your left side with you right hip directly over your left.
2. Bend your left leg to provide stability during the stretch and extend your left arm in line with your upper body so that you can rest your head on it.
3. Reach down and grab your right foot with your right hand.
4. Bring the right foot up towards your backside in a slow controlled manner until you can feel you can bring it back no further. Breathe out slowly as you stretch. You should feel a tightness in the muscle, but no pain. If the muscle that you are stretching is shaking, ease off a little until it stops.

5. When you have pulled the leg back as far as you can, hold the stretch for 2 seconds whilst continuing to breathe out.

6. When you release, fully straighten the leg to return it to the start position. This needs to be done for each repetition and applies to any stretch that you do. Breathe in slowly at the same time; this helps blood flow which provides nutrients and oxygen to the muscle tissue and fascia being stretched. It also allows metabolic waste products made during the stretch to be removed.

7. You have now completed one repetition. Do 10 repetitions and then repeat the same process (lie on your right side) to stretch the quadriceps of your left leg.

Stretching - Summary

Stretching always seems to be the poor cousin of CV and strength training; the first to be dropped if there's insufficient time to fit it in. I hope that by reading this section you appreciate that not making it part of your regime compromises your whole fitness. Think of all the components of exercise as parts in a jigsaw. They must all be in place to make the whole greater; flexibility is a big piece of that jigsaw!

Finally, you may want to consider trying Yoga and Pilates if you haven't already. Both are excellent for increasing your flexibility. You can either go to a class or choose to buy a DVD; there are also channels on TV dedicated to it. If you have not practiced Yoga or Pilates before, I would recommend going to classes to get first hand instruction. This will help you to master the exercises which you can then practise at home. When we watch videos it's very easy to think that we're doing what is on the screen and unintentionally do things incorrectly.

By attending a class when you begin, the Instructor can correct your technique to prevent bad habits and minimise the risk of injury. Once mastered, Yoga or Pilates are exercise systems that can be used for the rest of your life, don't usually need equipment and can be done virtually anywhere; I highly recommend them.

The Importance of Antioxidants and Exercise

To make the most of the exercise you do, it is very important to support your body nutritionally. When you are exercising you are applying the overload principle and putting greater physical demands on yourself and as a result your body will have a greater demand for nutrients. You therefore have to make sure that your diet and nutrition is as good as you can make it.

A major part of this is having a good supply of antioxidants that are crucial for general long term health and vital when you exercise. To explain why, I need to talk a little about what exactly antioxidants are and what they act upon that keeps us healthy, please bear with me.

In order to create the energy we need, our cells use oxygen to carry out a process known as cellular respiration. If you switched this process off you would drop dead within a matter of seconds, which is why cyanide is such an effective poison because it shuts down energy production in your cells. Unfortunately, by using oxygen we produce by-products called free radicals or oxidants. These set off a chain reaction which damages tissues in the body and can cause inflammation and soreness.

Apart from producing free radicals inside the body, you can also be exposed to them in many other ways including too much sunlight, pollution or eating food that has been subjected to excessive heat such as deep frying or burnt offerings on barbeques.

When you exercise you naturally use more oxygen. For example, during intense cardiovascular exercise you can use up to 12 – 20 times the oxygen you use when you are sitting down. This causes production of free radicals to go through the roof and although the body produces its own antioxidants that neutralise the free radicals it also requires additional ones from a good diet.

If you do not supply these, then your body will be overwhelmed by the sheer number of free radicals produced when you exercise intensively. These can then damage tissues and you will be more susceptible to soreness, injury and excessive inflammation.

There are many different types of free radicals and each one needs a specific type of antioxidant to neutralise it. You therefore need to make sure that you get as many antioxidants from your diet as possible. The basic rule of thumb is to eat fresh non processed whole foods and as many brightly coloured fresh fruit and vegetables (raw if possible as heat destroys antioxidants) as you can each day as these tend to have the greatest numbers and different types of antioxidants in them.

You can also supplement with a good quality antioxidant formula which will not replace the need for getting them from your diet but will greatly help to supply your body with the antioxidants it needs for quenching the excess free radicals produced by exercise before they can do damage.

PRINCIPLE 3: DO WHAT YOU LOVE .....CONSISTENTLY

The prime factor when planning how you are going to exercise is that you must do something that you enjoy! I know that sounds incredibly obvious, but you would be amazed at how many people take up a form of exercise that they think they *should* do, then find they lose interest in keeping fit very quickly!

What does exercise mean to you?

Do you get a fix from a good gym workout, love the high of a long run or do you tend to see exercise as a chore? Are team sports more appealing to you or do you prefer to dance, attend a fitness class or perhaps practise something like Yoga?

You don't have to be into playing sport or indeed, be an athletic person to get great benefits or enjoyment from exercise. And if you tend to see exercise as a chore then it's my aim by the end of this chapter to get you excited about your regular exercise!!

What's important to you?

The list below provides an at-a-glance view to enable you to evaluate what you're looking for in your exercise programme. Whether you already have an established regime in place or are new to exercise, this will help you ensure the types of exercise you choose fit with what's most important to you.

If **1** denotes **not important** and **10** denotes **very important**, circle the score that best reflects its current importance to you. If certain factors are not relevant to you, then change them or add in extra ones so that the list is tailored to your needs.

Date: ______________	Not important									Very important
Time efficient	1	2	3	4	5	6	7	8	9	10
Cost	1	2	3	4	5	6	7	8	9	10
Variety	1	2	3	4	5	6	7	8	9	10
Opportunity to socialise	1	2	3	4	5	6	7	8	9	10
Team sports	1	2	3	4	5	6	7	8	9	10
Competition	1	2	3	4	5	6	7	8	9	10
Losing weight	1	2	3	4	5	6	7	8	9	10
Cardiovascular fitness	1	2	3	4	5	6	7	8	9	10
Increasing muscular strength	1	2	3	4	5	6	7	8	9	10
Improving muscle tone	1	2	3	4	5	6	7	8	9	10
Becoming more flexible	1	2	3	4	5	6	7	8	9	10
Improving my balance	1	2	3	4	5	6	7	8	9	10
Being more coordinated	1	2	3	4	5	6	7	8	9	10
______________	1	2	3	4	5	6	7	8	9	10
______________	1	2	3	4	5	6	7	8	9	10

Consistency is key

When we're keen to move our fitness to a whole new level we can't wait to get started. However, we can often forget to consider factors that can get in the way when our enthusiasm has waned. By considering these upfront you can minimise their impact by choosing types of exercise that complement each other.

So, for example, you may love the energy and social nature of a Zumba class but after a long and stressful day it's losing its appeal especially as it's also dark, cold, windy and rainy outside. On such occasions you may prefer to stay indoors and practice some Yoga instead.

That expensive gym membership at the beginning of the year felt like a great idea to transform your fitness but work commitments are getting in the way of you being able to commit to those evening workouts so incorporating some HIRT (High Intensity Resistance Training) could be more practical and time efficient.

Common constraints to consistency

Listed below are common factors that can get in the way of exercising on a consistent basis. Review the list and tick those ones that apply.

❒ Travel time

❒ Time commitments

❒ Costs involved in membership or specialist clothing/equipment

❒ Attending at a specific time each week (e.g. irregular shift patterns)

❒ Insufficient variety leading to boredom

❒ The weather

❒ Recurring injury

❒ Not experiencing the benefits of exercise quickly enough

Exercise Options

Whether you are new to exercise and wondering what to try, are looking for another type of exercise to complement your current regime or simply looking for some variety; listed below, alphabetically, are some of the most popular activities with their advantages and disadvantages. Whilst some of the pros and cons are glaringly obvious it's amazing how we can easily overlook them when we're excited about trying something new!

Gymnasiums/Sports Centres

PROS

☺ Gyms provide the equipment necessary for you to work on CV, resistance and flexibility components of fitness.

☺ There are often many different types of class from beginners to advanced that will enable you to incorporate one or more of the essential areas that you need to regularly train.

☺ Fitness professionals are available for advice and guidance.

CONS

☹ Some people find the gym environment intimidating

☹ Numerous reps on gym equipment can a bit boring or simply a chore.

☹ It can be time consuming travelling to the gym and so difficult to fit into a busy schedule.

☹ Costs of membership can be high and not value for money unless you frequently make use of the facilities.

☹ Gym equipment does not always mimic natural movement.

Cycling

PROS

☺ An excellent form of cardiovascular exercise which also provides muscular endurance benefits.

☺ Being non-impact, your joints and muscle tissue are not subject to the same stresses as high impact exercise such as running; this makes it suitable for all ages.

☺ Provides excellent variety with an opportunity to enjoy the great outdoors either on or off road.

CONS

☹ There are initial costs of buying a suitable bike and safety equipment if you do not have them.

☹ Cycling can be difficult in winter and in inclement weather

☹ It does not provide any significant muscular strength or flexibility benefits.

☹ Cycling on busy roads can expose you to a lot of unnecessary pollution, can be stressful and even dangerous in heavy traffic so try and stick to quiet roads or less busy times of day whenever possible.

Calisthenics

Calisthenics is a form of exercise that uses your own body weight to provide a resistance training effect. Common calisthenics exercises are push-ups, pull-ups and squats.

PROS

☺ Even though calisthenics has been around for a long time, it has gained in popularity recently which means that there are plenty of videos to choose from on social media.

☺ You need zero equipment and it can be done literally anywhere. This makes it incredibly adaptable, zero cost and time efficient.

☺ Excellent for building muscular strength and endurance and can also help improve flexibility. Some more advanced routines (especially utilising HIRT) can also have a CV training effect.

CONS

☹ Calisthenics is not for everyone; and it is easy to pick up an injury if you are not used to exercising in this way. If you are a beginner it is a good idea to get some professional instruction to ensure that you start at the right level for your current state of fitness.

Cross Training

PROS

☺ This type of training combines two or more different types of exercise such as HIIT, HIRT, weight training and Yoga. This makes up for shortfalls in any one activity and provides a comprehensive form of training that covers all of the required areas to achieve optimum fitness.

☺ It is very popular in gyms owing to the varied equipment available and the motivational atmosphere of being part of a class. It can just as easily be done at home or outside with minimal equipment and is very adaptable.

☺ Cross training is one of the most effective ways of achieving first class health and fitness.

CONS

☹ If you are new to exercise it is easy to pick up an injury if you try to do too much at the beginning and it is best to seek professional advice and guidance to help you identify the best workout for your needs.

Dancing

PROS

☺ Dancing is one of the best forms of exercise I know and as it's fun many people do not even associate it with great exercise and the many positives that it brings to your fitness.

☺ As it's also social it gives us an extra incentive to keep it up.

☺ Provides excellent CV training, especially if you choose something like Latin American.

☺ Useful for developing muscular strength, endurance and muscle tone.

☺ Helps you to develop your flexibility, especially if you combine it with Yoga/Pilates.

☺ Fabulous for stimulating the brain (a great example of an exercise that helps maintain motor fitness for life) as you learn and master new moves

☺ Brilliant for improving your balance, agility, co-ordination, speed of movement and reactions, which is especially beneficial as we get older.

CONS

☹ Travel time and the cost of classes

☹ When busy schedules get in the way of regular attendance it's easy to feel behind the rest of the class, which can be a good excuse not to go! Try not to let that put you off - remind yourself that you're learning at your own pace. Even if you cannot get to a class you can always practise at home with a DVD or YouTube video if you have the space!

Running

PROS

☺ Running can contribute significantly to cardiovascular fitness and can also help improve muscular endurance.

☺ You can run pretty much anytime and anywhere (but avoid busy polluted roads).

☺ You can run on your own or with a running group or club.

☺ The only real cost involved is a decent pair of running shoes.

CONS

☹ It can be weather and season dependent unless you are a very committed advocate.

☹ You will need to complement running with a form of exercise that promotes muscular strength and flexibility.

☹ Even with quality running shoes, running is a high impact form of exercise and too much can have a negative impact on joints and muscle tissue, especially if you are not used to it or run too often.

☹ Running on busy roads means that your body is exposed to the harmful effects of pollution.

Swimming

PROS

☺ Excellent form of cardiovascular exercise. As it is non-impact it does not put stress on the joints, which makes it great for any age group.

☺ Provides muscular endurance benefits.

☺ It is not weather or season dependent and does not require any expensive gear unless you are going to buy a very special swim suit and goggles!

☺ It's easy to measure your progress as you become fitter - noting the number of lengths you can swim before you need a rest or the number of lengths you can do in a set amount of time.

CONS

☹ Swimming does not provide any appreciable muscular strength effect or flexibility benefits.

☹ Can be time consuming to travel to the pool so can be difficult to fit into a busy schedule.

☹ Chlorinated water can be very drying to your skin, can sting some people's eyes and some 'fun' pools do not often provide a conducive environment for swimming in a straight line! There is also the risk of picking up infections.

Walking

PROS

☺ Walking is a wonderful form of steady exercise, stimulating the lymphatic system and boosting the immunity.

☺ As many people enjoy a good walk it is a sociable form of exercise and it should be easy to find a fitness buddy to help you integrate it into everyday activities and your weekly plans.

☺ It is low impact so injuries are rare.

☺ Great exercise for people new to exercise or whose current health restricts them from more vigorous exercise.

☺ Not dependent on the seasons.

☺ Walking is very adaptable in that you can go for a long steady therapeutic ramble or a shorter speed walk which will give you more CV benefit. It can also give some muscular endurance benefits.

☺ Choosing different routes minimises the risk of boredom, a common factor as to why people don't maintain their fitness regimes.

☺ Apart from suitable footwear, there is no cost.

☺ Research has shown that walking in the countryside or in a park with trees is also therapeutic and can reduce stress levels.

CONS

☹ Apart from not providing any real muscular strength or flexibility benefits, there are no other real downsides to walking and it is one of the few exercises you can truly do every day for the rest of your life.

☹ In the winter months when the days are shorter you're more limited as to when you can walk in the daylight and as it's colder you may not wish to venture outside as often!

Yoga/Pilates

PROS

☺ These two forms of exercise can also be practised for the rest of your life and are among the most effective types of exercise.

☺ Both will help you to develop muscular strength, endurance, and are brilliant for developing flexibility and balance.

- ☺ They are also highly relaxing and can be an excellent way to de-stress.
- ☺ Yoga and Pilates have been shown to improve circulation and stimulate lymph flow.
- ☺ Whilst there is specialist equipment available, it is not essential, so you can do Yoga and Pilates almost anywhere and at any time you choose. An effective yoga session can be done in as little as 10 minutes.
- ☺ Classes are an excellent way to begin, enable you to learn the exercises/positions and ensure you are following best practice. You then could build on what you learn through DVDs and programmes or dedicated TV channels. This provides great flexibility for fitting around a busy schedule.

CONS

- ☹ With the exception of 'power Yoga' there is limited CV benefit.
- ☹ Attending weekly classes can be difficult when working irregular shift patterns.
- ☹ Attending classes in order to ensure you achieve the long-term benefits of Yoga or Pilates you will need to factor in the cost and time.
- ☹ Large classes can prevent the teacher from correcting incorrect technique so make sure you choose a class with smaller numbers.
- ☹ If you choose to practice Yoga or Pilates via DVDs or dedicated TV channels be extra vigilant that you are following best practice as it's very easy to think we're doing the same thing as the instructor!!

Assessing Options via Fitness Goals

You will naturally want to maximise the time you dedicate to exercise to achieve our personal fitness goals. The table below provides an at-a-glance view of the type of fitness benefits each provide so you can choose options that are going to be most enjoyable for you as well as achieve the desired balanced approach for long-term fitness and vitality.

******** **Great form of exercise for this**

******* **Useful contributor**

****** **Can bring some benefits**

***** **Limited benefits in this area**

	Callisthenics	Cross-Training	Cycling	Dancing	Running	Swimming	Walking	Weight Training	Yoga/Pilates
Cardiovascular Fitness	***	****	****	****	****	****	**	***	*
Muscular Strength	****	****	**	***	**	**	**	****	**
Muscular Endurance	****	****	****	***	***	****	***	****	*
Muscle Tone	****	****	***	***	**	**	**	****	****
Flexibility	***	***	*	***	*	**	**	*	****
Balance	***	***	**	****	**	*	**	**	****
Adaptable for HIIT	Yes	Yes	Yes	No	Yes	Yes	Yes	Yes	No
Adaptable for HIST	Yes	Yes	No	No	No	No	No	Yes	No

PRINCIPLE 4: LISTEN TO YOUR BODY – BE IN TUNE WITH IT

Whether you are exercising purely to stay fit and healthy or training for a sport, one of the most important things that you can learn is to tune into how you feel. I believe that to exercise or train over the long term and remain injury free whilst attaining great levels of fitness really is an art. Developing the ability to know when your body is ready for exercise or needs a rest is vitally important.

Pre-Fitness Checks

To give yourself the best chance of success, it's worth doing some 'pre-fitness checks': If you are going to be exercising under the guidance of a health professional they should cover all the necessary points with you before you start.

<u>1. Get your posture checked</u>

If you were having your dream house built, when it came to putting down the foundations it stands to reason that you would want it done properly to prevent subsidence and problems with the structure.

It is the same principle with exercise and posture; if your posture is misaligned, it can cause all sorts of problems when you embark on an exercise regime. If the solid foundation of good posture is not in place, when you try to build a fitter, stronger body it will exacerbate any weakness in your posture which is already there. With a lot of people this is usually in their back but it can just as easily be in the alignment elsewhere in the body such as the knees or shoulders.

Many people don't realise their posture is out of line. It is not until they start to get injuries or aches and pains during or after exercise that they become aware that something may not be right. This is because your body is brilliant at compensating and adapting.

For example, if you have a misalignment with your lower back your body may adopt a position that makes it easier for you to function without pain or restriction. However, this new position is usually not in natural alignment and may result in premature wear and tear to, for example, vertebrae or discs in your back.

Eventually your body can compensate no longer and it is usually when the added stress of exercise is imposed on a misaligned posture that something happens which stops you in your tracks such as a slipped or prolapsed disc in your back. This seemingly comes from nowhere but in truth it may have been developing for a long time, you simply won't have been aware of it.

It is therefore an excellent idea to get your posture checked. This can be done by a personal trainer, osteopath or chiropractor. They will be able to look at your posture and give you exercises that will either stretch tight muscles that are pulling posture out of line or strengthen weak muscles that are not supporting it as they should; a weak core is a common problem. Practising Yoga and/or Pilates can be great ways to strengthen and maintain your core muscles and improve posture.

2. Check your blood pressure and any medications

If you have not engaged in a structured exercise regime for some time, it is worth checking your blood pressure because of course it increases during physical activity. If you do not regularly have it checked or monitor it yourself, it is good policy to check to see whether it is within normal parameters.

If you have been diagnosed with high blood pressure (Hypertension) or low blood pressure (Hypotension), it is a good idea to speak to your doctor and inform them that you would like to start taking regular exercise. The good news is that a properly structured exercise regime will help to normalise blood pressure in the long term.

Similarly, if you are on any pharmaceutical medications you should inform your doctor of your intentions.

Working with Your Body

Here are 4 best practice tips to help you optimise your fitness regime:

1. Don't over train

As exercise makes us feel good it can be very easy to over train. It also seems logical that if we're doing something that's good for us, then the more we do the better it is. It can therefore be counter-intuitive to learn that over-training can result in you finding it much harder to achieve your goals and your fitness may actually regress to a lower level. Signs and symptoms of over training are:

☹ Increased muscle soreness after exercise which can also last for longer.

☹ Greater susceptibility to injuries.

☹ Insomnia.

☹ Fatigue.

☹ Increased resting heart rate (measure on first waking before getting out of bed).

☹ Increased susceptibility to illness (frequent colds, infections).

☹ Decreased motivation to exercise.

☹ Difficulty in increasing your level of fitness.

☹ Losing muscle (sarcopenia) through breakdown caused by excessive steady state exercise.

If you are experiencing any of these, you could be over doing it. Ease off on your regime and give yourself some extra rest days; you should not be exercising hard every day. In smart training and exercise, less is more. I cover this in more detail under **Principle 5**: **Less is More – smart training**.

2. <u>Avoid training when you are ill</u>

I have often seen people working out in gyms when they have a cold or a really bad cough. When I ask them why they are exercising when they are ill I often get responses such as “It’s not too bad, I thought I would sweat it out” or “I don’t want to disrupt my training because of a cold”. Well, the fact of the matter is that you already are disrupting it by continuing to exercise.

Any virus will be putting a strain on the body as the immune system deals with it. By using up further energy by exercising, especially intensely, you simply suffer for longer and usually get little or no benefit from the exercise.

My advice is, if you feel under par or have any signs that you’re coming down with a cold or cough, refrain from doing any hard exercise and rest for a couple of days. It never hurts to give your body a rest and not exercising for a short time will not impact your fitness levels. What it will do is allow your immune system to eliminate the illness more effectively and more quickly so you can get back to your usual exercise program a lot sooner.

You don't have to stop exercise all together; it depends on how you feel. But be honest with yourself; if you can go for a walk or do some stretching or other light exercise that's fine, but if you feel rough then have a complete rest for 2 or 3 days and see how you feel. In time you will get better at judging when to re-commence exercise after illness and will have better health because of it.

Also, do not beat yourself up if you get the odd cold or cough, everybody contracts the occasional virus. The time to be concerned is if you suffer from them very frequently (e.g. every couple of months); then you would need to look at ways to boost your immunity and look at the intensity of your exercise regime as you may be compromising your immune system by overtraining.

If you feel you are starting to come down with something treat it immediately with supplements that will boost the immune system. I use the following:

- ✓ Vitamin C 1000mg every four hours throughout the day. Continue this until the symptoms of the illness are gone. Don't worry about taking too much as taking multiple grams of vitamin C is perfectly safe. You can take it up to what is called bowel tolerance which is when you start to have loose stools; this is your body's way of telling you that you have reached your personal limit and when you should ease off the dose. Everyone is different but most people will not reach this limit taking 1000mg every 4 hours throughout the day.
- ✓ Echinacea is an herbal tincture that can be added to water and is very effective at boosting the immune system.
- ✓ Sliced ginger in hot water taken throughout the day is an excellent anti-viral and anti-bacterial remedy and also helps to soothe sore throats and any digestive upsets.
- ✓ Use garlic freely in cooking as it's a highly effective immune booster as well as having anti-viral, anti-bacterial and anti-inflammatory properties. You can also use supplements that use the active ingredient in garlic called allicin. Allicin boosts immunity and gives numerous other health benefits and can now be supplemented, giving you a concentrated dose. Just google allicin supplements.

3. Avoid exercises that aggravate an injury

It can often be tempting to keep exercising when you have got a niggling injury such as a sore knee because injuries are a nuisance and interrupt our daily routine. It is all too easy to strap up that knee and carry on in the hope that we can exercise through the injury somehow and it will go away and I have seen many people literally limping along, clearly in some discomfort, still exercising on an injury when they should be resting it.

If you can train around the injury and do a form of exercise that does not involve or aggravate it that is fine. But refusing to give it a chance to heal by exercising on it will increase the time it takes to put right and could turn it into a long term chronic injury.

Sustaining an injury is the last thing anyone wants but it does tell you that your body is not happy and that something needs addressing. What you have to ask yourself is not "why me?" but "what has caused this injury?"

By identifying the cause, whether it is for example worn out running shoes, lack of flexibility, exercising too intensely or misaligned posture, you can prevent it happening again.

4. Make sure you have adequate rest days

The idea of exercise is to build a fitter, stronger and more flexible body but in order to do this your body needs time to recover before you exercise again.

This is because all exercise is based upon the **overload principle**. This means that in order to train the body's systems such as the cardiovascular system or the muscular skeletal system, the system must be made to work harder than it is accustomed to working. It then needs time for the body to carry out the physiological changes as a result of this overload that will make it stronger.

Rest days are as important as doing the exercise itself and you need to ensure that you allow adequate days for your body to recover. This can be achieved by taking a rest day after a strenuous CV exercise session and then perhaps on the second day, carrying out a less strenuous exercise routine which exercises the body in a different way. So for instance, if you go for a hard cycle ride, have a rest day the following day with some stretching. Then on the second day after the hard session you might go for an easy walk or swim.

Rest days are equally as essential for resistance exercise as they are for CV training, if not more so if you are training hard in the gym. Muscles can take up to 5 to 6 days to recover from an intense resistance session so that particular group should not be targeted again for at least that time.

PRINCIPLE 5: LESS IS MORE – SMART TRAINING

Forget "No Pain No Gain"

In the past, it was generally thought that the harder and longer you trained or exercised the higher the level of fitness you would attain, which led to the culture of "no pain no gain". Happily, today, we know better than that, though I am still amazed at how many people still adhere to this philosophy, punishing their bodies relentlessly and expecting ever higher levels of fitness.

This is not the way to go, especially if you wish to carry on doing effective exercise for the rest of your life. As you get fitter and stronger you will inevitably be able to exercise for longer or with greater intensity if you wish, but whatever level of fitness you are currently at, the message remains the same. If you keep exercising for extreme periods of time (hours) with high intensity or steady state exercise and with insufficient periods of rest, you greatly increase the risk of:

- ☹ Sustaining injuries which can become chronic/long term.
- ☹ Burning out; ending up with long term fatigue of your nervous system.
- ☹ Prematurely wearing out joints leading to the possible development of osteoarthritis in later life.

This completely defeats the object! The point of exercise is to build up not to tear down! I have known people who have destroyed their bodies because they couldn't change their old mind set of "more is better" as it was so deeply ingrained in them. This often resulted in operations for musculoskeletal damage and permanent disability, which is why I'm so passionate about smart training. I am not saying that you should not use high intensity exercise regimes in your training (there are 2 examples coming up) just that they should not dominate and be used to excess.

So, what do we need to do? What is the smart way to train? Firstly, we need to establish what we want to achieve, what our fitness goals are and then use training methods that give us the optimum benefits for the least amount of time. These methods should allow us to hit our workout targets for CV and strength and then stop, walk away, rest!

Such training protocols will ultimately represent a new paradigm for many; but they are increasingly seen as the smart way to train, balancing short, highly effective workouts with equally important periods of rest.

Two of the best types which you may like to try if you have not already are detailed below:

1. High Intensity Interval Training (HIIT)

The fundamental concept with HITT training is that you exercise flat out.

This type of training requires short bursts of intense exercise with short rests in between and is known as anaerobic training. It is incredibly effective, though because of its intensity, it cannot be done every day. However, performing it just 2 days a week will give you results that are equal to and frequently better than doing steady state exercise 5 times a week!

<u>The incredible benefits of HIIT</u>

As you have probably guessed, I am a **BIG** fan of HIIT. I use it in my own training and incorporate it in the exercise programmes I've devised to help people apply the principles in this book. You can also use it in conjunction with steady state cardio if you wish; so for example, if you enjoy cycling whether it's for pleasure or competition, use HIIT to complement your existing exercise/training. I would definitely recommend that you use it because the benefits will help massively in attaining your optimal health and fitness for life.

The benefits of HIIT include:

☺ **Time Efficient:** It is very time efficient compared to traditional forms of CV exercise and can be done pretty much anywhere; all you need is an activity that enables you to work at maximum intensity.

☺ **Adaptability:** HITT can be adapted to pretty much any type of CV exercise (see the table at the end of Principle 3).

☺ **Activates Slow and Fast Twitch Muscle Fibres**. As HIIT exercises all the types of muscle fibre, it gives greater gains in cardiovascular fitness.

There are three different types of muscle fibre; these are known as slow twitch, fast twitch and super-fast twitch. Sprinters have more fast/super-fast twitch and distance runners more slow twitch fibres. Even though we all have a combination of these, people who only do steady state cardiovascular only work the slow twitch fibres.

Steady state exercise only works about 40% of your muscle fibres, including those in your heart muscle. By doing HIIT you can activate all of the different types of muscle fibre at the same time including the other fast twitch fibres that make up the other 60% of your muscle fibres. This is why you can do HIIT for 15 minutes and get greater improvements in your fitness than doing steady state aerobic exercise for 1 hour or more. Your health and fitness will therefore improve much quicker doing HIIT.

☺ **Weight Management:** It is easier to lose weight and keep it under control because recovery from HIIT uses lots of calories and activates genes for fat metabolism that help to use body fat for fuel. Also, the increased toned muscle tissue you develop will help you to control your weight even when you are not exercising!

☺ **Promoting the release of Human Growth Hormone:** HIIT promotes the release of a hormone called human growth hormone (HGH). It is known as the fitness or youth hormone and is responsible for cell regeneration and growth. HGH is at its highest in children and high in young adults and is one of the prime reasons for youthful vigour. Unfortunately, production of this hormone declines as we get older.

After the age of 30 this decline accelerates which means that we begin to lose all of the youthful benefits that HGH can bestow on us. The faster the decline, the quicker we lose the benefits, and there are many!

However, the good news is that we can increase production of this hormone if we use HIIT. So, what are the benefits that this wonder hormone can give us if we increase its levels in our body?

☺ HGH stimulates muscle growth and strength through changes to your DNA caused by the intensity of the exercise. So, we can improve and retain our strength and endurance as we grow older.

☺ If you play sports or just wish to be more athletic HGH can help you to increase your athleticism by enhancing the effects your exercise or any specific training that you do.

- ☺ But one of the most spectacular effects of increased HGH is that research is now indicating that it may help to slow down ageing. This is because it can reduce what is known as Telomere shortening. At the centre of each cell of your body (approximately 10 trillion of them) is the nucleus which houses the chromosomes that contain your DNA, the unique genetic code that makes you who you are. At the tips of these chromosomes are telomeres which protect the chromosome and your DNA from damage.

  Every time your cells divide, the telomere shortens. This is known as age related telomere shortening. When it has reduced to a certain length we die; depressing thought! However, increasing your production of HGH from doing HIIT may well slow the rate of shortening and therefore may help to prolong your lifespan.

  There is still more research to be done and telomere shortening is still not completely understood but the research so far is very promising and exciting. Incidentally, things that speed up telomere shortening are obesity, smoking, poor diet, nutrient deficiencies and toxins.

- ☺ **Healing and Repairing**: The ability of your body to heal and repair will be enhanced due to HIIT stimulating an increase in the production of human growth hormone (HGH). This can help recovery from exercise and help you to reach your fitness goals quicker. It can also help in recovery from health conditions and injuries.

- ☺ **Bone Strength**: HIIT helps to increase the strength of your bones. It does this because the increase in HGH stimulates the liver to convert it to a substance called insulin growth factor 1 (IGF1). IGF1 has growth promoting properties that act on special cells in your bones whose job it is to increase bone mass.

- ☺ **Toned Skin**: It can even help to keep your skin more toned and reduce wrinkles due to the actions of HGH.

- ☺ **Increased Energy:** You will also find that your energy levels improve. A major reason for this is that the number of mitochondria in your cells can be dramatically increased with HIIT. Mitochondria are the powerhouses of your cells and provide the energy to power your cells and body by producing a substance called Adenosine Tri-Phosphate (ATP). The more mitochondria you have, the greater your energy and the more robust your health will be.

☺ **Immune Function**: Your immune function will be improved. A major reason for this is thought to be linked to enhanced number and function of mitochondria.

Adapting to HIIT

It is very important that you adapt to HIIT. If you are new to HIIT but do regular exercise and have a good level of fitness, it still pays to slightly reduce the intensity for the first few workouts to give your body a chance to adapt. You may only feel like doing 1 session a week, this is okay, your body will adapt, don't rush it.

If you haven't exercised for a while, or don't do regular exercise it is a good idea to begin at a lower intensity (e.g. 70% max effort) and gradually build the intensity as your body adapts to the new training regime. This will vary from one person to another so it would pay to begin under the supervision of a health professional for guidance and encouragement. They can then assess when you are ready to work at maximum intensity.

This decision is of course down to you. However, I would thoroughly recommend doing this as it will help to ensure that you get the full benefit and avoid injury. The important thing is to be patient and let your body adapt to this new form of exercise.

Note: It has been discovered that consuming any kind of drink or food that is high in sugar within 2 hours of completing your HIIT will shut down the production of HGH that you have worked so hard to produce. So, you need to make sure that you avoid any drinks or foods high in sugar, which includes the fruit sugar fructose, which of course are found in fruit smoothies. It's also worth checking any commercially made exercise drinks as many of these contain sources of sugar such as glucose syrup.

Guidelines for effective HIIT

In order for HIIT training to be effective there are certain protocols that you need to follow.

Before You Start

- If you are on medication or have had health problems, you should consult a health and fitness professional before attempting HIIT.

Planning the Session

- Make sure that you hydrate properly before a HIIT workout, but avoid drinking large amounts of water too close to the workout (less than 30 minutes before)
- Vary the type of activity that you use for HIIT to increase the training effect.

Warming Up

- Make sure you warm up properly using the same activity that you are going to incorporate in the HIIT

Best Practice during the Session

- You must tune in and listen to your body when doing these workouts, especially if you are new to them. If you feel any strange sensations such as light headedness, dizziness or anything out of the ordinary, stop immediately. If you are concerned, get yourself checked over by a health professional, but it is most likely your body telling you that it is not ready yet to go at the intensity that you are working at; so reduce it for a while.
- You must go flat out - you will only get the full benefits of HIIT if you do this. In the example of HIIT that follows, if you are truly going flat out, at the end of the 30 seconds, you should be gasping for breath, unable to talk, sweating profusely (after 2nd or 3rd rep).
- As you need to exercise flat out, if you were doing the example HIIT workout for the first time, you may just manage 3 or 4 repetitions of 20 seconds. It does not matter; the important thing is to do what you can at 100% effort then stop if you can no longer sustain it. You will find that your progress with this type of training will be excellent and you will soon improve and be able to move towards completing the whole workout.

Warm Down

- Make sure that you warm down properly afterwards for at least 5 minutes so that your body can recover. It's a bit like a racing car doing cool down laps after running flat out.
- As with the warm up use the same activity that you used for the HIIT workout gradually reducing the intensity. This allows the blood pressure to return to normal and stops blood pooling in muscles (if you were to stop suddenly) which can help prevent any possibility of dizziness or feeling faint.

After the Session

- Make sure that you get good quality sleep (see chapter 2) and do not do another HIIT session for at least 48 hours. This is due to the time your body requires to fully recover from this intensive type of exercise. This limits you to a maximum of 3 HIIT workouts per week. Personally, I tend to alternate between 2 one week and 3 the next.

Example HIIT workout

Let's say you have chosen a static exercise bike for your HIIT session.

Duration	Exercise
3 minutes	It is very important to warm up and prepare your body for the intensive exercise you are about to do. So, you would cycle with gradually increasing speed for 3 minutes until you have a slight sweat, heart pumping faster so you are starting to get out of breath but you could still hold a conversation.
60 seconds	Start to ease off during the 4th minute before you begin the intensive workout.
30 seconds 90 seconds	At the start of the 5th minute, pedal as hard as you can for 30 seconds then slow right down or stop if you wish. Rest for 90 seconds. Repeat this cycle of pedalling hard for 30 seconds and resting for 90 seconds a further 7 times, so you are doing 8 in total.
5 minutes	Warm down

So, the actual length of the workout is 16 minutes plus your warm up and cool down periods, in this instance 25 minutes in total. However, of those 25 minutes, you are actually, only working flat out for 4 minutes!

Note: Cardiovascular training is not the only area where HIIT can be utilised. Modified versions of it can also be used with resistance training. You can use the principle in circuit training where you might combine calisthenics and exercise with weights and perhaps short high intensity anaerobic exercises such as sprinting on the spot for 20 seconds. The permutations are numerous; I have just given you one example of how it can be used.

HIIT - Summary

Prioritise HIIT training for your cardiovascular exercise/training. Types of exercise that can be adapted for HIIT training can be found in the at-a-glance comparison table “Assessing Options via Fitness Goals” at the end of **Principle 3. Do what you love .....consistently**

On the rest days between HIIT, you can do an easier steady state workout if you wish. Alternatively, you could do a resistance session on the days between HIIT and work on either muscular strength or endurance; or, just concentrate on core strength or flexibility, the choice is yours. It really depends on what you are trying to achieve and what you find best suits your requirements and your body. What works for one person won’t necessarily work for you so don’t feel you need to emulate someone else. This is where the advice of a physical trainer can be very helpful.

Although exercising as hard as you can sounds very extreme, it is only for very short periods of time and is all relative. To an athlete this may mean sprinting up hill; for a non-athlete or older person, walking quickly uphill could be an equivalent maximum effort.

Finally, if you find that HIIT is not for you that’s fine, it’s not for everyone, there are many other ways of exercising effectively that have been listed in this chapter. Experiment and find the regime that best suits you. I find that as people get more in tune with their bodies they instinctively find the exercise that suits them best and in so doing achieve amazing results.

2. Super Slow Resistance Training otherwise known as HIRT/HIST (High Intensity Resistance/Strength Training)

The philosophy of super slow is very similar to High Intensity Interval Training (HIIT) in that it allows you to achieve excellent benefits in a very short time and only needs to be done once a week. It also provides practically all of the same benefits of HIIT and can be used in combination with HIIT in your fitness regime to maximise your fitness. So, for example, you could do HIIT one week then Super Slow the next.

Because these exercises are performed extremely slowly, they produce a very quick deep fatigue in all of the different types of skeletal muscle tissue. This deep fatigue and the time that it takes to recover from it (typically between 4 to 7 days depending on your fitness level) is what helps to make the physiological changes that result in the development of exceptional muscular strength and endurance.

The incredible benefits of Super Slow

☺ It gives the same benefits as HIIT including time efficiency

☺ Because of the greater degree of muscular fatigue, it produces equal and often greater gains in strength and endurance than conventional weight training.

☺ It reduces the risk of injury because you are working slowly with lighter weights.

☺ It helps to reduce inflammation (see chapter 5) in the body. It does this by stimulating the body to produce cytokines, which are chemical messengers that help the immune system when fighting infections and modulating inflammation.

☺ Super Slow encourages the production from skeletal muscle of a specific type of cytokine called myokines that are anti-inflammatory. These enhance the insulin sensitivity of muscle cells helping to improve blood sugar control and all of the benefits that go with it (see chapter 5)

☺ It inhibits the release of a different type of cytokine from adipose tissue (body fat), especially around the trunk, which is pro-inflammatory. Although these are needed for immune response, we tend to overproduce them as a result of things like lack of exercise, poor diet and stressful lifestyle.

☺ It helps to reduce body fat efficiently, regardless of calorie intake (not an excuse to over eat!)

☺ It produces CV benefits equal to that of HIIT but in a different way. The benefits come from the massively increased volume of blood that is pushed back to the heart through the venous system by the slowly contracting skeletal muscles during HIRT exercises. This has the effect of increasing the stroke volume of the heart so that it can pump more blood with each stroke; enabling it to operate at a lower heart rate for a given workload.

☺ It stimulates the body to hold on to skeletal muscle (instead of succumbing to age related muscle loss) with all of the health benefits this brings (see generic benefits of regular resistance exercise)

☺ This type of exercise does not require you to warm up. Because it is carried out so slowly and with light weights the warm up is, in effect, built into the exercise. The first repetitions of each exercise serve as a warm up for the higher exertion that follows as muscle fatigue starts to set in.

☺ Super Slow does not require you to warm down. This is due to the nature of the way blood is pumped around the body during this type of exercise, which avoids pooling of blood in areas of the body such as the legs. This obviates the need to re-distribute blood flow by performing cool down exercise as is the case with other forms of exercise.

<u>Guidelines for effective Super Slow</u>

It's worthwhile considering the following protocols so that you get the maximum benefit from your sessions and adapt to this form of exercise.

Before You Start

1. If you are on medication or have had health problems, it's imperative that you consult a health and fitness professional before beginning.

2. As with HIIT, if you are new to resistance training or have not performed it for some time; it is important to monitor yourself closely and ease into this new regime. As these exercises are performed very slowly, it is extremely important to concentrate on your technique and hold your form.

   I would highly recommend consulting a health professional who specialises in Super Slow, who can tell you how to incorporate it into an existing fitness regime and advise you on technique. Doing so will help to ensure that you get the full benefit.

3. When first starting, it is best to begin with working on weights machines (especially if you are inexperienced with resistance exercise) as these give you more control over your movements as you start to fatigue. However, if you are experienced with training with free weights you can begin training with free weights straight away.

Planning the Session

1. It is best to use compound exercises so that you work the maximum number of skeletal muscles to exhaustion in the session such as squats or press ups. Please see examples below.
2. If you are a using a machine, set it up for a light load so that it is safer to work with (approximately 20-30% of what you usually work with). It may feel absurdly light to begin with but at the slow speed you will be working at it will soon get heavy.
3. If using free weights, again, use ones that are approximately 20-30% of the weights you typically work with.
4. A good test of the right weight/load for you is that you should be able to just perform 6 Super Slow reps before complete exhaustion.

Warm Up

No warm up is required, go straight into the session. See section on warm up in benefits.

Best Practice during the Session

1. The exercises need to be done slowly so that you quickly develop a deep fatigue in the muscles
2. A good time to aim for when starting out is 10 seconds on the concentric phase (when the muscles contract and shorten against an applied load) and 10 seconds on the eccentric phase (when the muscles lengthen against an applied load). So, if you are performing a press up:
    a. Eccentric Phase: You need to lower yourself slowly and smoothly so that your chest touches the ground just on the count of 10.
    b. Concentric Phase: The same applies as you push back upwards, slowly and smoothly over the count of 10 to the starting position.
3. Try to make sure that you avoid rushing past the most difficult point of the exercise. This keeps the speed of each exercise smooth and constant. It will become more difficult to do this as you fatigue.
4. Breathing during the exercises should be slow and continuous and performed through an open mouth. Don't hold your breath at any time

during the exercises. As it becomes more difficult and you approach muscular failure, breathe quicker and deeper.

5. When you reach the point of exhaustion your muscles will start to shake, this is quite normal and is a sign that you are doing the exercise correctly. When you reach a point when you cannot move against the load, try to fight against the load for a further 5 seconds.

6. As soon as you finish one set of exercises, move onto the next set without a break.

7. Although you want to make sure that you use the full range of motion in each exercise; try to avoid locking your joints at the end of each rep so that your muscles are under tension all the time. The total elapsed time that your muscles are under load for each exercise is known as time under load (TUL).

For example, if you are performing arm curls, avoid fully straightening your arms at the end of each rep. This ensures that your biceps are contracted all the time and have no rest between reps, leading to quicker, deeper fatigue

Warm Down

No warm down is required with this type of exercise, see benefits of super slow.

After the Session

1. Once you have completed the session, you must allow sufficient recovery time. This sort of exercise produces very deep muscle fatigue and the recovery time will vary and depends on the intensity of the workout. When you first start, recovery time will depend on the level of muscle fatigue you generate in the workout. Someone who is not experienced at weight training may easily recover after 3 days because they may not be able to train to the intensity required when they first start.

   A more experienced person may have pushed themselves harder during the workout and therefore have a greater post workout fatigue that requires 7- 10 days recovery. Although this sounds a long time between workouts it would be counter- productive to try to do another workout sooner. If you work the muscles too soon you will be undoing the good work that you have put into the session and holding yourself back from progressing. Remember, sufficient rest is as important as the exercise itself.

2. Do not try to mix a Super Slow workout with other resistance exercises or cardiovascular exercise in the same session; keep them separate. You will need to put all of your effort into Super Slow. Because it produces such a deep fatigue, it would severely compromise your ability to do any other exercise at the same time and be counterproductive.
3. If you have done a Super Slow session, avoid doing any other intense weight training in the recovery period.
4. As with HIIT, it is important to be patient while your body adapts to this new form of exercise - the results you will get will be worth the effort.
5. It is possible to mix Super Slow sessions with other types of resistance training. So, you could do HIRT one week (with approx. a week to recover) and then do another type of training the week after.

Progression

As you progress, the combined time that your muscles are under load in each exercise, will increase the stronger you become. So, if you did 6 reps to failure in 2 minutes you may progress to six reps to failure in 2 ½ minutes (going slower with each rep) as your strength increases.

The amount of resistance that you are using should increase (by a small amount) along with matching or bettering your time under load with each successive workout.

As you get stronger and do more intensive sessions you will take longer to recover, anything from 7 to 10 days or longer. If you find that you stop progressing, this is a sign that you need to insert more recovery days.

It is important to keep a record of your TUL for each exercise and the resistance used. This will allow you to gauge your progress over time, along with more obvious increases in strength.

Examples of HIRT Workouts – one for the gym and one for at home

Outlined below are two examples of a HIRT workout, one is for the gym and is best suited to people who do not regularly weight train or are new to weight training.

I've also included a workout that you can do at home. It's aimed at experienced exercisers who already have a good level of technique, muscular strength and fitness.

GYM WORKOUT (Please refer to the Super Slow guidelines)

- **Planning the Session**

The five machines that you will be using for the workout are:

1. Seated Row
2. Chest Press
3. Lat Pull Down
4. Overhead Press
5. Leg Press

- If you can, find a gym that uses NAUTILUS OR MEDX as the cam profiles on these machines are best suited for this kind of exercise. However, any quality machine will still give you excellent results.
- It is important to make sure that you are correctly positioned in each machine and that it is correctly adjusted for your size before you begin each exercise so if you are not familiar with the machines, make sure that you ask an instructor to help you.
- Set the weights to 20-30% of what you usually work with

Best Practice during the Session

- You will be working through these machines in the order shown, going straight from one to the next using the HIRT guidelines given above.
- Keep your core locked throughout each exercise.
- Try not to grip the handles of the machines too tightly.

HOME WORKOUT (Please refer to the HIRT/HIST guidelines)

1. Press Ups

- Correct technique is essential so ensure nice straight body, abdominals pulled in (core locked, see core training section), head in line with spine looking at the floor, hands shoulder width apart and hands angled inwards at approximately 45 degrees.
- Lower yourself gently and gradually to the count of 10 so that your chest touches the floor on 10 and then slowly push yourself up for the count of 10 for six reps.
- The last rep should be extremely difficult; if it is not, increase the difficulty by doing the rep slower or raising your feet on a box. If it is too hard to perform traditional press-ups at the beginning because of the reduced speed, put your knees on the ground with lower legs curled up or simply do less reps.

2. Calf Raise

- Stand on a step with feet shoulder width apart with the ball of your foot just on the edge of the step enabling you to lower your heel down as far as it will go.
- Lock your core.
- Whilst steadying yourself on a hand rail or wall, lower your feet so that your heels drop down as far as possible.
- When you have gone down as far as you can, immediately start to come back up.
- Going down and coming back up should take 10 seconds and be a smooth movement for six reps. If you find that you can do more, increase the intensity, make the movement slower, try it with a single leg or hold a weight (e.g. dumbbell).

3. Squats

- Go straight into the squats, lowering yourself down (so that your thighs are at 90 degrees to your lower legs and parallel to the floor) and slowly back up, both for the count of 10.
- Feet should be shoulder width apart angled slightly outwards, head up in-line with a straight back, core locked.
- Place the hands on the hips, across the front of your body or straight out in front of you.
- Try to do 6 reps, you may find that you reach muscular failure before this; but this is exactly what you want, rapid deep muscle fatigue. If you are not fatigued by the sixth rep, make the movement slower or use a small weight (e.g. barbell, kettle bell)

4. Bent-Over Row

- Stand with your feet shoulder width apart, bend over from the hips so that your upper body is about 45 degrees from upright with knees slightly bent and back straight.
- Lock your core
- Holding the weight at arms-length using a light weight (barbell or dumb-bells), slowly bend your arms, pulling the weight and drawing it up to your upper abdomen.
- Pause briefly then slowly lower it down to the starting position.
- Adjust the load so that you are totally fatigued by the sixth rep.

5. Overhead Press

- Stand with your feet approximately 2 shoulder widths apart with knees slightly bent.
- Lock your core
- With a light weight (e.g. dumbbell) in each hand, starting with the weights

at shoulder level, slowly press the weights above your head to the count of 10.

- Then lower the weight to the count of 10.
- As with the other exercises adjust the weight/load so that you can just perform 6 reps at the speed required.

Summary

Although I have concentrated on Super Slow as an example of resistance training; I want to emphasise, that this is just one of many other excellent types of training techniques that can be used to improve skeletal muscular strength and endurance.

Whilst I am obviously a fan, I use it in conjunction with other training protocols such as HIIT because I believe that no single one can achieve it all and that Super Slow can be complemented by using it with a mixture of different training methods. It comes back once again, to the main principle that this book is based on, synergy.

It also depends on what you are looking to achieve with your training. If, like myself, your goal is to achieve your best overall health and fitness so that I have the best quality and quantity of life possible, then I think that using a synergistic balanced approach in your training is the best way to go.

By challenging your body with different methods and training protocols, you can push your limits higher and attain your ultimate level of health and fitness.

If, however, you are training for a specific sport or activity, then you may want to tailor your training to mimic the actions required to do it. This is known as the Specificity Principle which incorporates training that results in a **S**pecific **A**daptation for **I**mposed **D**emand.

For example, if you want to train for a sport that requires explosive muscular contraction such as sprinting, then you could still use Super Slow as part of your strength training regime and then approaching your competitive season, make your training more sport specific with faster more explosive movements incorporating techniques such as plyometrics.

Super Slow is an excellent form of resistance exercise with many benefits, but, as with HIIT, it is just one tool in the box. As with all of the advice in this book it works more effectively when used together. If you would like to know more about this type of training I would recommend reading:

"Body by Science" by Doug McGuff and John Little.

Chapter 4 Summary

Principle 1: Don't underestimate what your body is capable of

Believe in the ability of your body to achieve amazing fitness

With the right support, your body can transform itself and it is never too late to start. Visualise; see yourself achieving your health and fitness goals. You are capable of things that you never believed possible. Be persistent and do not give up!

Develop core strength

Core strength is obtained by strengthening specific abdominal muscles which then allow you to perform exercise and everyday tasks more effectively whilst helping to support your lumber spine and protect you from injury. Two of the best types of exercise for developing core strength are Yoga and Pilates.

You don't have to be a "sporty" person to achieve great fitness

Anyone can achieve their health and fitness goals; it does not matter if you have never really considered yourself to be good at exercise.

Principle 2: Synergy & Balance

Combine different types of exercise for best results

Include aerobic (especially HIIT), strength and flexibility training in your regime in order to achieve optimal results.

Stay hydrated during exercise

Your performance during exercise can be impaired by losing as little as 2% of your body weight in water. It is vital to stay hydrated by sipping water before, during and after exercise.

Make sure you get a good supply of antioxidants

Support your exercise with antioxidants to help prevent soreness, inflammation and possible injuries.

Look after your nutrition

When exercising you are asking more of your body and consequently it has a greater requirement for nutrients. No matter how good your exercise regime is, it will be severely compromised if you don't support it with the right nutrition. You simply can't exercise your way out of a bad diet! The chapter on nutrition is, by some margin, the largest in this book. I have dedicated so much space to it because it is the cornerstone of your health and fitness.

Principle 3: Do what you love .....consistently

Focus on types of exercise that you love and enjoy

Sounds obvious but choose exercises that you really enjoy. This will help to ensure that you stay interested and do not look upon your regime as a chore.

Be regular and consistent

As with nutrition, the secret to achieving great health and fitness is to exercise regularly and consistently.

Develop the habit

I find that the biggest hurdle to anyone who is starting a new exercise regime is not the actual exercise itself but developing the exercise habit. Once you have achieved this, your health and fitness goals will be much easier to achieve and maintain. (Please see chapter 7 on Motivation)

Enjoy the benefits of your health

Once you have achieved great levels of health and fitness, make sure you enjoy it. You will be capable of enjoying many sports or other physical activities whatever your age and be able to live your life to the full!

Exercise with others

One of the best ways to achieve regularity, consistency and to develop your exercise habit is to exercise with others. This can be a class, through a club or simply with friends; the encouragement of others is a powerful tool.

Principle 4: Listen to your body – be in tune with it

Listen to your body

Learn to tune into your body and recognise when you can exercise more intensely and when it is best to rest or do an easier exercise session.

Get your posture checked

Taking time to check for and correct any postural problems will not only help prevent injuries but will make your exercise more beneficial.

Don't exercise around pollution

You are looking to build up your health and well-being so avoid exercising on busy roads. Exposure to pollutants will harm your body and make it more difficult to achieve your health and well-being goals.

Don't exercise intensely when you're ill

When you're unwell you need to avoid stressing your body unnecessarily, so be honest with yourself, if you are in doubt, don't exercise.

Look after injuries, don't ignore them

It is best to deal with injuries as soon as they happen. This will ensure that you recover fully and are back to full fitness quicker.

Principle 5: Less is more – smart training

Take adequate rest days

Allow yourself adequate time to recover from exercise sessions. You will make faster progress and achieve your fitness goals more quickly.

Don't over train

Recognise the signs of over training and ease off or adapt your training regime accordingly.

Don't beat yourself up if you miss a day or if you don't perform as you think you should

If you miss some days due to injury, illness, commitments, or simply have a mediocre exercise session don't get despondent. Everybody has these hurdles to overcome and you can recover any lost ground very quickly.

Final Thoughts

Whatever your fitness ambitions are, I hope that this chapter has given you some fresh ideas and useful pointers to help you go forward and make your fitness the best it can possibly be. Always keep in mind that there is always room for improvement and that your body is capable of achieving amazing fitness; believe that and not the naysayers!

Chapter 4 Review & Ideas For Your Action Plan

1. What areas of fitness would you like to focus on improving?

☐ Cardiovascular ☐ Flexibility ☐ Balance

☐ Muscular Strength ☐ Muscular Endurance ☐ Muscle Tone

Reviewing your current regime to what extent does it allow you to balance different types of fitness? Any tweaks required to achieve more balance?

2. In the "What's important to you?" exercise in Principle 3, what factors did you identify as most significant to you e.g. variety, competition, time efficient?

3. In Principle 3, reviewing the table "Assessing Options via Fitness Goals" did any forms of exercise stand out as being the most beneficial for you? And in reading through the pros and cons of popular forms of exercise were there any which appealed to you that you haven't tried before or that aren't currently in your fitness regime? For example:

☐ Callisthenics ☐ Dancing ☐ HIIT ☐ Super Slow

☐ Cycling ☐ Fitness Classes ☐ Pilates ☐ Walking

☐ Cross-Training ☐ Gyms ☐ Running ☐ Yoga

Chapter 5

The Incredible Power of Naturopathic Nutrition

This chapter is about the amazing power of nutrition and practical tips on how to make the most of the food you eat. Please be assured I'm not going to be preaching to you from some squeaky clean ivory tower about what and what not to eat. Life is for living and it's not about denying yourself foods you love. As with everything in life it's about balance.

Being clear on what constitutes a healthy diet can be challenging these days. We're constantly bombarded with contradictory information and news about the latest "super food" or miracle diet. What was good for us last year turns out to be the source of all ill health this year. Of course, there will always be new studies to challenge our current thinking and new things to learn.

There are, however, some fundamental principles that are worth knowing. My aim therefore in this chapter is to provide you with a practical tool kit to help you to make informed decisions about what's best for you.

We'll cover:

1. The Power of Nutrition

a. The power of nutrition and how it is often under-estimated in western medicine.

b. Naturopathic nutrition and why it's so effective

c. Optimum nutrition is vital to every function in your body

d. The power of synergy

2. Myths and Misconceptions

a. The perfect diet

b. Nutritional supplements

c. Cholesterol

d. Salt

3. Main Food Groups and Fibre

a. Protein

b. Carbohydrates

c. Fats

d. Dietary fibre

4. Three Powerful Practices for Optimising Nutrition

a. Food combining

b. Fasting

c. Detoxing

5. 3 ways to supercharge your long–term health:

a. Optimise your enzymes to supercharge your health

b. Control your blood sugar

c. Avoid, reduce/eliminate inflammation - major cause of disease

6. Pulling it all together

a. 21 Tips on making changes in your diet that stand the test of time

b. Your Quick Reference Food Table

c. Ideas for quick and easy nutritious recipes including menu planner and health benefits of the ingredients

SECTION 1. THE POWER OF NUTRITION

1A. THE POWER OF NUTRITION AND HOW IT IS OFTEN UNDER-ESTIMATED IN THE WESTERN MEDICINE.

It's always intrigued me that food and nutrition has been incredibly undervalued in modern western medicine. Nobody would argue that without food we would die, yet so little significance seems to be given to the quality of the food we eat and its role in the health and vitality of the human body. In most hospitals, for example, the food that is given to patients could not by any stretch of the imagination be considered of high nutritional value or quality. Patients would recover so much quicker and would stand a much better chance of avoiding complications if hospital nutrition was improved.

Doctors are required to take the Hippocratic Oath to uphold ethical standards yet this well-known quote from Hippocrates does not appear to form part of modern medical practice:

"Let food be thy medicine and medicine be thy food" Hippocrates

As you may be aware, training of medical doctors can take up to 10 years yet until recently the syllabus on nutrition was minimal. Whilst this is beginning to change it is important for us as individuals to take responsibility for our health. To invest time in learning about how best to obtain the nutrition we need to give our body the 'ingredients' it needs to keep as healthy as possible. And that's what this chapter is about.

I must admit at this point that 20 years ago in the mid 1990's I knew very little about nutrition. I tried to eat what I considered to be a reasonably healthy diet and thought that I was in pretty good shape. I was a Fire Fighter and exercised regularly to maintain a high level of fitness.

The only problem was that despite all this exercise I did not feel on top form. I was suffering from a combination of symptoms and conditions. Every summer I would get the most dreadful hay fever; I had suffered from this as a child but as I got older it just seemed to get worse. Every year it was the same, constantly blocked nose, uncontrolled sneezing and streaming eyes. I came to dread those summer months. I remember one year whilst driving on a long journey my nose was constantly streaming and it was so bad that by the time I reached my destination I had completely filled the passenger foot well behind the driver's seat with tissues!

If this was not enough, I had also started to suffer from severe fatigue. I would struggle to get up in the morning and feel un-refreshed from the night's sleep and by lunch time I would start to feel sleepy. Very often on my days off I would need to nap in the early afternoon and remember wondering why a supposedly healthy and fit Fire Fighter in his mid-thirties should have less energy than your average pensioner.

It was a suggestion from my wife Susan that proved to be not only a turning point in my long-term health and fitness; but the beginning of a fascinating and amazing journey that would ultimately teach me about the incredible health and fitness potential of the human body that is available to all of us.

Susan had been interested in nutrition for years after being diagnosed with rheumatoid arthritis and had managed to heal herself by changing her diet. She subscribed to a monthly magazine and suspected that my problems were because of my so called healthy diet and that a visit to a nutritionist may help me.

I agreed to go along out of a combination of curiosity and desperation. After my consultation, the nutritionist told me that along with other alterations to my diet, I had to give up eating wheat for a while as she was sure I had wheat intolerance. This is a very common condition where the immune system has an adverse reaction to certain food and drinks, in my case, wheat-based products (usually because of the group of proteins contained within wheat known as gluten, the most common of which is gliadin).

Gluten comes from the Latin for glue. It gives elasticity to dough, helps it rise, keep its shape and gives wheat products their chewy texture.

The trouble is that many people do not realise they have the condition as was the case with me. Very often, you will crave the very things that your body is having the adverse reaction to. I was told that I had to give up for a while, all bread and foods that contain wheat in them, which is a lot! It was at this moment that it dawned on me just how much bread I had been eating. The equivalent of a large uncut brown loaf every day! I was mortified, what was I going to eat? I would starve!

Well, I did manage to give it all up and the difference it made was incredible. Within 2 weeks I had gone from struggling to get out of bed at 9 am on my days off to bounding out of bed at 6 am full of energy. In the next year the indigestion I frequently experienced after meals was a thing of the past.

Over the next couple of years my hay fever symptoms gradually reduced until they completely disappeared and have never come back.

This had such profound effect on me that I decided to become a nutritionist and I chose the naturopathic route. This kind of story is very often the catalyst for many people deciding to train in nutrition.

1B. NATUROPATHIC NUTRITION AND WHY IT'S SO EFFECTIVE

The Oxford English Dictionary describes naturopathy as "the treatment of disease etc. without drugs, involving diet, exercise, massage etc." A Naturopath is a person who believes that the human body can remain in excellent health if it is provided with the optimum nutrition it requires together with a healthy lifestyle and environment. Our bodies want to exist in a healthy state, not an unhealthy one. The human body has evolved exquisitely over hundreds of thousands of years and has an amazing capacity for restoring health and maintaining vitality. Even a body in a long term chronic diseased state has the ability to heal itself. All it requires are the right tools to do so i.e. optimum diet, lifestyle and some time!

A naturopathic nutritionist simply provides the body with everything it requires and then allows nature to take its course. This is the best way to ensure you enjoy optimum health and longevity. You work with nature, not against it.

Allowing time for recovery from disease or illness is one of the cornerstones of the naturopathic philosophy. Despite what many people believe, the body you had a year ago is not the same body you have today. The cells in your body are constantly broken down and replaced at varying rates, depending on where they are located in your body. For instance:

- The cells lining your stomach are replaced every five days
- Your blood supply is replaced every three months
- The majority of the cells in your muscles are replaced every six months
- In a year, approximately 98% of the trillions of cells in your body have been replaced.

You get the general idea. This means that if we eat a diet with all the essential nutrients required for health and make sure that our lifestyle and environment is as healthy as we can make it, then we can, over time, replace the existing cells that make up our bodies with better quality ones. Better quality cells mean a better, healthier and more efficient body. But, we must be patient and wait for the changes to occur, there is no short cut, you have to wait for nature.

Unfortunately, our society is so frenetic that it does not want to wait for anything, we want it yesterday! This is why so many rely on pharmaceutical drugs to keep them going when they are ill. They don't have the time for being ill and they want instant relief from symptoms, which is understandable. Adverts on television every winter show some poor soul with flu and his colleagues are convinced he is going to miss that vital meeting. But when he takes his amazing medicine all his symptoms are miraculously gone! He turns up at the meeting smiling and looking full of health and vitality much to the incredulity of his colleagues.

Unfortunately, this is only a temporary fix as it treats the symptoms and not the underlying cause. In time they usually return in the same form or even something more serious because the more you suppress something the more likely it is to return.

We need to be patient! One of my great inspirations was a top research scientist on sport and physical performance called Dr Michael Colgan. For almost 40 years he advised numerous world champions in many different sports on nutrition and exercise and in his book Sports Nutrition Guide (2002) he draws a great analogy to the cell renewal I have talked about:

"Look at it this way. Without correct nutrition and training, the human body is like a neglected houseplant, dull, droopy, no sparkle. Given the right plant food, water, fresh air, light and TLC, the plant will perk up a bit. But you have to wait on Nature for the old defective leaves and stems to die off and new ones to grow, to see the real expression of its genetic makeup. In six months, the plant is sleek with budknots and the leap of life. With a couple of years of continuous care, it will grow to magnificence." Michael Colgan

So, in a nutshell, naturopathic nutrition is all about helping the body to help itself and giving it the tools to do so; being patient and keeping factors that interfere with this to a minimum.

1c. OPTIMUM NUTRITION IS VITAL TO EVERY FUNCTION IN YOUR BODY

It is impossible to achieve optimum health and longevity without optimum nutrition. It is like trying to run a racing car on the cheapest petrol and engine oil, it will not function very well, it will wear out quicker and chances are that it will be unreliable. So, if you want a top-quality body you must ensure that at least 80% of the time you eat food that is top quality and nutrient rich.

We have already talked about how your body replaces its cells over time, with each area of the body replacing cells at different rates. In order for this to happen effectively and give you improved quality of cells and health, you have to be in it for the long term. Eating well for a short time here and there will not improve your overall cellular function - consistency is key.

When you do this, over time, every organ in your body will be made up of more efficient cells and the function of the organs and bodily systems will also improve.

"If you have no time for complete and balanced nutrition, you better reserve a lot of time for illness." Michael Colgan lecture series 2000

This is not to say it will all be raw turnips and seeds from now on. As with all aspects of life it's about balance, but it goes without saying that the more nutrient rich food we choose the healthier our bodies will be.

1d. THE POWER OF SYNERGY

As mentioned earlier the guiding principles of this book are synergy and balance. I can't emphasise enough the importance of a synergistic approach to all areas of health and in particular, nutrition. I would therefore like to take a little time to look at synergy in a little more detail as this principle will help you achieve astounding results.

Nothing works on its own

When I work with a new client I always like to explain to them the reasons behind my recommendations and one of the most important concepts is that everything in nutrition works together. There have been numerous times when the mainstream media have announced the results of a study that claims that one particular nutrient has a preventative or therapeutic effect with respect to a disease or condition. What usually happens next is there is a big upsurge in interest as people start to buy the miracle nutrient.

There seems to be a mind-set, especially in orthodox medicine and the media that searches for a wonder nutrient or drug, a panacea that will cure diseases on its own; unfortunately, it does not work this way. We become susceptible to illness and disease through a combination (synergistic effect) of many different factors which include poor diet, stress, pollution, poor lifestyle choices and lack of exercise and the best way to promote healing and recovery is to treat them in the same synergistic way; looking at all the factors and making positive changes to them as is promoted throughout this book. In nutrition, there is no single magic bullet that will heal all.

Of course, there is nothing wrong with people wanting to take either preventative action against becoming ill or trying to improve a current condition or disease. But in many cases the supplement will be taken in isolation, often in conjunction with an unbalanced diet and therefore reducing its effectiveness. Nutrients work in combination with each other and it is the interaction of all the essential nutrients together that will give you optimum biological function and allow you to achieve your best health; ideally principally from your diet. Taking nutrients in isolation will not allow you to achieve the results you're looking for.

An example of this is Vitamin C which is one of the most commonly taken supplements because one of its most widely known and proven benefits is as an immune booster. It is great that many people want to take responsibility for their health and well-being, but Vitamin C would be far more effective if it was taken with other nutrients that are also required for optimum immune function.

To fully support the immune system vitamin C needs to be taken with bioflavonoids (many good vitamin C supplements will incorporate these), zinc, selenium together with vitamins A, B6 and E. The best way to accomplish this is to take your vitamin C in conjunction with a good quality, high strength vitamin and mineral formula and a quality antioxidant formula. You also need to think about supplementing essential omega fats as they also contribute to enhanced immune function.

So, although taking vitamin C is a positive step to improving your immunity, it will be greatly enhanced by the synergistic effect of taking it in conjunction with the other supplements.

I would like to stress at this point that I am a great believer in supplementation, but **not** in place of an optimum diet. They are, as the name suggests <u>supplementing</u> a healthy diet, not replacing it.

SECTION 2. MYTHS AND MISCONCEPTIONS

2A. THE MYTH OF THE PERFECT DIET

In my work as a nutritionist I meet people with very strong opinions about certain aspects of nutrition. One of the most common is relating to a healthy diet obviating the need for dietary supplements. I acknowledge that everyone is entitled to their opinion and respect them for it; however, I truly believe that achieving a perfect diet and obtaining optimum nutrition from it, is a myth in the 21st Century and here are some of the reasons why.

- SOIL DEPLETION - Intensive farming introduced widely in the 60's and 70's is now common practice and as a result, minerals in soils have become dramatically depleted. This makes it harder to obtain optimum levels of nutrients from the average diet.
- FOOD STORAGE – Modern food storage methods can often result in food on sale in supermarkets that appears to be fresh but may in fact have been in storage for weeks or even months, especially if it has been sourced from overseas. As soon as a food is harvested the clock starts ticking on its nutrient content. Obviously, the best time to eat it is straight away but we accept that this is not possible as it has to be stored and then transported to the point of sale. However, the longer this takes the fewer nutrients remain by the time it gets to your plate.
- FOOD PROCESSING – Many foods undergo some form of processing which helps increase shelf life but virtually destroys nutrients. For example, many processed foods contain refined grains stripped of their germ and fibre content such as white rice or pasta which is often marketed as a healthy choice but do little to contribute to your daily nutrient requirements.
- FOOD PREPARATION – Once you have bought your food if you then apply high temperatures to it as in baking, frying or roasting, the nutrient content is further reduced because the higher the temperature the more nutrients are destroyed.
- DIGESTIVE FUNCTION – When you have bought, prepared and consumed your food, the nutrients contained can only be efficiently extracted and utilised by your body if your digestive system is functioning optimally.

In addition to these factors that can affect everyone, there are certain groups in the population with greater nutritional needs who would benefit from supplementation.

- PRECONCEPTUAL, PREGNANT AND BREASTFEEDING WOMEN –

- A study from Harvard Medical School involving 18,000 women has shown that taking multi vitamins, particularly folic acid, can improve chances of pregnancy. Supplementing zinc has reduced the risk of health problems associated with low birth weight babies and the need for zinc increases during lactation.

  Pre-conceptual and early pregnancy supplementation of folate reduces the incidence of neural tube defects such as Spina Bifida. The Department of Health recommends that all women of child bearing age supplement 400 µg of folate daily – an amount that would be extremely difficult to obtain from diet alone.

- VEGETARIANS AND VEGANS - Vegetarians and vegans are susceptible to iron deficiency, as the most absorbable source of this mineral (haem iron) is from animal origin. They can obtain iron from non-haem sources, such as green vegetables – and a supplement of vitamin C would enhance absorption.

  Vegetarians and vegans who do not get sufficient exposure to sunlight may also need to supplement vitamin D, which is found in few foods, all of which are of animal origin, such as oily fish and full-fat dairy products. Vegans need to supplement vitamin B12, as this vitamin is only obtainable from animal sources or fortified foods, such as yeast extract.

- SMOKERS - Smoking generates enormous quantities of health-damaging free radicals, meaning that a smoker's requirement for antioxidant nutrients is greatly elevated. These include vitamins A, C, E and selenium. Indeed, studies have found that smoking lowers levels of vitamin C and beta-carotene, the antioxidant precursor to vitamin A.

  Cadmium, a heavy metal found in tobacco, decreases the bioavailability of selenium and depletes zinc levels in the body. Vitamin E is also thought to be at sub-optimal levels in smokers, as are B complex vitamins. There are probably few nutrients not seriously compromised by smoking, both in smokers and those regularly exposed to other people's smoke.

- DRINKERS – Although most people enjoy a tipple, alcohol depletes nutrients and adversely affects virtually every organ and system in the body. It interferes with magnesium metabolism and increases zinc and copper excretion. It upsets calcium and phosphate balance and interferes with levels of much-needed antioxidants, namely selenium, vitamin C and vitamin E. B vitamins are also lost through alcohol ingestion.

- EXERCISERS - Exercise requires greater nutritional support and this need increases the more you exercise. An example of this is the oxidative stress you create in the body (which increases with duration and intensity) as exercise uses oxygen, meaning free radical activity is increased. Prolonged exercise can overwhelm the body's antioxidant defences and result in increased post exercise soreness, inflammation and even DNA damage.

  Supplementation with antioxidants is thought to mitigate these effects. One example of this is a study that found post exercise inflammation in marathon runners reduced by consuming tart cherry juice twice a day, 5 days before, during and 2 days after running a marathon. They concluded this was because supplementing with the cherry juice increased the athletes' total anti-oxidative capacity, which reduced inflammation and aided in the recovery of muscle function.

  High sweat rates are another way that nutrients are lost from the body. This induces not only loss of water from the body but also iron, sodium, potassium and magnesium, which are lost in significant amounts.

- THE ELDERLY –The elderly can be a vulnerable group when it comes to malnutrition and deficiency, especially those who spend prolonged periods in hospital or care homes, as they frequently have little control over the quality of the food they eat. The problem is exacerbated by staff who may not be trained to recognise symptoms of deficiency.

  Low vitamin D levels, for example, are commonly found in the elderly. So too is calcium deficiency. This nutritional deficit means that the elderly are prone to fractures, and therefore time spent in hospital, which, as already mentioned is not the place to find the most nutritious of meals.

- CONVALESCENTS - When researchers studied the prevalence of malnutrition in hospital patients, they found that one patient in every five is malnourished – and that figure is thought to be an underestimation.

Malnutrition was also found to be associated with increased length of stay and development of infections, as well as disease severity. It gets worse: after major surgery, patients are at greater risk of malnutrition than most, partly because of the stress involved but also because of the increase in metabolic rate caused by the surgery.

2B. NUTRITIONAL SUPPLEMENTS

Some people say that taking supplements is a waste of money and just makes expensive urine. They believe you just need to eat a healthy diet and that taking supplements is unnatural. Yet modern living with exposure to pollution and the effects of stress are hardly natural! Supplementation is simply an effective way to complement our diet to help our bodies to thrive in the modern world. So, from my perspective, can any of us afford not to if we want to achieve optimal health and fitness?

In 2002, the Journal of the American Medical Association, for so long opposed to vitamin and mineral supplementation, stated that sub-optimal intake of many nutrients was common in the general population and was a risk factor for chronic disease, including heart disease, colon and breast cancer. According to the authors:

"... It appears prudent for all adults to take vitamin supplements".

Journal of the American Medical Association

Having studied under a range of experts on nutrition who have spent decades studying the research on the benefits of taking the correct dietary supplements I am convinced that supplementation can play a pivotal role in long term health and fitness. I have also seen amazing results in clients I've treated which could not have been achieved without the help of supplements.

I was a Fire Fighter for 30 years and up to the age of 54, when I retired, I had to maintain a level of fitness that enabled me to keep up with Fire Fighters who could be over 30 years my junior. I believe this would have been considerably harder without using supplements.

What supplements should I take and when should I take them?

Whether you are already taking supplements or thinking about taking them, the following tips will help you get the most out of them:

- ✓ It is best to prepare yourself for supplementing. You can do this by optimising your diet which will help to improve your digestion and create the enzymes necessary for effective absorption. Taking supplements in the hope of making up for a poor diet does not work. Also, depending on your current state of health, suddenly taking a supplement can promote a detoxification reaction which can make you feel unwell.

- ✓ It can be really useful to see a nutritionist as they will be able to tailor a supplement program unique to you that complements changes in your diet. Most people only think about going to see a nutritionist when they are ill, but you can get advice on your diet and supplements that will relate to your current lifestyle and specific health circumstances. The simple rule is, if in doubt over what supplements are best for you, consult a professional.

- ✓ Start by taking a multi-vitamin/mineral supplement. Avoid taking individual vitamins or minerals unless you are taking a general multivitamin/mineral. Remember, nutrients work together in synergy.

- ✓ Ensuring that you get the best supplements can be tricky if you do not know what to look for. Generally, the more expensive supplements are the better quality so avoid cheap supplements as the ingredients and formulation will not be the top quality you're looking for. So often the cheaper supplements are produced from chemical versions of the underlying nutrient rather than from natural ingredients, which, as well as being less effective, are often not easily absorbed by the body.

  However, just because a supplement is expensive does not guarantee that it will be effective, I have recommended some suppliers in the Useful Websites section at the back of the book.

- ✓ When taking supplements, for optimum results it is important to be consistent and take them every day. Leaving them out to remind you can help to develop the habit.

- ✓ Make sure that you read the labels so that you get the correct dosage and take the supplement at the right times. Many should be taken with food but not all.

- ✓ It is best to spread your supplements throughout the day if possible. For example, if you are taking more than two tablets or capsules of a multivitamin, Vitamin C or other supplements, taking them through the day ensures that your body has a continuous supply of extra nutrients. Of course, it is not always practical to do this and sometimes you may need to take them all at the start of the day, whilst this is not the ideal, it is better than not at all.

We are all unique biologically and therefore have unique nutrient requirements, which is why I would recommend that you see a nutritionist so that you can get a supplement program that is designed specifically for you.

This is especially important if you have health issues as simply supplementing in these circumstances without taking professional advice can cause complications. However, if you are in a good state of health and you have optimised your diet, here are some supplements that are worth considering:

1. Multi vitamin and mineral supplement

This will complement your diet and ensure that you are optimally supplied with all the nutrients you need for great health.

2. Antioxidant Formula

Most people could benefit from additional antioxidants, especially, as I have highlighted in chapter 4 if you exercise on a regular basis.

It is important to appreciate that we do actually need some free radicals because our body uses them for important biological processes. However, as with everything in health, it is all about balance and in modern life there are many factors that can push free radical production way in excess of levels that are beneficial to our health. These include:

a. Being over 40, the older we get the less efficient our bodies become at quenching free radicals with indigenous (produced internally) and exogenous (obtained externally from food) antioxidants.

b. Smoking

c. Working or living in polluted areas, such as along roads with lots of traffic.

d. Exercising regularly on or near busy roads (e.g. cycling, running, walking, playing other sports such as tennis).

e. Living or working around a smoky atmosphere (e.g. Firefighter)

f. Eating a diet lacking in fresh vegetables and fruit; less than one serving a day that covers the palm of your hand.

g. Eating fried, deep fried or browned/crispy food most days.

You should look for a formula that has a broad spread of antioxidants as these nutrients complement each other and work in synergy. Some manufacturers use a scale known as the ORAC scale (Oxygen Radical Absorbance Capacity). This is an indicator of the effectiveness of the product, the higher the ORAC number the better it is. Generally, you would be looking for an ORAC score of at least 5,000 per day.

3. Vitamin C

Vitamin C is essential to many functions in the body and is involved in the immune response. It is vital to skin and connective tissue and is a powerful antioxidant. As mentioned above, choose a supplement that includes bioflavonoids.

4. Essential fatty acid supplement

These tend to be found in oily fish such as sardines, anchovies, mackerel and salmon as well as vegetable sources such as flax seeds. High quality fish oil is good though Krill oil has been found to be a superior source of essential fatty acids. There are also blends which combine plant based essential fatty acids, one of the best is called Udo's Choice.

5. Aloe Vera Juice

Aloe Vera juice has many health benefits when taken orally. It has been proven to benefit the digestive and immune systems. It also has an anti-viral and an anti-inflammatory action. (Inflammation is a key cause of disease in the body).

6. Probiotic

A probiotic supplement will help to increase the number of beneficial bacteria in your digestive tract. This is crucial for your long- term health as these bacteria play a vital role in many systems including digestion and immunity.

7. Vitamin D

I want to go into more depth with respect to this vitamin and use it as an example of the need for supplementation.

Vitamin D is most well known as being essential for bone health and is also called the sunshine vitamin because of the skin's ability to make it when exposed to adequate amounts of sunlight. Historically vitamin D has not attracted a huge amount of attention but in recent years there has been a big upsurge of interest. This is because of compelling new research that shows that not only are many of us deficient, but this deficiency could be a major factor in the development of many disease conditions.

It is being recognised that by simply ensuring that we have optimal amounts of this vitamin, we may drastically cut the chances of developing a whole raft of conditions which include cardiovascular disease, osteoarthritis, osteoporosis and diabetes. It may also reduce your chances of depression, strokes, chronic pain, muscle weakness, muscle wasting and many types of cancer.

<u>What does vitamin D do?</u>

It promotes the absorption of calcium and phosphate from food and regulates calcium levels in the blood. When we have sufficient calcium in the diet this vitamin is fundamental in the development and maintenance of strong bones and teeth.

It helps to control insulin levels which in turn help to keep blood sugar stable.

It plays an important role in supporting the optimal function of the immune system, brain and nervous system.

It helps to support lung function and cardiovascular health.

What are the signs and symptoms that are associated with deficiency?

- ☹ If you suffer from depression it is worth having a vitamin D test. Research studies indicate that lower levels of vitamin D translated to a greater likelihood of depression.
- ☹ As you get older your ability to make vitamin D declines. This has been shown to be especially true for people over 50. So, the older you are the greater the chance of deficiency.
- ☹ If you are overweight, obese or a heavy person due to muscle mass, this increases your requirement of vitamin D compared to a slim person.
- ☹ Aches and pains in your bones may be caused by deficiency. It can be misdiagnosed as chronic fatigue syndrome (also known as myalgic encephalomyelitis ME) or fibromyalgia (pain or tenderness in muscle and bone).
- ☹ If you commonly find that you suffer from perspiration on your head this is an early sign of deficiency.
- ☹ If you have an under functioning digestive system or liver, this can affect your ability to absorb fats. Vitamin D is a fat-soluble vitamin and relies on our ability to absorb fats for its own assimilation into the body.

How can I check to see if I am deficient?

Every person is biologically unique and whilst one person is deficient, another may have adequate levels of vitamin D from the same lifestyle and circumstances. Therefore, the only accurate way to find out if you are deficient in vitamin D is to be tested.

This can be done through a simple blood test and you may even be able to get the test done free at your doctor's surgery. You can also get a test kit sent to your home which requires just a small blood spot sample from a finger. (See the Useful Websites section at the back of the book)

The optimal vitamin D levels should be between:

50 – 90 ng/ml	(nanograms per millilitre of blood) or
125 – 180 nmol/litre	(nanomols per litre of blood).

These are the two most common scales of measurement. If your test comes back as insufficient, use the protocols below.

Protocols to help ensure you get optimal levels of vitamin D

Sunshine

- ✓ The most natural way to attain optimal levels of vitamin D is through sunshine though depending where you live in the world this isn't always the most convenient way to source your vitamin D. Useful rule of thumb is that if your shadow is longer than you the sun is too low in the sky to make sufficient amounts of vitamin D.
- ✓ In the UK, where I live, it's only really possible in the summer months. During the summer it's best to get your sun in in the middle of the day between 10 and 3 o'clock. This is because the wavelength of light that your skin requires to make this vitamin (known as UVB) is at its highest. You also need to expose as much skin as possible if temperature and circumstances allow.
- ✓ In order to make useful amounts of vitamin D you need to be in the sunshine for between 15 and 30 minutes, in direct sunlight and not in the shade. Skin pigment can act as a natural sun screen so people with darker skin will need longer than people with pale skin.
- ✓ Try to avoid using sun creams during this time, especially ones with a greater SPF than 15 as they will block the UVB rays which your skin requires. You should not burn for this short time unless the temperatures are extreme as it has been shown that the wavelength of light that burns and damages skin, UVA, is produced in greater quantities during the early morning before 10am and later in the afternoon after 3pm.
- ✓ Sitting behind glass in the sun will prevent you making vitamin D because although UVA can pass through glass, the UVB rays needed cannot.
- ✓ If you have managed to get out into the sun at the correct time of day, try to avoid using soaps over those parts of the body that have been exposed. This is because a significant amount of vitamin D will be on the surface of the skin and takes around 48 hours to be absorbed. Showering with soap will unwittingly just wash away much of your vitamin D. A bit of a dilemma then. It depends on how warm you got, but if possible, just restrict washing to those parts that really need it so that you can maximise your absorption.

Food sources and supplementation

Winter months, inclement weather and pollution can all hinder your ability to get sufficient UVB rays. As an alternative you can get your vitamin D from certain foods and by supplementation.

- ✓ Healthy fats assist in the absorption of vitamin D, so try to consume them in your diet. You can get them from coconut fat, avocados, olive oil, a little butter, nuts, seeds, Krill oil supplementation and using Udo's Choice plant oil blend.
- ✓ Foods with good levels of vitamin D are oily fish (especially salmon, tuna, mackerel and sardines). Eggs and Portobello mushrooms also provide useful amounts.
- ✓ If you are vegan, there is less choice from foods that naturally contain Vitamin D. Portobello and maitake mushrooms contain reasonable amounts but you may benefit from looking at fortified foods as well. This can be a problem as many processed foods are fortified but not a healthy option. However, there are exceptions, such as almond milk which is frequently fortified and can be a useful replacement for cow's milk.

Factors to consider re supplementation

Taking a high-quality vitamin D3 supplement can be a good way to boost your levels of vitamin D but it is useful to bear the following in mind if you consider supplementation:

- ✓ It is a good idea to get your levels tested and seek the advice of a nutritionist who will be able to advise you of the best option together with a doctor if you are taking medication.
- ✓ Before considering supplementing, try to optimise your levels from sunlight and diet.
- ✓ You may need to take other supplements in conjunction with the vitamin D (multi vitamin/mineral complex). This is because it increases absorption of calcium which can lead to inadequate magnesium absorption.
- ✓ The current RDI set in the UK by the government for vitamin D supplementation is 400 IU (international units). This is woefully inadequate; designed to be at a level that supposedly prevents the symptoms of disease. This will prevent the onset of rickets, but little else; this RDI is nowhere near the amount required for optimal health.

If your test shows that your levels of vitamin D are low, then you need to supplement 10,000 IU to get up to optimum levels. This may take a few months and whilst you are doing this you should test every four weeks.

Once you have achieved the optimal level you can reduce your intake to 5,000 IU per day and continue to get yourself regularly tested. On an ongoing basis, it's wise to get tested at least once a year, although twice a year would be ideal.

Who might benefit from supplementation?

- ❒ All pregnant and breastfeeding women
- ❒ Breastfed infants may need to receive drops containing vitamin D from one month of age if their mother has not taken vitamin D supplements throughout
- ❒ People with darker skin tones as darker skin is more efficient at sun protection.
- ❒ People aged 65 years and over.
- ❒ People who have limited exposure to sun, for example if you work night shifts or spend most of your time indoors
- ❒ People who live in a part of the world where; for months at a time the sun does not rise high enough at midday to give you adequate UVB rays to make vitamin D. As mentioned above, a good way to assess this is to see if your shadow is longer than you are. If it is this means that the sun is too low in the sky for you to make vitamin D. In this case you should maximise your vitamin D from your diet and possibly take a supplement.

A final word

If you haven't done so already, I would strongly encourage you to get your vitamin D levels checked along with those of family and friends. There is growing evidence that not having optimal levels of vitamin D can have far more serious consequences for your long-term health than once thought. Some people may be able get optimal levels for free just by ensuring they get enough sun exposure. Making a few lifestyle and dietary changes together with possible supplementation to optimise your levels could potentially make a huge difference to your health and be one of the best decisions you ever make.

2c. CHOLESTEROL – NOT THE VILLAIN IT'S MADE OUT TO BE

Cholesterol, has, since a single flawed study in the early 1950's, been the scapegoat, the artery clogging villain, portrayed as a prime cause of cardiovascular disease (CVD) through misleading fear-based information. This has led to a monumental crusade to reduce levels in the body. It is so ingrained in our consciousness that the very mention of cholesterol causes most people to immediately think of heart disease!

Found in healthy fatty foods such as organic free-range eggs and butter, it has been tarred and feathered with the same CVD causing brush as saturated fat for many years.

Only in recent years is common sense starting to prevail and cholesterol is slowly starting to be seen, as a friend, instead of a sworn enemy that needs to be controlled at all costs.

Approximately ¾ of your cholesterol is made in your liver, so why would the body make so much if you didn't rely on it for optimal health? Only about ¼ comes from the diet.

Cholesterol plays a vital role in many areas of well-being including:

☺ The formation of healthy cell membranes, crucial to the function of the trillions of cells in the body.

☺ Cholesterol is used by the body to heal and repair damage.

☺ The manufacture of synapses in the brain, these are connections between nerve cells (neurones). It is these connections that allow cognitive function such as thinking, learning new things and memory. It is also crucial to the structure of the brain neurones themselves and the nervous system.

☺ It is used particularly in a fatty substance called myelin which wraps around and insulates the structures of the brain and nervous system, a bit like insulation around electrical wires. If it starts to breakdown we start to lose brain and nervous system function (multiple sclerosis). Myelin also nourishes and protects every structure in your brain and nervous system - and it is made up of 20% cholesterol! In fact, your brain contains about 25% of the cholesterol in your body.

☺ A precursor in the manufacture of bile acids which play a vital role in dietary fat breakdown and absorption as well as the absorption of fat soluble vitamins A,D,E,K. Your body actually re-absorbs the cholesterol to re-use it once the bile has done its work, it's that important.

☺ The manufacture of sex hormones such as testosterone, progesterone by the sex glands and stress hormones such as cortisol and adrenaline by the adrenal glands.

☺ The production of vital vitamin D from sunlight interacting with cholesterol in the skin.

This is by no means a complete list of the roles cholesterol plays in the body, but I hope it gives you an appreciation that if we try to limit it artificially, these processes and others start to suffer.

Your body is very good at controlling levels of cholesterol according to its own needs. These levels will go up and down according to the environment inside your body. For instance, it is used by the immune system, so if you are fighting a viral infection or bacterial infection the level in the blood will go up. It will also increase if we are under physical or psychological stress. Also, if inflammation is high in the body due to damage/injury, levels go up because cholesterol is used to heal and repair. Alternatively, if we are happy, relaxed and in good health cholesterol will adjust to optimal levels.

Different types of cholesterol

It is now well known that HDL Cholesterol (High Density Lipoprotein) is beneficial to health. Conversely, it is also thought that all LDL cholesterol (Low Density Lipoprotein) is bad for health. However, there are 2 different types of LDL:

1. Large Particle Type A

This is known as fluffy LDL and is beneficial to health

2. Small Dense Particle Type B.

This is the one that can cause problems and increase coronary heart disease (CHD) risk.

Checking your coronary heart disease (CHD) risk

When it comes to looking at cholesterol as an indicator of coronary heart disease risk, ratios are far more important than the total level. Here are 2 useful ways to check your coronary heart disease risk:

1. Ratio of HDL to total cholesterol

In the U.K. you can get a test through your doctor's surgery that gives you your serum cholesterol levels or they can be included in a more general blood test that can also check, for example, levels of Vitamin D.

When you receive your results it's important to calculate the ratio of HDL cholesterol to the total cholesterol as this is considered an accurate measure of your risk of Coronary Heart Disease.

<u>Calculating the ratio:</u>

Divide the HDL figure by the total cholesterol (HDL/Total cholesterol).

The result should ideally be above 24%.

2. Triglyceride/HDL ratio

Another accurate indicator of potential CHD risk is your triglyceride/HDL ratio. Triglycerides are found in foods such as eggs, fish and dairy and are also made by the liver. They are used to transport fat in the blood and can be broken down and utilised for energy or stored as body fat. They are an essential part of metabolism but as with everything in the body, it's all about the right balance. High levels of triglycerides in the blood can reduce your levels of HDL cholesterol and the Triglyceride/HDL ratio is a good indicator of this.

<u>Calculating the ratio:</u>

Divide the Triglyceride by the HDL (Triglyceride/HDL)

The result should ideally be less than 2%.

How can we maintain optimal levels of cholesterol for health?

If your doctor is concerned about your cholesterol you may be advised to take statins. Statins are prescribed frequently these days and can cause their own problems with side effects such as:

☹ Depression

☹ Dizziness

☹ Cognitive impairment including memory loss

☹ Reduction of levels of Co-enzyme Q10 in the body

☹ Decreased immunity

☹ Liver problems

☹ Increased risk of nerve damage (polyneuropathy)

If you are considering taking statins research them carefully to make sure it is the best option for you. Ideally discuss with your doctor the viability of choosing the natural route first by following the protocols in this book by optimising your diet, exercising regularly and reducing stress levels. In particular:

✓ Exercise on a regular basis, HIIT is particularly useful

✓ Try not to drink more than one unit of alcohol a day

✓ Avoid smoking

✓ De-stress and nurture yourself (see chapter 6)

✓ Make sure you get plenty of good quality Omega 3 fats (Krill Oil is excellent for this)

✓ Drastically decrease or better still, eliminate grains and sugar from your diet

✓ Try to eat a substantial part of your diet raw (more on this later)

✓ Eat healthy fats, raw and from organic sources

✓ Reduce your weight if over-weight

In Summary

The message that is emerging from the latest thinking concerning cholesterol is that it is not something to be feared. In fact, too little cholesterol can have dire health consequences. Health is all about balance, and so it is with cholesterol. We need to get the right balance of HDL and the types of

LDL. For the majority of us, the most natural and effective way to do this is through comprehensive lifestyle changes. These will enable you to keep your cholesterol balanced in the ideal ratios for your health; something that only your body knows how to do best.

2D SALT IS NOT BAD FOR YOU!

Salt is essential to life as it contains sodium and chloride, which cannot be made by the body. It forms part of our blood, sweat, tears, lymphatic fluid and extracellular fluid. Together with other trace minerals found in natural salt, sodium and chloride play a vital role in many biological processes including;

- ✓ The functioning of neurones in the brain
- ✓ The passing of signals to muscles that initiate movement
- ✓ Supporting adrenal function
- ✓ Helping nutrients to enter cells and regulating the water both within and surrounding the cell for optimal function
- ✓ Maintaining and regulating blood pressure in conjunction with a diet high in vegetables and good hydration
- ✓ Enhancing the action of digestive enzymes and the absorption of nutrients
- ✓ Helping to regulate sleep
- ✓ Helping to prevent muscle cramps
- ✓ Helping to promote vascular health
- ✓ Helping to promote sinus health

How did salt get such a bad press?

One of the first flawed studies that led to promoting low sodium diets was carried out in 1997. It concluded that a diet low in salt could control blood pressure. This led to salt being demonised. However it was later found that the reason for the decrease in blood pressure was not less salt in the diet but less fructose. More recent studies have shown that salt actually helps to regulate blood pressure and that low salt is as detrimental to health as too much.

Choose the type of salt you consume wisely

Some salt does deserve a bad press as it is harmful to the body. Whilst all salt contains sodium and chloride not all salt is the same. It's therefore imperative that we choose the type of salt we consume wisely. The salt that is bad for you *is processed table salt* and should be avoided.

Table Salt 97% sodium chloride 3% manmade chemicals

- When you look at what is done to the salt before it goes to market you can understand why table salt wreaks so much havoc with health. Part of the processing involves heating it to 1,200 degrees Fahrenheit, which unsurprisingly, changes the chemical structure.
- Manmade chemicals are also added as moisture absorbents and flow agents to stop the salt clumping together. These are toxic and do not belong in the body, having nothing in common with natural salt.
- As table salt is stripped of nutrients it lacks the synergistic elements required to keep things in balance so impairs bodily processes.

Natural Salt 84% sodium chloride 16% trace minerals

- As it is unrefined, and processing is kept to a minimum, it retains its original chemical structure and trace minerals.
- Natural sea salts are popular now. Examples include Brittany sea salt and Hawaiian sea salt, known as Alaea salt. However, increases in pollution levels in oceans can mean that some sea salts contain heavy metals.
- My favourite natural salt is Himalayan Crystal Salt. As the name suggests it is mined in the Himalayas and is as free from heavy metals and industrial toxins as it is possible to get. This salt is pink in colour and a nutritional goldmine. In addition to sodium and chloride it contains 84 trace minerals that play important roles in a wealth of bodily processes including thyroid, adrenal and immune function. It has more potassium than other natural salts, which helps to balance the sodium potassium ratio essential to health.

Tips for Salt Intake

✓ Replace table salt with Himalayan Crystal Salt both on the table and during cooking.

- ✓ Avoid or cut down on processed foods.
- ✓ If you eat out a lot, ask the restaurant to prepare your meal without table salt. You can then add sea salt at the table, and if this is not provided, take your own Himalayan salt.
- ✓ Even though natural salt is very beneficial, it is important not to overdo things. As with everything in health it's all about balance.
- ✓ A useful way to regulate salt intake is according to how much you drink, so a ½ tsp for every 2 litres of water is about right.
- ✓ Try to spread your salt intake throughout the day.
- ✓ If you are engaged in intensive exercise and sweating heavily or live in a hotter climate you will need more salt and the equivalent water.
- ✓ If you overdo your intake (too high a salt to water ratio) your body will tell you; it will result in swelling due to water retention and your weight will increase. Just increase your water intake and stop taking salt for a short while (a day is usually enough) to allow the water to wash the excess salt out of your body.

SECTION 3. The Main Food Groups and Fibre

Although most people are aware of the main food groups, I think that it is important to understand their function, so you can appreciate the vital role they play in keeping you healthy.

We are bombarded with often conflicting and confusing information about protein, carbohydrates and fats. It is therefore not surprising when many people, confused about what they should and should not eat, just switch off and I completely understand this frustration

Now, at this point I would love to be able to tell you that there are infallible methods that you can use that would guarantee you always received precisely the right amounts of these food groups from your diet. Unfortunately, this cannot be achieved because there are just too many variables that affect how much each person manages to absorb and assimilate into their body.

It is far better, in my opinion, to have a basic set of ground rules that you can easily apply. These will give you the means to make informed choices so that you can achieve the right balance from your diet with reasonable accuracy.

They will also help you to ensure that your diet provides you with the best quality nutrients.

3A. PROTEIN

The word protein comes from the Greek word "proteos" meaning the first one or most important one and proteins are certainly the most important building blocks for the human body. Every one of the trillions of cells that make up you is heavily dependent on protein for its structure and function. Protein is used for growth, repair, and maintenance of good health through countless metabolic interactions.

It is the second most abundant compound in the body after water. A large proportion is found in muscle (43% on average) with significant proportions being present in skin (15%) and blood (16%).

It is obviously beneficial to include the best quality proteins in your diet. This will ensure that you will be able to build better quality cells which in turn will give you a better, healthier and stronger body.

How much protein do you need?

The recommended daily intake is based on what is called the Reference Nutrient Intake (RNI). The RNI is defined as the amount of a nutrient that is enough to meet the requirements of the majority of the population. Only a minority of the population will need more than this amount e.g. elite athletes, pregnant women.

The RNI for adults is 0.75 grams of protein per kilogram of bodyweight per day. However, current research now suggests that it is prudent to modify this slightly. The ideal intake should be 0.75 grams of protein per **LEAN** kilogram of body weight. Your lean body weight can be calculated by finding out your percentage body fat and subtracting it from your total body weight.

There are numerous ways to calculate percentage body fat. Two of the most commonly used are:

Body fat calipers - These are used to pinch folds of skin at various sites on your body and then extrapolate a body fat percentage by putting the readings into a formula. Calipers can be bought very cheaply on the internet and this method does not take long and is pretty accurate.

The measurement method - This works by measuring the circumference of your neck, waist, hips and sometimes other body parts such as wrist and forearm. These figures are then put into a calculator together with your gender and height. This is not as accurate as the caliper method but is quicker and more convenient (there are lots of measurement calculators on the internet) and is okay to use for determining daily protein requirements.

Once you have established your body fat percentage you can use the simple formula below to work out your approximate daily protein requirements.

LEAN BODY WEIGHT IN KG × 0.75 = DAILY PROTEIN REQUIREMENT IN GRAMS

Using this formula, you can work out your approximate requirements which will then help you in consuming adequate amounts of good quality protein per day. However, you should treat this number as a guide and not an absolute. This is because we are all biologically unique and our protein requirements differ from one person to the next. There are also other factors that alter an individual's requirements such as age, current state of health, gender and level of daily physical activity, the quality of the protein and how you cook it.

How do you know you're getting the right amount?

This can be done in two ways. Firstly, by fully utilising the information on food labels you will be able to get a good idea of the protein content of many foods. Secondly, for those foods that do not have nutrition labels you can make use of one of the many nutrition apps now available. These allow you to calculate total protein intake (see Tip 19 in section entitled "Pulling it all Together"

You can then adjust it up or down as necessary. Also, after a short while you will come to learn how much protein is in your regular diet and can work it out in your head without using a label or app if you wish to.

I know that all of this seems like an incredible faff, but it really is important to make the effort to get a reasonably accurate idea of your protein intake. This is because not getting enough quality protein in your diet will prevent your body from achieving optimal health.

Also, there is an upper limit to how much protein your body can actually use, and new research suggests that consuming too much daily protein on a regular basis may well be counterproductive to long term health. When you consume too much protein your body has to remove nitrogen waste (which comes from the breakdown of protein) from your blood and this stresses your kidneys. There is also research that suggests that excessive protein intake could be a major factor in accelerated ageing and the development of diseases such as cancer. As with anything in nutrition we must find a good balance and eating an excess of any essential macronutrient is not better and can be just as counterproductive as not eating enough.

If you are in training or just play a lot of sports, it is of course possible to calculate your theoretical daily protein intake extremely accurately by using a tracker app all the time. In general though, you do not have to go to these lengths and it's not something that I do. Just use the figure you have calculated as something to aim for and you'll be fine– please don't obsess about achieving the figure exactly!

Top tips for getting the right quantity and quality of protein

✓ Eat organic sources of protein whenever possible. This will ensure that they are free from pesticide residues in the case of plant protein foods such as flax seeds. It will also avoid the growth hormones and antibiotics that are routinely given to factory farmed animals in their feed, residues of which can find their way to your plate.

✓ Check for the Soil Association or other well-known trusted marks on packaging. If a food is certified by these bodies, it is a symbol of the quality of the organic farming. This is important as organic farms can vary greatly in their standards.

✓ When preparing your meals try not to overcook your protein as this damages the protein structure, making it more difficult for your body to use it effectively. It also forms substances that cause inflammation in the body which is a prime cause of premature ageing. Frying, grilling and roasting are methods that are worth avoiding or at least reducing. Try boiling, steaming, steam frying or cooking for longer at a lower heat or eating raw when possible.

✓ Use packaging to identify the protein content of foods. This will help act as a guide to you eating the correct amounts per day as worked out from the RNI.

✓ Proteins are made up of 20 amino acids. We can make 13 of these ourselves. The remaining 9 we must get from our diet which is why they are called essential amino acids. It is therefore a good idea to eat a broad selection of protein foods that will ensure that you receive all 9 from your diet. This is especially important for vegans and vegetarians. Proteins that provide all the essential amino acids are known as complete protein foods.

✓ Protein from animal sources contain all 20 of the essential amino acids needed by the body. Great sources of animal protein include:

☺ Chicken and turkey

☺ Red meat (in moderation)

☺ Eggs

☺ Fish such as wild salmon, mackerel, sprats, herring, sardines, anchovies. Try to avoid frequently eating fish bigger than salmon on a regular basis, such as tuna. Although a great source of protein, it is a large fish and the bigger the fish, the further up the food chain it is and consequently the higher the pollutants that are likely to be found in the fish such as mercury. So, regular intake of fish such as tuna and swordfish should ideally be restricted or ideally avoided.

✓ Try to have at least 2 days a week where you get your protein from non-animal sources; this will help to promote beneficial alkaline conditions for improved health (see section 5c on inflammation). There are some vegetable sources of complete proteins; others must be eaten in combination to ensure all 9 essential amino acids are provided. Great vegetable sources are:

Complete protein food	**Complete protein combination**
☺ Quinoa	☺ Rice and beans
☺ Chia Seeds -great in smoothies	☺ Hummus and pitta bread
☺ Tofu-made from soya beans	☺ Spinach salad and almonds
☺ Hemp -great in milk or powder form	☺ Avocado and bean salad

✓ Consider using a protein powder supplement such as whey or pea protein as a source of high quality complete protein. They are very versatile and can be mixed into juices if, for instance, you need a quick nutritious meal in the morning. They can also be used in soups, porridge and pretty much anything else and are well worth using for their quality and convenience. They also make it much easier to keep an eye on your daily protein intake.

✓ Don't eat excessive amounts of protein. Going over your optimal amount by 5 or 10 grams occasionally is okay but regularly exceeding it by say, 50% or more is not a good idea as this may have serious consequences for your long-term health. You will find that it does not take many high-quality protein foods to reach your protein requirement for the day. It should also be remembered that most foods including vegetables and fruits have varying amounts of protein in them. This can be small, but the accumulation of these can quickly add up.

  So, for instance, if you eat a lot of vegetables, this could substantially contribute to your daily requirements. It is therefore not just being deficient in protein that we should be concerned about, it is also getting too much! Current research suggests that it is okay to go up to 1 gram of protein per gram of lean body weight per day, but I would personally not recommend going higher on a regular basis.

✓ Try to spread out your protein intake throughout the day as eating your daily protein requirement in one meal may result in you not being able to absorb it as efficiently as eating smaller amounts throughout the day. 30 grams at one sitting is currently considered to be a good guideline.

✓ Aim to have a maximum of approximately 20% of your diet made up of healthy protein.

✓ Consider using an app to manage your protein intake, at least in the beginning (see Tip 19 in section entitled "Pulling it all Together"

3B. Carbohydrates

Carbohydrates are made up of carbon, hydrogen and oxygen molecules. The name actually means watered carbon or carbon with attached water molecules.

You may already be aware of classifications of carbohydrates into simple and complex. But just to summarise, simple carbohydrates that are made up of simple sugars are very rapidly digested and absorbed into the blood stream making it very difficult to maintain a balanced blood sugar level (more on this in the section on how to control your blood sugar). Examples of these are white and brown sugar, honey, fruit drinks and bread, especially processed white bread.

Complex carbohydrates are a healthier choice as they are absorbed more slowly and help to keep your blood sugar stable. Examples of these are whole fruit, green vegetables, nuts, beans and lentils.

The main health benefits of including complex carbs in your diet are:

☺ **Vitamins and Minerals**

They provide a great source of essential vitamins and minerals such as B vitamins and iron. High-fibre fruits and vegetables, such as berries, artichokes and cabbage are an excellent source of antioxidants, which aid in preventing many diseases such as cancer and heart disease.

☺ **Improved Digestion**

Complex carbs provide fibre which helps to keep blood sugar stable and healthy bacteria to proliferate in the digestive tract. It also helps bulk up stools and eases their passage out of the body helping to prevent constipation.

☺ **Fuel**

Complex carbohydrates are perhaps best known as a source of energy for your body, providing continuous steady levels of energy throughout the day. Whilst it is reasonable to use them as a source of energy recent research suggests that we should not rely on them as our primary fuel and should encourage our bodies to use healthy fats instead (see section on fats)

How much carbohydrate do you need?

As is the case with protein, we should consider the individual biological factors that dictate what your optimal carbohydrate intake would be. These include age, gender, body composition, how active you are and your current state of health. The bottom line is that we all have unique requirements.

So, once again, it is important not to become obsessive about measuring total carb intake as it is time consuming and not very practical.

The key point is that you try to ensure that you eat mostly the complex variety and limit the less healthy simple carbohydrates in your diet. Try to work on a ratio of at least 90/10 in favour of the complex carbs. Ideally aim to have most of your complex carbohydrates from vegetables.

If you do this and combine it with regular exercise you will be taking a big step towards optimal health.

Top tips for carbohydrates

✓ Try to eliminate or at least limit your intake of simple carbohydrates as much as possible. They are most often found in heavily processed and refined foods such as confectionary (e.g. cakes, biscuits, chocolate). But a simple rule of thumb that I use is this; anything that comes in packaging or a box is more likely to contain simple carbohydrates.

Look at the ingredients, they are listed in descending order of content in the food, with the first being the largest component. Sugars, syrups, fruit juices, fruit purees, molasses, jams and jelly are all examples of simple carbohydrates. Latest research has confirmed that they are a prime cause of most diseases, especially heart disease and cancer.

You can get an approximate idea about the amounts in packaged foods by looking at the labelling. This will state how many carbohydrates there are per 100g e.g.

Curry Sauce: Carbohydrates 8.3g of which sugars 4.9g

From this we can see that over 50% of the carbohydrates in this curry sauce are made up of simple carbohydrates and when checking the list of ingredients sugar is there, which you may not have expected in a jar of spicy curry sauce! It's so easy to miss these sugars so getting in the habit of checking labels can be useful. Adding lots of fibre rich vegetables to the curry and serving it with wholegrain rice will tip the balance in favour of complex carbs. Ideally though avoid as many products as you can where simple carbs comprise are a higher proportion.

✓ Most types of mass produced bread even those that appear to be 'healthy' have been shown to spike blood sugar levels as quickly as granulated sugar. They have also been linked to leaky gut syndrome and increased inflammation. If you want to eat bread, try to ensure you choose organic wholemeal bread with the minimal number of ingredients that match as far as possible the recipe if you were making it at home.

Many of us are over reliant on bread as it's convenient and satisfying. Rather than follow the "give us this day our daily bread" see it as a once or twice a week treat. A useful way to ensure that you don't consume too much is to slice up a loaf and put it in the freezer then you can take a couple of slices during the week rather eat it all before it goes stale.

✓ A healthy alternative is kamut bread or give it its full name, kamut khorosan wheat. This can be ordered online or purchased from health food shops. This ancient grain, unlike modern hybridised, genetically altered modern grains, has been shown to be beneficial in helping to reduce inflammation, is not implicated in leaky gut and does not spike the blood sugar. If you really want to eat bread I would recommend eating this and moving away from modern genetically altered grains.

✓ Try to eat mainly complex carbohydrates. These are found in natural whole foods that already come with their own fibre which helps slow the rate of absorption into the blood such as green leafy vegetables; basically, anything that comes in nature's own wrapper and is not processed.

✓ Eat carbohydrates with protein or a healthy fat if possible. They will help to slow the speed that they are digested and absorbed into the blood helping to prevent fluctuations in your blood sugar. Aim to have approximately 30% of your diet made up from complex carbohydrates.

✓ Chew your food thoroughly; the digestion of carbohydrates starts in the mouth.

✓ Try not to rely on complex carbohydrates as your main source of energy. By this I mean don't let carbohydrates dominate meals. Meals should always include a good source of protein and healthy fats.

✓ Listening to your body is perhaps the best indicator of achieving the right carbohydrate levels for you. If you feel great and full of energy you are getting it right.

✓ Consider using an app to manage your carbohydrate intake until you get a good idea of the carbohydrate content of your regular diet. (see Tip 19 in section entitled "Pulling it all Together")

3c. Fats

Fats are probably the most misunderstood food group of all. There is so much confusion over what fats are good and which ones are bad because over the years we have been told different things; sometimes due to new research and other times from clever marketing by companies wanting to portray their produce as healthy.

Fat has been demonised and portrayed as a direct cause of obesity and high cholesterol, but this is very simplistic and untrue. In fact, if you get your intake of fats right it helps you to improve many areas of your health. These include; maintaining healthy levels and types of cholesterol, improving your insulin sensitivity which helps control your blood sugar and making it easier to lose weight and keep it off!

Fats are used in numerous ways in your body:

☺ Provide a concentrated and efficient source of energy; it is now recognised that it is better for your body to use fat as its primary source of energy rather than carbohydrates.

☺ Building blocks for cellular walls.

☺ Essential part of a variety of hormones and hormone like substances.

☺ Make us feel satiated more quickly than carbohydrates. They also help to control appetite by slowing down food absorption, so that we can go longer without feeling hungry.

☺ Act as carriers for important fat-soluble vitamins A, D, E and K.

☺ Used for the conversion of carotene to vitamin A and for mineral absorption.

☺ Involved in growth

☺ Help give your skin a smooth healthy texture

☺ Help reduce inflammation

☺ Help to control blood pressure

☺ Involved in the immune response

☺ Essential for the function of the brain (which is made up of over 60% fat), nervous system and for psychological well-being.

☺ Provide cushioning against physical shock in the skin and around the organs.

This is by no means a complete list of all the functions that fats are used for in your body, but it gives you some idea of how vital they are to our well-being. Ensuring that you get the right types of fat in the right quantities will play a massive role in helping you to attain optimum health and longevity.

There are three different types of dietary fats; monounsaturated, polyunsaturated and saturated.

Monounsaturated fats

These fats can be made by your body from saturated fats so are not essential like polyunsaturated fats. Known as Omega 9, the most abundant is Oleic acid which is found in animal and vegetable fats. Omega 9 is one of the most common fats in human breast milk and one of the most abundant fatty acids in the body. Although our bodies can make Omega 9 it is also useful to include good food sources in a balanced healthy diet. Their benefits include:

☺ Helping to reduce inflammation

☺ Increasing insulin sensitivity

☺ Lowering your risk of heart disease and stroke by decreasing the bad type of LDL cholesterol and increasing good HDL. The Mediterranean diet associated with a lowered risk of these conditions is high in these fats from things such as olive oil.

☺ Boosting energy levels

Good organic food sources of Omega 9 and especially Oleic acid are:

✓ extra virgin olive oil

✓ avocados

✓ almonds

✓ cashew nuts

✓ macadamia nuts

✓ sunflower seeds

Polyunsaturated fats

Most fats can be made in our body if required but there are some, known as the essential fats that we cannot make and must obtain from the diet. These are the polyunsaturated fats Omega 6 and Omega 3.

Most of the tissues in your body are made up of monounsaturated and saturated fats and you only require small quantities of polyunsaturated fats. However, these small quantities play a crucial role in your long- term health and wellbeing:

☺ Vital component of cellular membranes

☺ Energy production

☺ Haemoglobin production (the protein in red blood cells that delivers oxygen from the lungs to the tissues of our body)

☺ Help fatigued muscles to recover after exercise (help turn lactic acid into water and carbon dioxide)

☺ Help to regulate many functions within your cells

☺ Stimulate growth

☺ Fat loss

☺ Reduce inflammation and speed up healing

☺ Keep skin smooth

☺ Help to maintain correct blood pressure

☺ Help to reduce water retention

☺ Enhance immunity

We tend to get a lot more Omega 6 than Omega 3 in our diet due to Omega 6 being found in many processed foods and oils (such as vegetable oil). These are invariably damaged during the manufacturing process and have a disastrous effect on our health. Unfortunately, it is very easy to unwittingly consume too many Omega 6 fats without realising it. We therefore need to ensure we consume natural wholefoods and supplements that provide the highest quality, undamaged Omega 6 and Omega 3 fats in the correct ratio of 4:1 which is the optimal ratio for health.

Great whole food sources of these fats, are:

- ✓ Organic eggs
- ✓ Sardines, anchovies, sprats, mackerel, wild salmon.
- ✓ Organic freshly ground flax seed.
- ✓ Organic chia seeds
- ✓ Organic walnuts

Saturated fats

With respect to saturated fats, the latest research has proven that the old theory about them being bad for your health is not true. Whilst it is true that eating any saturated fats that have been processed such as in confectionary can harm your health because of their chemically altered unnatural structure; eating natural, healthy sources of saturated fats do not cause heart disease or raise the levels of the unhealthy type of cholesterol.

In fact, they can have many health benefits:

- ☺ Provide the building blocks for cell membranes, hormones and hormone like substances
- ☺ Carriers for the important fat soluble vitamins A,D,E,K
- ☺ Provide satiety, making you feel full quicker and for longer so you will tend to eat only what you require.
- ☺ Substances in saturated fats can be antiviral
- ☺ Help with the absorption of calcium
- ☺ Help with the manufacture of Vitamin A in the body

- ☺ Help your body to keep your cholesterol at optimal levels by assisting it to make healthy types of cholesterol and block its manufacture of the unhealthy type.
- ☺ Provide a very efficient fuel for your body, especially your brain. Latest research recommends that our diet should be made up of a greater percentage of foods that contain healthy fats rather than complex carbohydrates. Aim for approximately 50% from healthy fats and 30% from complex carbohydrates. This will, in conjunction with intermittent fasting, which I cover later in the chapter, and the right types of exercise encourage your body to use fat as fuel which has a whole raft of health benefits. These have been shown in studies to include:
  - ☺ Lower percentage of body fat
  - ☺ Easier weight control
  - ☺ Maintenance of healthy blood pressure
  - ☺ Improved insulin sensitivity which helps in the prevention of diseases and conditions associated with ageing.

It is important to point out at this point though I am sure that you already appreciate, that these saturated fats cannot be from any old source. They must be from natural sources which have not been processed or refined and should also be organic whenever possible.

Great sources of healthy and natural saturated fat include:

- ✓ Organic free range eggs
- ✓ Organic avocados
- ✓ Organic coconut fat/oil
- ✓ Organic butter
- ✓ Organic plain live cow's, goats, sheep's or coconut yoghurt
- ✓ Organic olives/olive oil
- ✓ Wild salmon fillets (organically reared if farmed)

Simple rules to follow for fats

The following tips will help you to choose the right fats and suggest ways to make sure you get healthy fats in the right balance.

1. Getting the right fats in your diet

Do:

- ✓ Do not overcook foods high in Omega fats because you will damage the delicate structure which can turn them from health enhancing fats into fats that harm your health. So, poach or boil eggs and avoid frying and scrambling. The same goes with fish -steaming or poaching will help retain the important healthy properties of these fats. Avoid frying or cooking in the oven. If you do choose to oven bake cook at a maximum of 140 degrees.
- ✓ You can also get your essential fats from supplementing them. The best form of animal-based oil is Krill Oil (tiny crustaceans that are the favourite food of many whales), you can also take a good quality fish oil but current research suggests that Krill Oil provides a better source of essential fats.
- ✓ If you prefer a plant origin supplement you can take flax seed oil. An excellent plant-based blend is Udo's Choice which can be purchased at good health food stores or bought online. Taking either one of these will help to ensure you get the correct quantities and 4 to 1 ratio of Omega 6 to Omega 3 essential fats.

  If you don't like the taste of the oil you can take it in capsule form instead. The advantage of capsules is that they are more convenient and transportable. Though please be aware that taking oils in liquid form allows you to supplement a larger quantity (one tablespoon) more easily and is more cost effective.
- ✓ It can be useful to alternate between plant derived and Krill based oils to widen the variety of beneficial fats you consume. For example, taking Krill one day and Udo's Choice the next.
- ✓ Use only organic fats/oils if possible.
- ✓ Organic butter can be used in the diet in moderation, especially if you are active as it provides a good source of energy. It also contains fatty

acids used by the colon that are anti-carcinogenic, antimicrobial and antifungal.

- ✓ Oils that can be used in food/salad dressings are extra virgin olive oil, coconut oil, avocado oil and flax seed oil.
- ✓ Coconut fat can be taken off the spoon as part of a meal or between meals. It sounds a bit weird, but the taste is okay (and this is from someone who grew up hating the taste of coconut). Coconut has many health benefits that include providing a source of healthy saturated fats and being anti-viral, anti-fungal and anti-bacterial. It also helps optimise your cholesterol levels in favour of healthy types of cholesterol, promote heart health, reduce the chances of strokes and strengthen your immune system. Take two to three teaspoons of coconut fat per day.
- ✓ Work on having up to 50% of your diet made up of foods that incorporate healthy fats (essential omega fats, but predominantly natural sourced saturated fat and monounsaturated fats). Foods such as avocados and eggs provide a great natural balance of all the healthy fats that you require.

Try to give up, avoid or reduce:

- × Avoid margarines if you can. Although they seem healthy, most will have been processed and heated at some point in their manufacture. Although many contain vegetable oil, omega or polyunsaturated fats, these will have had their structure damaged and will be harmful to your health.
- × Also, look for hydrogenated fats which are artificially made saturated fats (unnatural and damaging to your health). There are some specialist margarines that claim to be healthy, but read the labels carefully before buying. Rule of thumb is that the more the ingredients needed to be processed the less likely it will be healthy.
- × Commercial vegetable oils which have been touted as healthy because they are vegetable in origin should be avoided at all costs. They will have been damaged by being processed and wreak havoc with your health.
- × Be wary of the statement cold pressed; although this infers that no heat has been used in the extraction process, in many instances it means that

no external heat has been applied to the pressing process. However, industrial presses and processing can still raise the heat levels that cause damage to the fats. Instead use organic extra virgin olive oil, which is the only oil that will not have been damaged by excessive heat or by the chemicals used in industrial processing of oils such as seed and vegetable oils.

× Avoid any processed foods containing polyunsaturated or hydrogenated oils (chemically processed/refined saturated fats) e.g. hydrogenated palm oil.

2. Storage

Do:

✓ With fish oil and flax seed oil make sure that you keep them in a fridge, put the top on as soon as you have taken your oil and ensure that they come in dark glass bottles. Light, heat and air degrade the delicate omega fats in the oil making them go rancid so to prevent this you should limit their exposure as much as possible.

✓ Oils, such as Udo's Choice, will be in dark bottles and have been subjected to very low heat during manufacture and protected from oxygen and light. This ensures the oil retains all of its beneficial properties. It should state that it is unrefined on the label.

Try to give up, avoid or reduce:

× Avoid any oils that are in clear glass bottles. The delicate molecules in omega fats react to light passing through the glass and go rancid.

3. Cooking

Do:

✓ Try to eat oily fish raw or cook on a very low heat, poaching or steaming is best. Avoid frying fish and if baking, ensure the temperature is no higher than 140 degrees.

✓ The safest way to fry if you wish to do so is to use butter or coconut oil as these are stable fats and will not produce harmful by-products when heated. You can also add a little water to create steam which lowers the temperature to about 100 degrees and helps to protect the essential omega fats of the food that you're cooking.

Try to give up, avoid or reduce:

- × The golden rule with monounsaturated or polyunsaturated fats is not to heat them if you can avoid it, especially polyunsaturated. Heat damages the structure of the fat molecules and turns them from healing fats into ones that harm your health.

3D. A Few Words about Dietary Fibre

Fibre is the indigestible portion of plant foods and there are two types, soluble and insoluble. Soluble fibre is found in such things as beans, nuts, cucumbers and berries and can be broken down until it becomes a gel like substance in the small intestine. This slows down digestion making you feel satiated for longer and may help to slow the breakdown of carbohydrates and absorption of sugars which helps avoid blood sugar spikes.

Insoluble fibre is found in foods such as dark green vegetables, green beans, carrots and does not dissolve but passes into the large intestine unchanged. Here, it helps to bulk up and soften your stools so that transit time is reduced for healthy elimination. Fruit and vegetables contain both types of fibre.

Other benefits of dietary fibre:

- ☺ Heart health: Research has found that those who have a consistent high fibre intake can reduce their risk of developing heart disease by up to 40% and their risk of a stroke by 7%.
- ☺ Weight loss and management: Fibre can assist in this because it makes us feel satiated sooner and for longer and helps to control blood sugar.
- ☺ Skin health: By improving intestinal health, the condition of your skin can improve because very often problems in the bowel can be expressed in rashes or spots on the skin as your body attempts to rid itself of toxins.
- ☺ Protection from diseases of the colon: Dietary fibre (especially insoluble) may drastically reduce your risk of haemorrhoids and diverticulitis, an inflammatory condition of the large intestine.
- ☺ Reduction in the incidence of gallstones and kidney stones.

☺ Fibre provides fuel for beneficial bacteria which are vital for optimal function of your digestive system and immune system.

How to ensure you get enough quality fibre from your diet

✓ Eat a wide variety of fruit and vegetables daily so that you get a good amount of both types of fibre. Try to bias this towards vegetables with 6 portions of vegetables if possible and 3 of fruit.

✓ Resist the urge to use grains as your main source of fibre. Vegetables are a far superior source of fibre and contain high amounts of vitamins and minerals. Also, overuse of most grains, especially modern hybridised types, promotes acidity and inflammation in the body, can damage the lining of your gut leading to leaky gut syndrome and all the health problems associated with it. Over reliance on grains can also increase your chance of suffering from diseases such as diverticulitis.

There are however, some ancient grains that do not have the same negative effects on health. Spelt is one such grain; another, as previously mentioned is kamut. Unlike modern grains, kamut has no detrimental effects on health and has been shown to have anti-oxidant properties.

✓ If you have been diagnosed with digestive problems such as leaky gut or diverticulitis or you experience symptoms described in the digestion chapter e.g. bloating or abdominal pain, then it is best to eliminate fibre for a period. This is because insoluble fibre can feed bacteria in the bowel. This is great if it is predominantly good healthy bacteria but bad if it is unhealthy bacteria. The fibre feeds either, so this could cause unhealthy bacteria to flourish.

It is best to see a nutritionist who will be able to work with you to help rebalance your gut flora with friendly bacteria. They will also help you to monitor and regulate the re-introduction of a high fibre diet once this has been achieved.

SECTION 4. 3 Powerful Practices For Optimising Nutrition

This section is an introduction to food combining, fasting and detoxing. All three practices can be really useful ways to get the most from the food we eat and help our bodies to be more efficient, which in turn can transform our energy levels and sense of vitality. They suit some people more than others, so you may wish to experiment to see if any of them work well for you. Be prepared to feel fully-charged!!!

4A. An Introduction to Food Combining

If you have ever experienced bloating, sluggishness, indigestion or heart burn after particular meals it may be worth considering food combining. I used to suffer from terrible indigestion when I was younger, which ruined eating out at restaurants and the pleasure of favourite meals. It was only when I went to see a Nutritionist that I discovered the reason for the constant discomfort that seemed to follow every meal.

Apart from having a poorly functioning digestive system, I was also combining foods that were having their own personal battle in my digestive system, which resulted in my discomfort. In my case, it was usually a starchy food such as bread, combined with a protein rich food that caused the problem.

When I applied the principles of food combining it made a huge difference to my ability to digest foods properly and improve the overall function of my digestive system. Best of all, no more painful indigestion!

The principle of food combining is simply considering the way that different types of food are digested and eating them in combinations that assist in this digestion.

For example, in my case, combining starchy bread with meat in a delicious chicken sandwich! What I was unaware of was that these two foods are digested in completely different ways. The body starts to breakdown the starches in the bread in the alkaline environment of the mouth with an enzyme called amylase contained in saliva.

Once this is swallowed it passes through the stomach which has an acid environment that stops amylase from working. Not until the starches pass into the alkaline environment of the small intestine does the digestion continue with more amylase secreted by the pancreas.

In contrast the protein of the chicken requires the acid environment of the stomach which activates the protein digesting enzyme pepsin. If we have foods that require an alkaline environment for digestion and eat them at the same time as foods that require acidity, neither gets digested properly in the stomach. They then pass into the intestine partly undigested, which can cause all sorts of problems. Signs that this is happening can be:

☹ Indigestion

☹ Acid reflux (heartburn)

☹ Intestinal gas

☹ Dysbiosis

Another example is fruit. If this is eaten with main meals, maybe as what is thought of as a healthy dessert it can again cause problems. Let's say that a high protein course has just been eaten and is busily digesting away in the stomach. We then eat our healthy raspberries for dessert. They then arrive in the stomach and cannot make their way through to the small intestine because it is full of protein being digested in its acid environment.

They would normally pass through an empty stomach in about 30 minutes but instead get trapped in the stomach for up to 4 hours or more. So, they sit there and start to ferment or rot which will feed undesirable bacteria in the gut and interfere with the digestion of the protein.

The premise behind food combining is that during our evolution we simply did not eat foods in the combinations or amounts that the modern world now allows us to do. This means that our digestive systems have not evolved to cope with eating foods that require completely different methods of digestion at the same meal.

Of course, most food has a degree of protein and carbohydrate contained in it, but the principle of food combining is to avoid eating foods together that have concentrated protein or starch in them. For instance, meat (protein) and potatoes (starch).

<u>Simple tips for effective food combining</u>

✓ Eat fast fermenting fruits on their own, as a snack away from main meals. They should be consumed at least 30 minutes before a meal and you should wait at least 2 hours after a meal before consuming them. Most soft fruits ferment quickly once ripe. Examples of these are peaches, plums, mangoes, papayas, berries, cherries, melon and strawberries. There are a few exceptions of fruit that can be eaten with starches such as apples and pineapple which contains bromelain, a protein digesting enzyme that can help in its digestion; but it is far simpler just to keep all fruit away from meals.

✓ Try to avoid eating high starch foods such as potatoes with high protein foods (sausage and mash). Ideally, things such as potatoes, wheat, rice, oats, pasta and bread should be eaten separately to meat, poultry, eggs, cheese, milk, yoghurt, fish and shellfish. At first not as easy as it sounds, but it's only habit that makes us combine them.

✓ Protein foods can be eaten with vegetables. Root vegetables (not spuds!), green leafy vegetables such as kale, spinach, cabbage and all types of salad are okay.

✓ Starchy foods can be combined with vegetables.

✓ If you decide to try food combining it is a good idea to plan your meals and decide exactly what you are going to eat. It can be all too easy if we are in a hurry to default to old food combinations. Having a planned menu will help prevent this until we get used to our new dietary regime.

Food combining can be a useful technique to incorporate into your health regime. Even if you have not suffered from digestive problems and find that you have no problem combining the food groups mentioned, I would urge you to give it a try. It could help to improve further the condition and efficiency of your digestive system.

This does not mean that you have to completely give up combining certain foods, just consider perhaps making that bacon sandwich an occasional treat rather than an everyday staple.

4B. An Introduction to Fasting

Fasting has been receiving a lot of publicity in the last few years. What has been found is that in a very short period it can literally transform your health. People have discovered that they can lose weight and control it more easily. They are also able to control their blood sugar levels more effectively because fasting helps optimise insulin sensitivity. One of the biggest noticeable benefits of this is that people notice that they have a lot more energy.

Other benefits of fasting include:

☺ Large increases in human growth hormone (HGH) which is equated with turning back the ageing clock by allowing your body to more effectively repair and build a stronger you, increasing muscular strength and muscle tone. It has also been reported to make skin firmer, reducing wrinkles. (For more information on the benefits of HGH, refer to the section on HIIT in chapter 4)

☺ No longer craving stimulants or sugary snacks

☺ Normalizing ghrelin levels, also known as "the hunger hormone" which helps to control your hunger and prevent over eating or binging.

☺ Reduces oxidative damage by free radicals which are a major cause of inflammation and the development of disease.

☺ Helps your body to use body fat as fuel instead of sugar helping you to control your weight effectively. It also reduces the likelihood of developing diseases associated with using sugar as energy such as heart disease and cancer.

☺ Helps your body to adapt to use substances called medium chain triglycerides (MCTs) found in saturated fat, as fuel, especially if you include a reasonable amount of healthy saturated fat in your diet. MCTs are especially rich in coconut oil.

  - MCTs have been identified in new studies to be a more efficient and healthier fuel for your body than carbohydrates (especially simple ones that are loaded with sugar). This does not mean that you should not eat complex carbohydrates (such as those found in vegetables) but that you should not rely on them as your primary source of energy.

  - MCTs are used by your liver to produce substances called ketones which are the preferred fuel for your brain.

☺ Fasting also helps improve brain function by increasing production of a natural protein in the cells of the body called Brain Derived Neurotrophic Factor (BDNF). When this happens, studies have shown that the brain can make new cells and improve the physical connections between those cells. This helps to improve learning ability and memory. It can also maintain the health of neuromuscular junctions which transmit nerve impulses to your muscles. By doing this it is possible to maintain a greater efficiency and strength in muscles as we grow older. Increasing levels of BDNF may also provide a protective effect from Alzheimer's and Parkinson's disease.

There are quite a few theories as to why fasting has been shown to be so beneficial. The most practical to me is that when we fast, our body has a chance to divert the substantial energy required for digestion to maintenance and repair. Another theory that is interesting and seems plausible to me is that we are programmed from an evolutionary biological standpoint to deal with feast or famine. During our evolution, we had to hunt for our food and never knew when the next meal would come, so human biology adapted itself to deal with these periods of no food and continue to function effectively. Today we have an uninterrupted supply of food available to us which has changed the way we eat. Consequently, when we fast we are simulating feast and famine which works with our evolutionary biochemistry.

Fasting Methods

There are three distinct intermittent fasting methods at present, these are:

INTERMITTENT ALTERNATE DAY FASTING

This requires you to fast every other day and on the days that you do not fast you eat a normal healthy diet. On fasting days, it is recommended that you limit your calorie intake to 500 to 600 calories.

INTERMITTENT 5:2 FAST

This method involves eating normally for 5 days and then for 2 days a week reducing your calorie intake to 500 to 600 calories. Recommendation is 500 calories for women and 600 for men.

TIMED INTERMITTENT FASTING

This involves timing when you eat every day. So, for example, you eat your meals in a time window during the day (e.g. 11am to 7pm). This allows your body to fast for approximately 16 hours in this example. You can of course vary this time to suit, but what this method allows you to do is to establish a continuous everyday fasting regime.

This method also seems in line with our 'body clock' which has 3 cycles of roughly 8 hours each. Medical research suggests that the body responds well to eating between midday and 8pm when the body is in its assimilation phase. After 8pm and before 4am the body tends to focus on repair and maintenance. Between about 4am and noon, the body is getting rid of toxins and waste products, so the last thing that it really needs is to divert substantial energy away from this process to digestion.

Choosing the best method for you

Any of these methods will produce health benefits. You may wish to experiment to find out which one fits into your life the best.

I use the timed approach as it means that I do not have to restrict calorie intake to 500 to 600 calories a day, which can prove difficult on days I'm really busy or maybe eating out. I've got used to not having an early breakfast now and it saves me time in the morning when I need to dash out the door! It also means that I don't have to vary my diet on different days of the week, which would take far too much planning for me.

Fasting is not for everyone

Fasting is of course, a personal choice and is not for everyone. Some people do not like the idea of fasting as it does not fit into their lifestyle or do not react well to it. That is fine; fasting is simply another tool in the box (albeit a very effective one) and you can simply choose to concentrate on making your lifestyle and diet as healthy as possible; you will still get amazing health benefits.

People who need to avoid fasting or use caution

If you are on medication it is best to check with your GP before you try one of the fasting regimes. If you are suffering from Hypoglycaemia (low blood sugar), or diabetes it is best to consult a GP and also a nutritionist who will be able to advise you on the best way forward.

If you are pregnant or nursing, it is also best to avoid fasting and concentrate on optimising your nutrition to ensure that your baby gets all the essential nutrients it needs.

Tips for fasting

- ✓ On 5:2 and alternate day fasts which require calorie restriction, it is best to place emphasis on vegetables, especially leafy green vegetables and quality sources of protein as these will make it easier to limit your calories.
- ✓ Bear in mind that if you are using the 5:2 method, you are likely to be fasting for anything up to 60 hours (including the nights before and after your 48 hours fasting); even with an alternate day fast you can be fasting for over 36 hours before you go back to normal eating.

Even with the timed fasting you will go about 16 hours either side of your normal eating time window. For this reason, if you are finding it difficult to keep on any of the fasts you can slowly build up over a couple of weeks, the amount of time you fast for until you reach the desired time frame.

- ✓ Once you have begun your fast regime it will take time to see the benefits so stick with it and be consistent. You need to wait for nature to make those biological changes that will manifest in the health benefits. Everyone being biologically unique, some people will experience those changes quicker than others, but they will happen.
- ✓ If fasting is new to you, be mindful of any reactions or symptoms that might occur. Listening to your body and not rushing things is important. If you are getting any symptoms such as extreme fatigue or headaches it may be that you are going too quickly, and you should temporarily reduce your fasting hours or stop and concentrate on your daily nutrition. This will help prepare you and you can then try again at a later date if you wish.
- ✓ Find someone else who also wants to try fasting, who you know will be supportive. Then you can support each other and increase your chances of success. It can be challenging when you first start so having other people you can turn to for support can be very helpful. You could search for a fasting Facebook group or start one of your own.
- ✓ Keep a log of your progress; writing down changes in how you feel and any physical changes in your body after beginning fasting can help you to see progress and keep you motivated.

Most people I know who have integrated fasting into their lives have adapted really quickly and didn't experience any side effects so don't necessarily expect to experience any problems. Listen to your body and tune into whether it feels right for you.

4c. An Introduction to Detoxing

When I studied naturopathic nutrition we learnt a lot about detoxification, why it is necessary, how the body carries out this process and the protocols that should be followed to ensure that it is done successfully.

In recent years detoxing has become common practice with many people including high profile celebrities promoting it. Many books on detoxing and articles in magazines have heralded it as a quick fix that you can do in a couple of days.

This can lead to people viewing it as an easy way to offset a less than healthy lifestyle or instantly erase the damage done by overindulgent eating or frequent binge drinking. Detoxification regimes that last two or three days achieve little in such a short period and to be successful, a longer time is needed.

A time frame of one to two weeks could be all that is needed for people in good overall health. In the case of ill health a couple of months is not uncommon and in some more extreme circumstances (especially if there is a severe health problem) this could be a lot longer.

This does not mean that your life has to stop during this time and you should live like a monk! A good nutritionist will control the process so that you do not have any ill effects enabling you to carry on your everyday life as normal.

Detoxification is a very useful way of promoting long term health and fitness, but it must be done properly, used in the right context. The underlying purpose of detoxification is to enable our cells to get rid of toxic substances which impair their biological function.

Source of Toxins

A toxin may be defined as any compound (formed when two or more atoms form chemical bonds with each other) that has a detrimental effect on cell function or structure. Toxins come from a variety of external and internal sources:

☹ Food

☹ By products of unhealthy types of bowel bacteria

☹ Waste products of metabolism

☹ Interaction of environmental toxins (pollutants) with tissue components.

Avoiding Aggravation

It is possible to experience unpleasant reactions known as 'aggravation' when the toxins released from the cells cannot get out of the body. These include headaches, fuzzy thinking, nausea, aches and pains throughout the body or worse. These reactions can occur if the detoxification happens too quickly for the body to cope with or if the liver, kidneys or bowels are under-functioning. It can be compared to dustbins overfilling with rubbish and not being collected – not a great environment to live in!

What are the benefits of a successful detox?

Detoxing helps the body get rid of a substantial amount of toxins allowing the cells to function more efficiently. This means that all tissues and systems in the body benefit, which can result in:

☺ Improvement or eradication of illness

☺ More energy

☺ Better-quality sleep

☺ Improved digestion

☺ Clearer skin

☺ An overall feeling of well-being and vitality

Tailored Detox Regimes

Although this is something that you can do for yourself, if you are in ill health, I would highly recommend that you see a nutritionist who can guide you through all the processes necessary to help improve your health and achieve meaningful long-lasting results.

As to how long you will need to detox for, is a question that can only really be answered by a nutritionist reviewing your personal circumstances because everyone is biologically unique; people have different levels of toxic load so will need regimes tailored specifically for them.

If you are reasonable healthy with no health conditions and are looking for a 'spring-clean' then a 2-week detox can be done without a health professional. However it's important to follow the protocols outlined below so that you can maximise the benefits and avoid any potential side effects or reactions.

If you experience any of the aggravation symptoms outlined above, feel strange or unwell increase the amount of water you are drinking and ease off the regime. If this happens, it is advisable to consult a nutritionist who will be able to advise on the best course of action for your specific circumstances.

Below are the essential criteria and protocols that you need to consider if you decide you would like to try a 2-week detox.

Getting Prepared for a Detox

Taking the time to put a few things in place before you start can help to make the whole process run more smoothly. You need a plan as this will help remove obstacles that could derail your detox, make it easier for you to complete it and get the greatest benefits for your efforts.

✓ Try to choose a time when you are not too busy in your life. Not always easy I know but if you try to a detox when you have a lot going on it can make sticking to it much harder. An ideal time might be when you have some time off from work with minimal commitments and when you are relaxed. You need to choose a time when you have the best chance of being able to rest as this will greatly help your body to detox effectively and you to stick with it.

✓ Many think of January to do a detox at the end of the Christmas and New Year indulgences and there is nothing wrong in doing it at this time. From a naturopathic point of view the best time is in spring or autumn. However, if you take a little time to prepare, good results can be achieved at any time of year.

✓ Find someone to do it with you or just make sure that you have supportive people around you. This can be invaluable if you have a difficult couple of days.

✓ Get healthy ingredients in so that you have got them already and hide anything that might tempt you during your detox.

✓ Try to make sure that the main routes of detoxification are supported <u>before</u> you do a detox e.g. liver, kidneys, digestion. This will make it much more effective and drastically reduce the chances of aggravation occurring. If you currently eat healthily, are physically fit and have an efficient digestive system then your main routes of detoxification should be fine.

However, if you're knew to focusing on your health and well-being you may want to follow the tips and guidance in this chapter, the digestion chapter and the fitness chapter before thinking about a detox.

During the 2-week detox

The following points should be born in mind during your detox.

- ✓ Make sure that you get plenty of quality sleep as your body will need time to carry out detoxification. Aim for a good 8 hours (10pm -6am is ideal) although you may need longer (see chapter 2)
- ✓ Support your liver; it is one of the main organs of detoxification along with the kidneys and will be working hard during the 2 weeks. You can take Milk Thistle in capsule form or as a tincture; this will give good liver support (Take as directed). You should ideally not have alcohol as this places an added burden on your liver.
- ✓ Drink plenty of quality water (see chapter 2) as this will support your liver, kidney and digestive function. Water dilutes toxins and helps your body to excrete them efficiently. You cannot do an effective detox if you are dehydrated and you will be more likely to suffer from adverse symptoms and side effects. Water is perfect, but you can use fruit and herbal teas if you need some variety.
- ✓ Try not to drink tea or coffee (I love them both so I know how tough it can be to give them up for a while). Caffeine is after all an addictive toxin and will place an additional burden on your liver.
- ✓ Cut out foods that place a burden on your digestive system. Of course, everyone is different but common protagonists are dairy products, wheat and any foods that contain gluten.
- ✓ Try to eat as much food raw if possible, e.g. salads, juices as this will provide your body with the best supply of nutrients.
- ✓ Eat as many superfoods as you can e.g. all types of berries, melons, peaches, papayas, kiwi, mangoes, grapefruit, red grapes, beets, spinach, sweet potato, cucumber, kale, watercress, bean and seed sprouts.
- ✓ Eat these foods to help support and cleanse your liver: garlic, citrus fruits, broccoli, avocado, green leafy vegetables, turmeric and walnuts.
- ✓ Consider fasting, as this will help in the detoxification process.

- ✓ Consider supplementing to give your body all the nutrients it needs.
- ✓ Take light to moderate exercise every day. Try to avoid intense training during the 2 weeks as your body will be using considerable energy in the detoxification process.
- ✓ Skin brush every day (see chapter 2) as this will help lymph flow and aid in the detox.
- ✓ Having a hot bath with Epsom salts can help to draw toxins out through your skin. Skin brushing before you get in will also help.

A smoothie and a juice that you can use during your detox

It is highly beneficial to use juices and smoothies during your detox. They will save you time, are in a state that helps your body absorb nutrients quickly and best of all because no heat is applied they are packed with nutrients (especially enzymes that are destroyed very easily when any heat is applied).

I recommend making a fresh juice every day. Ideally drink straight away though it's possible to keep in the fridge for later or for the next day if time is tight or you don't particularly enjoy washing up the Juicer too frequently (not my favourite job!).

<u>Note</u>: If you have never used juices or smoothies before, introduce them gradually over a couple of days. They have a strong eliminatory effect and have been known to cause sudden detox reactions such as sudden onset of diarrhoea.

<u>Smoothie</u>

1 x half of an avocado (use a whole avocado if you wish)

1 x half of lemon freshly squeezed juice

1 x handful of spinach

3 x slices of ginger root

A handful of fresh mint

2-3 scoops of a flavourless protein powder (optional)

Place in blender and top up with filtered water.

Juice

2 x whole peeled and diced beetroot

3 x slices of ginger root

1 x whole apple

1 x half of lemon freshly squeezed juice

1 x half of tsp of turmeric powder (optional)

Put through a juicer and top up with filtered water to dilute if desired

Meals

It's useful to plan your meals so it's easier to stick to eating cleansing foods. There are many recipes that can be used during a detox and a wealth of inspiration and inspiration to be found online. I have also marked detox friendly recipes at the end of this chapter with (D).

After your detox and going forward

At the end of your detox you should be feeling appreciably better than when you started. The most noticeable improvements are usually such things as more energy, clearer thinking and a general feeling of increased overall well-being.

A detox should not need to be carried out very often, perhaps once or twice a year. As with the other tips and suggestions in this book, I hope it will prove to be a valuable addition to your toolkit.

Summary

A detox regime properly prepared for and carried out can make a huge contribution to long-term health and wellbeing. Short term benefits include feeling great with amazing amounts of energy, vibrant skin, and even improved psychological health.

In fact, a detox done correctly can improve just about every system and function in your body and bring your fitness up to levels you did not think were possible. But it should not be thought of as a cure all, simply another tool at our disposal to kick start the journey to optimal health and fitness.

For more in depth information on detoxing there are 2 books that I would recommend reading:

"Detox Handbook" by Dr Jennifer Harper

"The 9 Day Liver Detox" by Patrick Holford

SECTION 5. 3 Ways to Supercharge your Long-term Health

In this section we'll look at how to:

5a. Optimise your enzymes to supercharge your health

5b. Control your blood sugar

5c. Avoid, reduce/eliminate inflammation - major cause of disease

5a. How to Optimise Your Enzymes to Supercharge Your Health

The Oxford English Dictionary describes an enzyme as *"a substance which is produced by an organism and serves to control and promote a specific biochemical reaction"*

Enzymes catalyse biochemical processes in your body by speeding them up. Without them, these reactions simply could not happen at body temperature and they are critical to every biochemical reaction that takes place. Examples of processes they are involved in include:

☺ Digesting food

☺ The absorption of oxygen

☺ Helping to reduce inflammation

☺ Getting nutrients into your cells

☺ Carrying away toxic wastes in the detoxification process

☺ Helping to dissolve blood clots

☺ The optimum regulation of hormones

☺ Slowing the ageing process

☺ Helping to fight infections and to heal wounds

☺ Breaking down fats in your blood, regulating cholesterol and triglyceride levels

By accelerating physiological reactions, they also lower the energy that is required for these reactions to occur. If you have a deficit of enzymes, it affects the efficiency of every cell in your body and therefore every system and organ. It is therefore vital that you maximise your intake and production of enzymes if you want long term optimal health.

There are 3 types of enzyme:

1. Digestive
2. Food based
3. Metabolic

Digestive enzymes are produced in the body to breakdown food so that it can be absorbed into the blood stream. For example, lipase breaks down fats, protease breaks down protein and amylase breaks down carbohydrates.

Food based enzymes exist in natural wholefoods, most notably raw foods and can assist in the digestive process. For example, bromelain formed of two protein digesting enzymes is found in pineapples.

Metabolic enzymes are found inside the cells of your body. They are involved in numerous crucial functions such as energy production, the formulation of new proteins and the detoxification process.

What can deplete or reduce the effectiveness of enzymes?

- Metabolic and digestive enzyme production decreases as we age.
- Enzymes are very susceptible to pH, so if you have a lifestyle and diet (little or no exercise and a diet high in processed foods) that promotes acidity in the body, enzyme activity is greatly reduced.
- If you are not getting enough enzymes from your diet your body has to work harder to produce more digestive enzymes which can in turn have a knock-on effect on your body's ability to produce metabolic enzymes.
- Too much heat in cooking can destroy naturally occurring enzymes in foods.
- Stress can adversely affect your ability to produce digestive enzymes which then affects absorption of food-based enzymes
- Use of pharmaceutical drugs such as antibiotics

How can you help to ensure that you have optimal levels of all types of enzymes?

- ✓ Ensure that you eat as much raw, organic food as possible such as salads that are rich in naturally occurring enzymes. A good way to consume raw food is to juice it, which also makes it easier to assimilate. You can start your meal with a small glass of vegetable juice.

  When you cook, avoid using excessive heat; this is because cooking easily destroys the delicate protein structures of enzymes. As a general rule, you should aim to keep temperatures to no more than 100 degrees F (the temp of boiling water) if possible. Steaming is the best option for vegetables.

- ✓ You can supplement with digestive enzymes (as mentioned in chapter 3)
- ✓ You can also supplement with what are called systemic enzymes. These must be taken between meals so that they are not used in digestion. They can then be absorbed into the blood and help to reduce inflammation in the body.
- ✓ Try to ensure enzyme supplements are from microbial sources as these have proven to be more potent and effective than animal derived enzyme supplements. It is best to seek the advice of a nutritionist before supplementing with enzymes.
- ✓ Take action to reduce your stress levels.
- ✓ Don't over eat as this places a burden on your body to produce more digestive enzymes which then takes away energy needed to produce metabolic enzymes.
- ✓ Eat a natural wholefood alkaline diet as far as possible to keep the pH of body tissues in the optimal range for enzyme activity.
- ✓ Chew your food well; this helps digestive enzymes in the mouth to start to break down carbohydrates more effectively before they are swallowed. It also sends signals to the pancreas which helps it to produce sufficient digestive enzymes for optimal digestion.
- ✓ Avoid chewing gum as this fools the digestive system into producing digestive enzymes and wastes the enzymes and the energy that it takes to produce them.

- ✓ Eat enzyme rich foods such as sprouted seeds and legumes, extra virgin olive oil, coconut oil, avocados, raw honey, pineapples, papayas, kiwis, mangos and grapes.
- ✓ Taking action to optimise the levels and function of the three different types of enzyme in your body is an incredibly effective way to optimise every aspect of your health.

5B. How to Control Your Blood Sugar

Having a very sweet tooth presented a bit of a problem when I trained to be a nutritionist and started to practice as I believe that if you are asking someone to give up or limit foods which include the processed sugar found in simple carbohydrates and processed foods then you really should set an example yourself.

So, I developed ways to help myself limit these foods but at the same time still enjoy the odd treat. I will cover these tips later in this section but firstly I want to explain why it is **ABSOLUTELY VITAL** to your long-term health and wellbeing that you eliminate or at least limit your intake of sugary foods.

Sugar has a bad rap these days and nice though it is to eat, its reputation as a food that can severely damage your health is thoroughly deserved. It has been called a metabolic poison and if you consume too much that's exactly what it is. Increased sugar intake in western society is behind many of the modern-day diseases.

Excess consumption has contributed to the obesity epidemic and is a major factor in heart disease, cancer and type 2 diabetes to name but a few. It is also a major factor in promoting inflammation, accelerated ageing and all the health problems that go with it.

A prime reason why this happens is to do with the hormone that is involved in controlling blood sugar called insulin. It is the job of insulin to keep your blood sugar under control by getting glucose out of your blood and into your cells to be used as fuel.

If this is done efficiently, you have a steady blood sugar and feel full of energy, your mood will be good, you stop craving sugary foods and you are much more able to lose weight and keep it off. Many people also find that their memory and concentration improves with less likelihood of anxiety and depression.

The trouble starts when we eat simple carbohydrate foods and consume sugary drinks which spike our blood sugar. Then your body has to produce more insulin to counter the rocketing blood sugar. It tends to over produce insulin in these situations which in turn causes your blood sugar to plummet below the optimal level. You then feel tired and have another quick fix stimulant which spikes your blood sugar again. This is repeated throughout the day in a constant yoyo effect.

In time, your body loses the ability to produce enough insulin and insulin also becomes less effective at its job. This is known as decreased insulin sensitivity or insulin resistance and is a prime factor in the development of many modern disease conditions including cardiovascular disease and cancer.

Balancing your blood sugar is therefore one of the most important things that you can do to ensure your long-term health. Our bodies depend on a steady and even blood sugar level and it is vital to ensure that this is maintained. You can also dramatically reduce your susceptibility to blood sugar related diseases and you will age slower!

This is another time when it is important to listen to what your body is telling you. There are many signs and symptoms that will tell you if your blood sugar control is not all that it should be. Be honest with yourself when you look at the following list; I know that I would have ticked at least half of these twenty years ago.

- ❒ Do you feel tired and have trouble in waking up in the morning?
- ❒ Do you need stimulants such as coffee, tea, cigarettes or energy drinks to get you going in the morning and at regular intervals throughout the day?
- ❒ Do you have energy slumps after meals if you don't have a stimulant?
- ❒ Do you have a short fuse or react disproportionately to stressful situations?
- ❒ Do you crave sweet treats at regular intervals throughout the day or after a meal?

- ❒ Do you have difficulty in maintaining your concentration?
- ❒ Do you suffer from headaches?
- ❒ Do you suffer from mood swings or get depressed?
- ❒ Do you crave chocolate, cereals, cakes, biscuits, bread, and pasta?
- ❒ Do you drink a lot of sweet fizzy drinks or fruit juices during the day?
- ❒ Do you find it hard to go more than 4 hours without food? For example, become irritable or feel shaky?
- ❒ Do you lack the energy to exercise?
- ❒ Do you have less energy than you used to?
- ❒ Do you find it hard to maintain a steady weight even though you exercise regularly and don't eat excessively?

If you ticked more than 3 of the above, it may be that you have some degree of blood sugar fluctuation. The more you tick the greater the likelihood that this is a problem for you.

However, regardless of how many you ticked, everyone can benefit from the following tips to maintain stable blood sugar.

How to ensure you effectively control your blood sugar

<u>Try to give up, avoid or reduce</u>:

- × Avoid sugary processed (simple carbohydrate) foods because they are absorbed into the blood stream very rapidly and are like rocket fuel, releasing glucose far too quickly and causing your blood sugar to go up rapidly. The body then reacts to bring it under control quickly as it needs to be within certain parameters. Unfortunately, this can often lead to a dip in blood sugar which manifests in any of the symptoms above.
- × Reduce, or if possible, avoid eating grains such as wheat, barley and rye. Although publicised as healthy many types of grain can increase your blood sugar to harmful levels quicker than a bar of chocolate! In the section on how to achieve your optimum diet at the end of the chapter I highlight which grains to avoid and which ones can be eaten in moderation.

- ✗ Some people find it useful not to have sugary snacks or drinks in the house so that they're not tempted by them; this includes me.
- ✗ Try to avoid having sugary snacks with caffeine drinks such as coffee, tea or energy drinks that contain caffeine. Having this combination quickly destabilizes your blood sugar. The caffeine effectively supercharges the already destructive effects of sugar on your health.
- ✗ Avoid sugary canned drinks such as energy drinks or colas.
- ✗ Be aware that many products have added sugar, so check the labels.
- ✗ Limit the amount of alcohol that you consume because it encourages insulin production which can destabilise blood sugar. Also, many alcoholic beverages contain large amounts of added sugar.
- ✗ Avoid all sweeteners if possible, you don't need them; it's only a habit. If you traditionally have a sweetener in a drink, try gradually reducing it over a couple of months. You will eventually give it up altogether. I did this and when people accidentally put sweetener in my drinks after I had quit, it tasted so sickly sweet, absolutely disgusting.

<u>Do:</u>

- ✓ Make your 1st meal of the day as nutritionally complete as possible. Try to make sure that you include foods that will provide all the main food groups.
- ✓ Eat complex carbohydrates found in unprocessed wholefoods. These will also have insoluble fibre which will help to keep your blood sugar stable.
- ✓ Include some form of protein in your meals (e.g. fish and vegetables) to help control the speed of absorption of glucose into the blood stream. This will help to avoid blood sugar spikes by slowing down the rate of absorption. So instead of the peaks and troughs you will be able to maintain an even blood sugar.
- ✓ Eat as and when you feel you need to and try to avoid over eating or eating out of habit when you are not even hungry. Everybody is different, and you will find what works best for you. Fasting can really help you control your appetite.

- ✓ Do some sort of exercise everyday if possible as this plays a big role in long term blood sugar control.
- ✓ Take a high strength multi vitamin/mineral supplement each day.
- ✓ Indulge yourself from time to time just make sure it's not daily! Again, it's all about balance and it helps to prevent cravings for sugary treats. If you're meeting a friend for coffee or going out for a meal just enjoy it – a little bit of what you fancy is good for you after all! So, there's no need to be the pious one in the restaurant ordering the raw carrot sticks.

  It's very easy for people to start feeling guilty about eating certain foods. Our 'relationship' with food is a huge topic in itself. Simple rule of thumb is if at least 80% of the time you're eating healthily there's absolutely no need for guilt; just try not to go completely berserk with the 20%!
- ✓ When you do choose to treat yourself try to pick the highest quality products you can, such as organic chocolate or organic coffee.
- ✓ If you have a treat, try to have it with a meal that has a balance of protein, complex carbohydrates and healthy fats. Although still not ideal, this is better than just simple carbohydrates on an empty stomach!
- ✓ A teaspoon of cinnamon with food each day has been shown to be very effective at balancing blood sugar.
- ✓ Eat a low GL diet. GL stands for Glycaemic Load and is a measure of the quantity of carbohydrates found in particular foods and the quality; low quality processed carbs will quickly affect your blood sugar whilst high quality complex carbs will not. The tables work by listing all foods according to quality and quantity of carbohydrates. It provides a numerical score for each food so that you can see which foods are good for blood sugar control and which are not.

  The higher the score the worse the food. By using GL tables, you can build a diet that will help keep your blood sugar stable with all the benefits that this brings. (See Further Reading)
- ✓ Eat more healthy fats in your diet such as those found in coconut, avocado and eggs. Your body will be able to control its blood sugar much more effectively if you are using fats as your prime source of energy rather than carbohydrates. One reason is because healthy saturated fats

from foods such as coconut have been shown to help improve insulin sensitivity.

✓ Consider fasting (see section 4b) as this is one of the most effective ways to help your body to adapt and to optimise blood sugar control.

5c. How to Avoid, Reduce or Eliminate Inflammation

Inflammation is one of the key factors in ill health and disease. Most of us have experienced inflammation at some time in our lives. Whether this is from a physical injury, soreness after exercise or a disease condition ending in "itis" such as arthritis, laryngitis, tonsillitis, it usually goes hand in hand with varying degrees of pain.

The natural desire of course is to be free of this pain as quickly as possible so that we can get on with our lives. One of the most common ways of rapidly achieving this is to take pharmaceutical painkillers or Non-Steroidal Anti-Inflammatory drugs (NSAID).

Whilst the fast relief they offer in the short term from, for example, a sports injury is useful, continued use can be linked with many side effects such as:

☹ Nausea

☹ Vomiting

☹ Diarrhoea

☹ Indigestion

☹ Abdominal pain

☹ Gastritis

☹ Duodenal or gastric ulcers

☹ Allergic reactions (such as a rash)

☹ Worsening of asthma symptoms from bronchospasm

☹ Headaches

☹ Dizziness

☹ Fluid retention (bloating)

☹ Raised blood pressure

What should also be considered is that the relief provided by these drugs is only temporary which often means that you have to keep taking the drug for continued relief. This is because the pain relief is achieved by blocking the chemical pathways in your body that produce the pain and inflammation. Since pain is our body's way of telling us something's wrong, by taking pain killers we are literally telling our body to shut up, which is obviously not an ideal long-term solution.

Another concern over taking pain killers such as Non-Steroidal Anti-inflammatory Drugs (NSAIDs) is that many can be addictive. This has been shown by reports of some people who when stopping use of NSAIDs after as little as three days have reported symptoms of withdrawal.

The long-term use of NSAID is clearly not an option if you are looking for optimal health and longevity. If you have taken pharmaceutical drugs for pain relief or to reduce inflammation for a long time, it may be worth consulting your doctor to explore the best option for you.

The ideal alternative is to eliminate the source of the inflammation and pain through preventative measures and on the occasions when it does occur, to treat it with natural sources of pain relief, which are covered further on in this chapter.

What's the Role of Inflammation and Why Does It Cause Pain?

Although inflammation and the associated pain is often looked upon as a problem and something to be eliminated, it has a part to play in the natural healing process. Pain is your body's way of communicating with you that inflammation is present in your body whether on the surface or internally. This is good in the short term as it allows you to recognise that there is a problem and to take action in dealing with the root cause so that it does not occur again.

It is also a natural part of the immune function, promoting swelling around damaged tissue cells which isolates them from further damage. It also produces chemicals which initiate antibodies (white blood cells) to protect the site from further attack from antigens (foreign bodies such as bacteria and toxins).

However, if pharmaceutical painkillers are continually used to mask the pain, the inflammation may become long term and chronic. This may lay the foundations for the development of many disease conditions such as arthritis and joint problems, osteoporosis, cardiovascular disease, diabetes, obesity, Alzheimer's disease, asthma and cancer.

A great alternative to pharmaceutical painkillers are hop alpha acids which as the name suggests, are derived from hops. In trials, they have been shown to reduce pain from 30 minutes after the first dose and be the equivalent of taking 2 capsules (400mg) of Ibuprofen but without the side effects.

However, it should be borne in mind that although this provides relief of symptoms, long term use is not recommended over addressing the root cause of the pain.

WHAT CAN YOU DO TO AVOID OR ELIMINATE EXCESS INFLAMMATION?

The good news is that there are many things that you can do to avoid developing inflammatory conditions and the pain that goes with them:

1. <u>Avoid using non-prescription pharmaceutical drugs if possible</u>

Let me just say at this point that I believe that there is a place for painkillers as emergency treatment. If I break my leg, it is fair to say that I will be in a lot of pain and will be only too glad of the relief that these substances will provide.

What I do not believe in is the continuous use of them to treat every day ailments such as headaches or more serious conditions such as arthritis. In such situations drugs tend to cause more problems than they solve. On every set of instructions that come with a drug you will find a set of possible side effects. Some are listed as common and others less so, according to statistics. All of these side effects without exception occur because the drug does not belong in your body and your body recognises this and produces reactions to it.

I think that Michael Colgan, one of my role models put it best in his 2002 book All New Sports Nutrition Guide:

"*The best example of the toxicity of man-made molecules is prescription drugs. These chemicals are all man made and never existed on earth before the 20th century. Why have they grown to such prominence? One reason is the futile arrogance that man can design better than nature. A second is our archaic laws, which decree that you cannot patent naturally occurring chemicals. Without patent protection, there is little profit in selling them as prescription medicines. To make their chop, pharmaceutical companies have to throw man-made wrinkles into the chemistry, wrinkles that wreak havoc with nature's design of man.*

All this stupidity occurred in the last 100 years. But evolution takes millennia. So, the human body has had no time at all in evolutionary terms, to develop the mechanisms to deal with man-made drugs. They were not on earth during human evolution and are mostly invisible to the body's defensive chemistry. (Although they have potent effects in reducing surface symptoms of disease, every man-made drug is toxic to the human system.")

I realise that many people will be reliant on drugs for health conditions, but my advice would be to see a nutritionist who can then work with you and your physician over time to address the underlying causes of your health problems. This will hopefully lead to you stopping or at least reducing your reliance on long term medication and the side effects that they produce.

2. <u>Get the right balance between acid and alkaline in your body</u>

Acid and alkaline are measured using the pH scale. If you are unfamiliar with this, very briefly, the scale runs from 0 to 14. With 7 being neutral, that is, neither acidic nor alkaline. Everything below 7 is increasingly acidic, so for example the hydrochloric acid produced in the stomach is very acidic and has a pH of between 1.5 and 3.5. Conversely, everything above 7 on the scale is increasingly alkaline.

To work at an optimum level, your body needs to control the balance between acidity and alkalinity very precisely. For example, your blood needs to be slightly alkaline (7.4) and your body has very effective ways to maintain this and the pH balance throughout your body.

Most bodily tissues and fluids prefer to be neutral or slightly alkaline with notable exceptions such as parts of your digestive system for example your stomach and the surface of your skin (approximately 5.5).

Unfortunately, many people's bodies are unbalanced with the majority having too much acidity (metabolic acidosis) with most not even realising. This is usually due to a combination of different factors in our lives which interfere with our body's ability to effectively control the pH balance of the fluids, cells and tissues that make us!

Factors that can cause metabolic acidosis

- Poor diet choices (e.g. excess sugar)
- Stress (see chapter 6)
- Environmental pollution (see chapter 2)
- De-hydration (see chapter 2)
- Smoking
- Alcohol
- High caffeine intake
- Antibiotics
- Inadequate oxygenation of tissues e.g. shallow breathing (see chapter 2)
- Lack of exercise (See chapter 4)
- Poor chewing and eating habits
- Excessive exercise

These factors can lead to the disruption of vital mineral levels in the body, affecting its ability to heal and assimilate vitamins and minerals from the diet and supplements. This can then disrupt homeostasis at a cellular level, compromising your ability to maintain an optimal pH balance.

The resulting metabolic acidosis then creates an environment that leads to inflammation and pain and has been linked to the development of most health conditions and diseases.

What are the health symptoms/consequences of metabolic acidosis?

Short term

- ☹ Inflammation
- ☹ A lack of energy or chronic fatigue
- ☹ Allergies and asthma
- ☹ Skin problems
- ☹ Ulcers
- ☹ Weight gain
- ☹ Frequent viral infections
- ☹ Joint problems such as frozen shoulder
- ☹ Muscular tightness and pain
- ☹ Chronic back pain
- ☹ Headaches

Long term

- ☹ Rheumatoid arthritis and osteoporosis
- ☹ Kidney stones and renal disease
- ☹ Hormonal imbalance such as hypothyroidism
- ☹ Cancer
- ☹ Diabetes
- ☹ Fibromyalgia
- ☹ Heart disease
- ☹ Multiple Sclerosis
- ☹ Stroke

Now, I can appreciate that this makes pretty depressing reading, but the good news is that there are a great many things that you can do to drastically reduce acidity and the inflammation that goes with it!

However, an important thing to bear in mind is that what we are looking to do is to **re-balance** the acid/alkaline in our body in favour of alkaline, but not to completely eliminate acidity; some acidity is good. It's just unfortunate that many of us have too much of it!

When you achieve this, inflammation and pain will disappear or at the very least be massively reduced! As a result, your health and well-being will take a huge turn for the better.

How can you achieve optimal pH in your body?

Try to give up, avoid or reduce:

- Any processed foods because without exception, they will all promote excess acidity. This means fast foods, confectionery, anything that has an ingredients label that reads like a chemistry experiment (very long list with things you have never heard of and have difficulty in pronouncing) and sugar in all its forms. Also, foods can expose you to hormone disrupting chemicals that leach from soft plastic packaging (e.g. cheese, meat or fish shrink wrapped); difficult to avoid I know as so much food seems to be wrapped in plastic these days!
- An excess of animal-based protein in your diet will also predispose you to acidity. So, for instance, dairy is okay maybe two or three times a week but eating it in excess e.g. milk, cheese (unfortunately hard mature cheese is particularly acid forming), yoghurt everyday can create too much acidity in your body. Another example would be red meat. There is nothing wrong in treating yourself once or twice a week with good quality organic meat if you wish but eating it too often will make it more difficult to get that optimal alkaline environment in your cells.
- Try to avoid eating excessive amounts of animal-based protein. If you eat meat most days, consider reducing your intake and replacing it with vegetable sources of protein. (see next section)
- Try to limit the amount of grains that you eat. Too many grains, especially wheat, oats and rye create acidic conditions in the body.
- Since alcohol promotes acidity in the body, try to keep your consumption reasonably low, no more than 1 unit a day
- Some types of cooking create acidity in foods that are not themselves acidic. You should avoid cooking with very high temperatures, so frying and high temperature baking/roasting is something that should not be used very often, if at all. You need to also be careful not to burn food, for instance when toasting or barbecuing.
- Reduce your exposure to external toxins from pharmaceutical drugs, cigarettes, environmental pollution (both in and outside of the home),
- Protect yourself from exposure to internal toxins caused by gut bacterial imbalances (dysbiosis). Please see chapter 3

- ✗ Try to limit stress as much as possible. Be aware of what causes you to feel stressed and look at ways to reduce these factors (see chapter six)

Do:

- ✓ It's a good idea to try to aim to have at least two days a week where you get your protein from vegetables sources (e.g. quinoa, tofu, nuts, seeds, lentils).
- ✓ Make sure you stay adequately hydrated throughout the day. (See Chapter 2).
- ✓ Get most of your complex carbohydrate intake from vegetables especially dark green leafy ones such as Kale or Spinach.
- ✓ Eat fruit as a snack, as pretty much all have an alkalising effect.
- ✓ Make sure you get enough quality sleep to help your body carry out its healing and repairing processes. See section on sleep in Chapter 2.
- ✓ Exercise regularly, but don't over-do it, making sure that you include HIIT (if you have not used it before, at least give it a try) and all the other components discussed in chapter 4 in your regime.
- ✓ Take up fasting.
- ✓ With respect to getting the right balance, we can use fruit and vegetables to help neutralise the acidity; for example, if you were having chicken which is particularly acidic, you could counteract that acidity by having plenty of green vegetables with it. As I said, we can have some acidity in the diet and some acidic foods are nutritious foods such as organic eggs, walnuts, mussels or oily fish. So, we can if we wish, keep these in our diet to enjoy their health benefits as long as we counter balance their acidity with alkaline food.
- ✓ Practice deep breathing (see Chapter 2)
- ✓ Make sure your diet has the correct levels of Omega 3 essential fatty acids and low in processed damaged fats. Many people are deficient in Omega 3 but have more than enough Omega 6. It is therefore a good idea to ensure that you get the correct ratio of Omega 6 to Omega 3. For optimal health, this is approximately 4:1. A good way to do this is to take a quality Krill oil supplement which will help to ensure you get these essential fats in the right ratio.

✓ Take Spirulina as a powder supplement every day. A nutrient rich superfood derived from blue-green algae, it is alkalising and anti-inflammatory.

✓ Juice vegetables (a great way to counter-balance acidic foods) especially dark green leafy ones such as spinach, kale and cabbage, also cucumber and celery. These are high in alkalising minerals such as potassium and magnesium. Beetroot, carrot, apple and ginger are also great to throw into the mix.

✓ An effective way to keep the tissues in the body alkaline is to eat as much raw fruit and vegetables as possible. Whilst it can sound unappetising there are some excellent books on raw diets to help create delicious meals. After all, the way we prepare our food is largely a result of habit so it's useful to experiment. Crudité, coleslaw, salads and juicing has been helpful to me. Also, vegetables don't lose their alkalising properties if you lightly steam them for a couple of minutes.

✓ Make sure that you effectively control your blood sugar.

3. <u>Make sure that you get enough antioxidants</u>

Antioxidants are our defence against highly reactive and damaging molecules known as free radicals. The action of free radicals is very pro inflammatory and is a major cause of ageing and disease from wrinkles to heart disease and cancer.

There are different types of free radicals and different types of anti-oxidants to neutralise them. Antioxidants work in synergy and so it is important when supplementing to take a synergistic mix. Avoid taking them in isolation as they can actually be detrimental to your health. For example, Vitamin E and Co-enzyme Q10 are 2 antioxidants that work together. After Vitamin E has neutralised free radicals, Co-enzyme Q10 is required to regenerate the antioxidant potential of Vitamin E after it has reacted with free radicals.

The following tips will help you obtain optimal levels of antioxidants.

Try to give up, avoid or reduce:

× Try to avoid over cooking as too much heat destroys many antioxidants

× Avoid excessive exercise, e.g. ultra-endurance, doing high intensity exercise every day. (See antioxidant section in chapter 4).

- × Avoid exercising near or being around pollution such as busy roads
- × Don't smoke and avoid being around people smoking.

Do:

- ✓ Consume plenty of brightly coloured fresh vegetables and fruit every day. Blues, greens, yellows and reds, the more diverse the colours the better. A simple way to do this is a large salad.
- ✓ Juicing is another great way to get a concentrated antioxidant hit. You can mix vegetable and fruit juices for extra potency.
- ✓ When you have vegetables with a meal, try to ensure that at least half your plate is vegetables.
- ✓ Berries are a great source of antioxidants and the darker the colour the better. Freezing them will allow you to have a ready supply.
- ✓ Take an antioxidant supplement to complement those in your diet.
- ✓ Take a good multi vitamin/mineral supplement to support the action of the antioxidant supplement.
- ✓ Take vitamin C, a key antioxidant separately from the other supplements to get the required amounts (aim for at least 1000mg daily).
- ✓ Snack on fruit and raw nuts that are high in antioxidants; good examples are pecans, walnuts and hazelnuts
- ✓ Many herbs and spices have potent antioxidant properties which is highest in the fresh form rather than powdered. Try ground cloves, ground cinnamon, oregano, turmeric, ginger and garlic.
- ✓ Organic green loose-leaf tea is one of the most powerful antioxidants yet discovered. To help the antioxidants to be absorbed drink with a slice of lemon.
- ✓ If you like a little wine, then drinking a small glass of red can give you some antioxidant benefit as it contains an antioxidant called Resveratrol. You can also get it from red grape juice (dilute to reduce sugar content). Resveratrol is also available in capsule form which will give you a concentrated dose.

SECTION 6: PULLING IT ALL TOGETHER.

I hope that this chapter has built on your existing knowledge and given you some ideas for changes you may wish to make to attain long-term health and vitality. I've gone into a lot of detail as I think the more we understand and appreciate the role of nutrition the more we are more likely to be successful in establishing and maintaining a healthy diet.

It's all about balance

As is the theme of this book it's all about balance. It's not about being too rigid and regimental. Aim to achieve a diet that is as healthy as possible for at least 80% of the time. For most of us living in the real world that 10 to 20% gives us the flexibility for meals out and holidays.

The only time I encourage 100% compliance is when a serious health issue needs to be resolved. Once you have attained a good state of health, your body can cope with the occasional indulgence but what people usually find is that after they have enjoyed their treat, they want to quickly return to the diet that makes them feel great.

However, if you want to do the 100% compliance, that's brilliant.

Making gradual changes

Of course, it is important to make the necessary changes in a diet to achieve your desired level of wellbeing. However, I find that this can be achieved and maintained far more easily by steady gradual changes. Making small changes one step at a time can make a huge difference and is more likely to be sustainable over the long term.

6A. 21 TIPS FOR MAKING CHANGES IN YOUR DIET THAT STAND THE TEST OF TIME

Tip 1: Avoid immediate drastic changes to your diet

I have spoken to many individuals who have made sudden radical changes to their diet that prove to be too much of a shock to the body. They very often feel worse (quite often because of a detoxification reaction or aggravation) with symptoms such as headaches, aching joints, digestive upsets and fatigue. Examples of when this can happen are going straight into eating large amounts of raw food or juicing if you are not used to it. If you experience adverse reactions to dietary changes it is prudent to reduce the rate of change which should alleviate the problem.

Tip 2: Plan your meals before shopping

After a long day at work when the last thing you want to be thinking about is slaving over a hot stove it can be really easy to rely on takeaways or ready meals, we've all done it. Fine from time to time but ideally you want such options to be the exception rather than the rule. I've found that having healthy ingredients indoors for putting quick but tasty meals together can be incredibly helpful in resisting the temptation.

It's easy to equate healthy eating with plain and boring, but it doesn't have to be, I promise! There are some great health focused cookery books about these days that are worth flicking through for inspiration and to add some variety. I've included some of my favourites at the end of this chapter.

I find that taking a little time to think of the meals I want to make, enables me to identify exactly what you need and saves lots of time when shopping. A little planning goes a long way and makes it far easier to adapt to healthier eating.

Tip 3: Eat organic whenever you can

In my experience, organic food tastes better and you have the advantage of not having to worry about what chemicals have been used to grow it. Supermarkets have a wide range of organic produce these days. The Soil Association logo provides extra reassurance that the produce has been grown to strict organic standards.

You may also wish to try one of the weekly organic box schemes. As well as saving time I find that it encourages me to eat a wider range of produce and try new vegetables I've not come across before. It's made me more creative in the kitchen and it's great to know that it's locally sourced and rich in nutrients.

Vegetables not grown organically, although still very good for you, do not share the same nutritional quality as organic. This was proven by recent research published in the British Journal of Nutrition carried out by Newcastle University. Organic produce was found to have greater levels of antioxidants without increased calories and reduced levels of harmful cadmium and pesticides.

It is interesting to note that some organic produce was found to have pesticide traces, probably due to contamination from non-organic producers.

An important point here is to always give your food, especially fruit and vegetables a good wash. You can buy special washes that you spray onto fruit and vegetables and rinse off or simply adding a little vinegar to a bowl of water and rinsing is also very effective.

Unfortunately, this is not a fool proof method for removing chemical residues for produce that has not been grown to organic standards. This is because it depends on what type of pesticide the food has been grown in. If it is a contact pesticide, this can be washed off safely from the surface of the plant. However, if the pesticide used is what is called a systemic pesticide, it will have been absorbed into every part of the plant and cannot be removed by peeling or washing.

As we have no way of knowing what type of pesticide has been used, the default safe solution is to buy organic if you want to eat food that is free from chemical contamination and nutrient rich.

Tip 4: Eat locally sourced fresh seasonal produce where possible

Eating locally sourced produce ensures that it tastes great and has more of its nutritional goodness intact; both of which deteriorate during prolonged transit and storage. Also, it will often work out cheaper as it has not incurred travel costs.

Eating seasonal food is important. Before we developed the technology to move food vast distances and to store it for months, we evolved over millennia eating in line with the seasons. So, in winter we ate bulkier and dense produce such as root vegetables that gave us a good source of complex carbohydrates and enabled us to put on a few extra pounds to fuel us through the coldest months of the year. Then in the summer lighter foods designed to cool us down in hot weather and keep us hydrated such as leafy greens, fruits, berries, cucumber, watermelon etc.

In the 21st century, even though foods are available out of season I believe that this works against our natural evolutionary seasonal cycles. If we endeavour to eat local foods in season, the majority of the time, we will be more in sync with our bodies and in turn facilitate the natural healing process. So, it makes sense to leave the strawberries for the summer rather than adding them to our Christmas menus!

Finding local producers near you that provide seasonal produce and may offer delivery services has never been easier – farm shops, farmers' markets and on-line delivery schemes are becoming ever popular. I use a local farm shop that stocks fabulous products.

In terms of delivery schemes, I use Riverford who deliver weekly locally sourced organic seasonal produce. Their produce is excellent – I've managed to convert many friends who weren't previously fans of veg to include more veg on their plates now as it tastes so good!

If you have time you may wish to grow your own fruit and veg either in your garden or on an allotment. It's a great way to keep fit too!

Tip 5: Storage

The way we store our food not only determines how long it lasts but more importantly how much goodness is left in it by the time we eat it. It's worth planning meals around what needs eating first, whenever possible.

To prevent deterioration from light it's better to choose oils such as olive oil and avocado oil in dark bottles.

With essential fat supplement oils such as flax seed oil or fish oil, keeping them in the fridge helps prevent deterioration from heat and light.

If it's not clear how best to store it, then I find the simple rule of keeping it in the fridge works well.

The following table shows how long to store common fruit and vegetables.

Fruit/Vegetable	Room Temperature	Cool Dark Place	Fridge
Apples, pears	3 to 5 days		
Asparagus			1 to 3 days
Avocados	3 to 5 days		
Bananas	week or more		
Beetroot		week or more	
Broad beans			3 to 5 days
Broccoli			3 to 5 days
Cabbage			week or more
Carrots			week or more
Cauliflower			week or more
Celeriac			week or more
Citrus Fruit	week or more		
Courgettes			1 to 3 days
Cucumber			week or more
Fennel			week or more
Jerusalem artichokes		week or more	
Leeks			week or more
Mushrooms			1 to 3 days
Pak Choi			3 to 5 days
Parsnips			week or more
Peppers			week or more
Potatoes		week or more	
Spinach			1 to 3 days
Spring greens			3 to 5 days
Squash	week or more		
Swede			week or more
Tomatoes	week or more		

Tip 6: Maximise nutrient content by choosing the right cooking method

To make the most of healthy ingredients it is important that you prepare them so that you lose the minimum of nutrients. The most nutritious way to eat your food is in its raw state such as in salads but this can sometimes cause digestive upsets if you are not used to eating raw food. If this is the case it is best to start by lightly cooking until your body adapts to your new dietary regime; the best ways are steaming, poaching and boiling as they apply less heat (the more heat you apply the more nutrients get damaged and lost). The water used in these cooking methods contains valuable nutrients so it's worth keeping to add to a juice, smoothie or as a basis for a soup.

Of course, there are times when we prefer to bake or roast. Just bear in mind that to get the most nutritional benefit the less heat you apply the better, so use these cooking methods in moderation and not as your default method of cooking.

Tip 7: Prepare food for when you have less time to cook

As with the shopping, planning ahead can help to prevent you from falling back on less healthy alternatives when you're hungry and don't have time to prepare. Making and freezing meals at the weekend for the week ahead can be really useful when you know you'll have limited time for cooking in the evenings. My wife will quite happily lose herself in her cooking listening to a play on the radio for a couple of hours but if this is not your thing (it's not my idea of fun!) here's a few other options I've found work well that you might like to try:

- ✓ When cooking recipes that freeze well double the ingredients so that you have sufficient to freeze for another meal. Make sure you label the containers carefully though unless you like a surprise meal for supper!
- ✓ Become creative with leftovers! For example, if you have too many steamed new potatoes you could keep some to bulk up a salad the next day.
- ✓ Deliberately cooking extra of certain ingredients can also be a useful. For example, cooking extra vegetables can be useful for numerous dishes such as vegetable curry or a soup, or a pilaf with quinoa.
- ✓ Cook two meals at the same time to free up the following evening; great to know when you're on your way home from work all the hard work is already done!

Tip 8: Give juicing a try

The popularity of juicing has exploded in the last few years and I talk to many people who enthusiastically tell me how much better they feel since they started juicing. I enjoy experimenting with different combinations. The benefits include:

✓ Providing your body with a nutrient dense liquid that is easy to assimilate.

✓ Being made from raw ingredients many important vitamins and enzymes which are easily destroyed by the heat of cooking remain intact.

Juicing can be useful if you have limited time to prepare a meal, especially if you put some protein powder in with a little live yoghurt. Adding an avocado provides lots of incredible nutrients and makes the juice really creamy, a great snack or light meal when you're pressed for time.

There are many great books available with excellent advice and recipes or you can experiment with your own. But if this is your first-time juicing, listen to your body and take note of any apparent symptoms which could be a detox reaction or a blood sugar spike.

A few points to bear in mind:

✓ It is wise to start slowly with small amounts if you are new to juicing. This is because as any naturopath will tell you, juices have a strong elimination effect. This means that they can promote detoxification reactions in your body, which, you might think, is a good thing, but it depends on how it manifests itself. I have known people have quite severe and sudden reactions as a result of going straight into juicing say twice a day. These have ranged from sudden onset of diarrhoea to bad headaches and mood swings.

✓ If you are using fruits, be aware of the high sugar content in the form of fructose that can have a big impact on blood sugar. If your juicer keeps the fibre in the juice this will help to slow down absorption of the fructose into your blood. I tend to use vegetables mostly when I juice as they have less of an effect on blood sugar.

✓ To obtain maximum nutritional content, drink as soon as it's ready.

Tip 9: Add variety to your diet

Variety is the spice of life. It is all too easy to find things that you like and eat them too often; I know that I've been guilty of this. The problem with this is that you restrict the amazing variety of nutrients that are available to you with a diet that includes a diverse range of different foods. You can also become stale and bored with your food so to avoid this, try to eat as varied a diet as possible and try new foods. As already mentioned, eating seasonally is a good way to do this. With our box scheme, we do not specify which vegetables are delivered each week, so it is always interesting to see what we get, and it makes us try new things. One thing I've found useful to do is to experiment with at least one new recipe a week.

Tip 10: Try to avoid bingeing or over eating

Most of us have binged on food at some time or another. Maybe because we were very hungry, or we have been mad about a favourite food. Whatever the reason, bingeing makes it hard for your body to maintain an even blood sugar throughout the day.

If you decide to try fasting which I would highly recommend you do, you will find that your blood sugar control and regulation of your hunger improves. As a consequence, you will be able to go for longer without food, not feel hungry and avoid the temptation to binge.

Bingeing can also overload your digestive system making you feel bloated and uncomfortable. If you eat large quantities of food, your digestive system can struggle to produce enough digestive juices and enzymes to effectively break down and efficiently digest all the food. The result is that you may get some food that has not been properly broken down passing into the small and large intestine which can cause problems as discussed in chapter 3.

Tip 11: Take your time when eating your food

This is not always easy because of the fast pace of modern life; however, it is a good habit to get into. Eating quickly invariably means that you do not chew properly so the process of carbohydrate digestion which starts in the mouth does not begin as it should. This can also impact on the digestion of protein in the stomach as it's simply not broken down sufficiently. Your stomach does not have teeth; it needs you to do the chewing!

Also, if you eat quickly you will not feel satiated which means that you are more likely to eat more than you need to get a feeling of fullness. This is because your body produces hormones during a meal which tell your brain when you have eaten sufficient food which then makes us feel that we have eaten enough. It takes approximately 15-20 minutes for these hormones to work and if we eat too much food too quickly we can easily over eat. I am certainly guilty of this so need to remind myself to slow down.

Tip 12: Read food labels

Food labels must be provided by the manufacturers by law. Please make sure that you read them, especially if you are thinking of trying a product for the first time. Basic rules of thumb include:

- ✓ The fewer the ingredients the better, try to choose products with a minimum number of ingredients.
- ✓ The ingredients are listed in direct proportion to the amount so if unhealthy ingredients are at the top of list you know it's not going to be a particularly nutritious choice.
- ✓ Look out for ingredients that sound like food rather than the contents of a chemistry lab!
- ✓ It goes without saying but look for ingredients that seem logical to be in the product. It's amazing how much sugar is added, for example, even in products you'd least expect to be sweet, like a ready-made sandwich!

Tip 13: Listen to your body to perfect your diet

Whilst there are fundamental guidelines about which types of foods are beneficial, we are all biochemically different so there is no perfect diet that suits everyone. It's therefore crucial that we listen to our body so that we can adjust our diet accordingly in order to gain the optimal sense of wellbeing and health we are seeking.

For example, soya is a great source of vegetable protein and contains therapeutic phytoestrogens. However, it doesn't suit everyone as some people find it very hard to digest and can end up with stomach aches and digestive upsets.

Note: A lot of soya is genetically modified so if you are including this in your diet, be very careful where you source it from. Make sure that it is certified organic by a reputable organisation such as The Soil Association.

Tip 14: Be flexible in when and what you eat

Some of us have a tendency to divide our meals into recognised parts of the day as a consequence of how we were brought up. I can remember growing up with the usual three meals a day and that's just the way it was. Breakfast was always cereal and the main meal was always in the evening, kept warm for hours if I arrived home late by which time there were unlikely to be any nutrients left!

It's easy to get into rigid habits that can be difficult to fit around busy lifestyles. This is where some forward planning can help overcome everyday snags and make it easier to apply the concepts in this chapter. I found I was eating huge meals late at night. So now, when I know I'm going to be home late, I try to plan ahead and either have ingredients in for easily prepared light meals or have my main meal at lunchtime so I only need a quick snack in the evening. When I'm out and have needed to skip breakfast or lunch I try to make sure I have some nuts and seeds handy to keep hunger at bay.

When I was a Fire Fighter it could be very unpredictable as to when we got the opportunity to eat. I therefore took food that could be eaten at any time and did not require further preparation. That gave me the flexibility to ensure that I could eat nutritious food and avoid resorting to unhealthy alternatives too frequently.

Breakfast is considered to be the most important meal of the day and rightly so, as the name suggests you are breaking a fast, so it needs to be as nutritious and balanced as you can make it so that your body can replenish its nutrients after hours of not eating. Some people like their breakfast at a certain time and find that it sets them up for the morning, while others may eat something because they think they ought to but are not really hungry. Then there are those who find the thought of food first thing in the morning makes them feel a bit queasy. Everyone is different and there are no hard and fast rules about when you should eat the all-important first meal of the day. The best indicator is how you feel and comes back again to listening to your body.

However, if you do eat early in the morning, it is best not to eat until you have fully woken up. You cannot expect your digestion to be ready immediately, so it is best not to eat for at least 1 to 2 hours after waking if you can. I realise for some this might not be practical. For example, some pharmaceutical drugs that need to be taken first thing may also need to be taken with food. Do what's right for you, but if you are able to leave a couple of hours before eating in the morning, your digestive system will be appreciative!

Personally, as I use intermittent timed fasting, I use the 8-hour eating window which starts with the first meal at 11am. Before trying fasting I used to eat my breakfast early and thought I'd have trouble adapting. However, I found that I soon got used to eating later. If you're someone that isn't particularly hungry first thing it may be worth giving intermittent fasting a try.

There is also the habit of what we tend to eat according to the meal. This is most noticeable with breakfast, where over the years the food manufacturers have spent untold millions trying to convince us that we simply cannot start the day without one of their amazing cereals!

However, when you look at these breakfast cereals they are often loaded with sugar and other simple carbohydrates as well as being grains which together give a big sugar hit; which, as we have seen, is very bad for the blood sugar and our long-term health. Many grains are also acid forming and make it more difficult to achieve the predominantly alkaline conditions that are a foundation of good health.

There are of course some excellent healthy cereals available that do not affect blood sugar and are not acid forming. But even with these it is easy to eat them every day because they are convenient. Also as we're often in automatic pilot in the mornings, it's easy to get into the habit of having the same thing every day for breakfast so it's useful to think about creating some variety. Might sound rather odd, but I quite often save some of my evening meal from the night before. This saves time and as it usually contains vegetables and a quality protein it is a great first meal of the day. If you want to add some variety to your breakfasts I hope some of the recipes in Section 6c will give you useful ideas.

By being inventive it is possible to get an amazing mix of meals throughout the day which breaks up the traditional format and gives you the opportunity to experiment and to optimise your health and well- being.

Finally, it can be challenging to keep up with the latest research. What was last year's superfood is now being heralded as unhealthy and to avoid! It can be hard to keep up so it's really important to keep flexible as well as open to trying new things. Building flexibility into our eating habits is a great way to succeed in maintaining a healthy diet.

Tip 15: Try to avoid eating too late

Obviously, there are times when this may be difficult such as when we eat socially but most of the time it is not a good idea. This is because your body naturally wants to divert its resources to maintenance and repair and then start to detox whilst you are asleep. It cannot do this efficiently if it is burdened with diverting a lot of energy towards digestion. So, as a rule it is best to try not to eat less than 3 hours before you go to sleep or 4 hours if it is a large meal.

Tip 16: A quick way of estimating portions and size of your meals

I am certainly guilty of eating too much at times. It's easy to load up the plate when you're hungry or when it's a favourite meal. It's best to finish your meal feeling as if you could eat a little more if you wanted to, but don't **need** to. A useful way not to feel uncomfortably full or to over burden your stomach is using your palms as a measure:

Serving Size **Palm of your hand**	One portion of food should fit easily in the palm of your hand. This should only cover the palm not the whole hand and should not be piled up so that it is falling off!
Meal Size **Cupped Hands**	You should be able to fit your meal into both of your hands cupped together.

Tip 17: Treat yourself

There is absolutely nothing wrong with eating less healthy foods occasionally. I believe that treating yourself is important and helps to keep you motivated. The treat can of course be anything you fancy but try to make it a good quality treat if possible (e.g. if you have chocolate try to make it organic) and they should also be occasional (part of the 20% of the 80/20 rule). In any case if you have something all the time it fails to remain special and a treat. As the saying goes "if there's always biscuits in the tin, where's the fun in biscuits!"

Tip 18: Make changes you want to implement gradually

As mentioned at the beginning of Section 6, it's important to make changes gradually as there's more chance that they will stand the test of time. When we've made the decision to eat more healthily it's easy to obsess over everything and to be too stringent. If the changes are too sudden and feel arduous it's less likely that you will succeed in the longer term. Some people find it easy to make changes quickly whereas others need more time – do what feels right for you. As long as you remain committed and patient you will succeed.

Tip 19: Using an app

As I'm sure you're aware there are now many Apps available that help you to track different components of your diet.

Apps allow you to monitor the main food groups and see the exact percentage of protein, carbs and healthy fat you are eating and enable you to adapt the amounts to achieve your goals. Apps can also offer an almost infinite variety of information on vitamins, minerals and other nutrients and I know that many people find these extremely useful. Of course they're not infallible – they are another resource in the tool kit.

One that I have tried is **cronometer.com** which is free to download. This app works out what nutrients you are getting each day, sets fitness goals and helps you to integrate other lifestyle factors such as exercise into your health regime. In fact, it allows you to go into every tiny aspect of your nutrition and diet. This can be useful if you need to address a serious health issue or wish to train for a sport or some other physical challenge. However, I feel that it is easy to become too obsessive about achieving the exact amounts of every nutrient in your diet every day.

You may wish to give apps a go and you may find they work well for you. I prefer to use the simple rules that I have set out in this chapter to keep me focused and on track.

Tip 20: Review your intake of raw food

Whilst we are aware of the virtues of raw food for achieving the best possible health, eating a diet made up of 100% raw food is not practical or desirable for many of us. You may wish to review your current intake of raw food and look to increase the amount you eat gradually. If it's currently 10% aim to build up to 20%, and over time work up to 50%.

I find this is achievable in the summer months. In winter you may wish to include more raw veg through juicing, coleslaw or crudité for warmly spiced dips. I urge you to give it a go; you will be taking a huge step towards a long and healthy life.

Tip 21: Be patient, persistent and consistent!

I appreciate that there is an awful lot of information to take in from this chapter and that this can take time to implement. The key is to apply the information with consistency, keep at it and be patient– you'll be amazed at the results you'll achieve.

6B. Your Quick Reference Food Table

The following table represents a balanced diet with some latitude for treats etc. To get the optimum benefits you need to bias towards the green section as much as possible. This will help to ensure that your diet is alkalising, helps to keep blood sugar in balance, provides you with high quality protein, complex carbohydrates and healthy fats and gives you all the essential nutrients your body needs to thrive.

Don't be concerned if trying to stick to the green section looks a bit draconian, this is just to identify the ideal. I know that in the real world this can be challenging to maintain and there is nothing wrong with combining foods from the green and amber sections in the proportions stated below with occasional use of foods from the red section.

GREEN

Eat these foods freely, they should form **at least 40% of your diet**; the more of these foods you include in your diet, the better your health will be. Ideally, they should comprise 80% of your diet.

AMBER

Eat these foods in moderation, they should make up no more than 40% of your diet. Ideally, you should limit their intake to 20%.

RED

You should try to limit or exclude them as much as possible and at the very least restrict them to **no more than 20% of your diet**. If you want to occasionally treat yourself, try to make sure it is organic if possible. For the best results, you should consider eliminating these foods from you diet altogether.

You can progress at your own pace according to practicalities and how you feel, making your own informed choices with respect to working towards the ideal diet that suits your unique biological requirements.

GREEN Eat these foods freely

Vegetables & Herbs

Artichokes
Asparagus
Aubergine/Egg plant
Basil
Beetroot
Broad beans
Broccoli
Brussels Sprouts
Cabbage
Capsicum
Carrot
Cauliflower
Celery
Chard
Chilli
Chives
Coriander
Courgette
Cucumber
Dandelion
Endive
Garlic
Green Beans
Kale
Kelp
Leeks
Lettuce
Marrow
Onion
Parsley
Peas
New potatoes
Pumpkin
Radishes
Runner Beans
Spinach
String Beans
Swede
Sweet potato
Watercress

Fruit

Avocado
Fresh coconut
Grapefruit
Lemon
Lime
Tomato

Grains

Amaranth
Brown rice
Buckwheat
Chia
Kamut
Quinoa
Spelt

Beans and Pulses

Chick peas
Lentils
Lima
Mung
Pinto
Red
Soy
White

Nuts and Seeds

Almonds
Coconut
Flax
Pumpkin
Sesame
Sunflower

Oils

Avocado
Coconut
Flax
Krill
Olive
Udo's oil blend

Drinks

Almond milk
Filtered water
Goats milk
Green tea
Herbal teas
Spirulina juice
Wheatgrass juice

Fish

Freshwater fish
Ocean fish
Wild fish

n.b. ideally choose fish that fit on your plate. Larger fish like tuna can contain high degrees of mercury

Non-animal proteins

Tofu

AMBER Eat these foods in moderation.

Fruits	**Dairy Products**	**Oils**
Apple	Butter	Sunflower
Apricot	Cottage Cheese	
Blackberry	Yoghurt	**Drinks**
Blueberry	Whey	Tea (max 3 per day)
Cantaloupe		Rice milk
Cranberry	**Grains**	Soy milk
Currants	Brown rice	Tap water
Fresh dates	Oats	
Grapes	Rice pasta	
Nectarine	Wild rice	
Orange		
Papaya	**Beans**	
Peach	Black beans	
Pineapple	Kidney beans	
Plum		
Strawberry	**Nuts**	
Sweet cherry	Brazil	
Water melon	Cashew	
	Chestnuts	
Animal Products	Hazelnuts	
Eggs (up to 6 per week)	Pecan	
Game	Walnuts	
Lamb		
Poultry		
Shell fish		

RED Limit these foods as much as possible

Grains

Rye bread

Wheat based products including:

- White and wholemeal breads
- White and wholemeal pastas
- Noodles
- Pizza

Animal Products

Beef

Pork including bacon

Rabbit

All processed meats including:

- Sausages
- Burgers
- Faggots
- Luncheon meat
- Corned beef
- Canned meats

Nuts

Macadamia

Peanuts

Pistachios

Oils

Commercial vegetable oils

Cooked oil

Margarine

Oil exposed to heat, light and air

Snack Foods

Biscuits

Chocolate

Confectionary

Crisps

Drinks

Alcohol

Carbonated water

Cocoa

Coffee

Colas

Decaffeinated drinks

Energy drinks

Flavoured waters

Milk

Pasteurised juice

Sports drinks

Sauces

Brown

Ketchup

Mayonnaise

Mustard

Pickles

Tabasco

Tamari

Wasabi

Sweeteners

Artificial sweeteners

Carob

Corn syrup

Fructose

Glucose syrup

Honey

Maple syrup

Processed sugar

Saccharine

Sucralose

6c. Ideas for Quick and Easy Nutritious Recipes

When we're busy it's easy to rely on convenience foods so the aim of this section is to provide you with some ideas for quick, easy and nutritious recipes.

Menu ideas for a week

The meal planner that follows provides some ideas for a week that are both quick to prepare, tasty and healthy. Whilst the planner is structured around the traditional 3 meals a day, you may find that you only require 2 meals with perhaps 2 snacks throughout the day, everyone's different.

The first meal of the day can be any time of your choosing, so if you have decided to give fasting a go this may not be until late morning, especially if you choose to use the intermittent timed fasting method.

The important thing is to make sure that this first meal is as nutritionally complete as you can make it; incorporating high quality protein, essential/ healthy fats and some complex carbohydrates if you wish.

Cooking tips to maximise nutritional content:

- ✓ Use organic ingredients whenever possible
- ✓ Use butter or coconut oil instead of olive or vegetable oils when sautéing as they are heat stable and will not form harmful by products when heat is applied. You can also steam fry which reduces the temperature and will also help to protect the nutritional value of the food. Just add a couple of table spoons of water when the butter or coconut oil has melted.
- ✓ Chopping or slicing garlic activates the healthy nutrients in garlic. To retain these, add garlic towards the end of cooking for the last 5 to 10 minutes. Avoid microwaving or boiling uncrushed whole garlic bulbs as these de-activate the health benefits.

Menu Planner - quick and nutritious ideas for a week

Recipes marked with an asterisk are included in this chapter.

Day	Breakfast	Lunch	Supper
Monday	Poached eggs on grilled portobello mushrooms	Beetroot, rocket, apple and cashew nut salad*	Salmon and quinoa risotto*
Tuesday	Protein porridge*	Prawn and avocado salad*	Poached eggs with root veg and crushed seed dressing*
Wednesday	Yoghurt with nuts, seeds, cacao nibs and chopped fruit	Lentil soup*	Grilled fish with French beans, potatoes, broccoli 1
Thursday	Avocado and chia smoothie*	Salmon Caesar Salad*	Rice pasta with feta + sundried tomatoes*
Friday	Yoghurt, berry and chia pot*	Veggie Nicoise*	Chickpea curry* 2
Saturday	Smoked salmon kedgeree*	Smashed avocado on toasted spelt bread with crumbled feta	Sea bass with salsa verde on a bed of mash and spinach* 3
Sunday	Sweet potato, wilted spinach and poached egg *	Lentil shepherd's pie	Crudité,* oat cakes or toasted spelt bread with smashed avocado, houmous* and mackerel pâté*

Notes

1. cook extra potatoes and green beans for tomorrow's Caesar salad
2. cook extra rice for tomorrow's Kedgeree
3. make double the mash for Sunday lunch

Ideas for quick and nutritious recipes

Breakfast:	Protein porridge	(D)
	Avocado and chia smoothie	(D)
	Yoghurt, berry and chia pot	
	Sweet potato, wilted spinach and poached egg	(D)
	Smoked salmon and watercress kedgeree	
Snacks:	Ultra-quick grab and go avocado	(D)
	Lentil soup	(D)
	Crudité	(D)
	Houmous	(D)
	Smoked mackerel pâté	
	Handful of nuts and seeds	(D)
Salads:	Beetroot, rocket, apple and cashew nut salad	(D)
	Prawn and avocado salad	(D)
	Salmon Caesar salad	
	Veggie Caesar salad	(D)
	Veggie Nicoise	(D)
Meals:	Poached eggs with root veg & crushed seed dressing	
	Salmon and quinoa risotto	
	Chickpea curry	(D)
	Rice pasta with feta and sun-dried tomatoes	
	Sea bass fillets with salsa verde, mash and spinach	
	Lentil shepherd's pie with sweet potato mash	(D)

(D) = Can be used in a detox

Breakfast: **Protein porridge** Serves 1

Preparation time: 5 to 10 minutes

This is one of my favourite snacks as it is very quick to prepare and requires minimal cleaning up afterwards! Porridge is often associated just with breakfast though I love it when I need a warming snack. It also is a very nutritious and complete meal with complex carbohydrates for great energy levels, good protein content and essential omega fats from the nuts and seeds.

<u>Ingredients</u>

50 g porridge oats (gluten free if possible)

20g pea protein powder

350ml milk – to reduce dairy intake you may wish to try coconut, almond or hazelnut milk though my favourite for porridge is vanilla rice milk.

1 tablespoon of plain live yoghurt (cow, goat, sheep or coconut)

1 apple chopped

1 tablespoon of nuts and seeds

Sprinkle of cinnamon powder

1. Stir the protein powder into the porridge oats to avoid lumpy porridge.
2. Add the milk and heat gently for around 5 minutes, stirring from time to time to stop it sticking to the bottom of the pan.
3. Once served top with the yoghurt, apple, nuts, seeds and cinnamon.

Breakfast/Snack: Avocado and chia smoothie Serves 1

Preparation time: 5 minutes (35 minutes includes soaking chia seeds)

This makes a great start to the day and is also an excellent post exercise snack.

Ingredients

1 ripe avocado

750 ml coconut milk

1 teaspoon vanilla extract

1 teaspoon cinnamon

1 teaspoon chia seeds

250g of fresh or frozen mixed berries such as raspberries/blueberries

1. Soak the chia seeds in 250ml of coconut water for 30 minutes. Soaking the chia seeds before making the smoothie sprouts them which makes all the fabulous nutrient content of these seeds available for digestion.
2. Place a peeled and stoned avocado into a blender together with the remaining 500 ml of coconut milk.
3. Add the berries, vanilla extract, cinnamon and soaked chia seeds.
4. Blend until smooth and consume immediately. If you want to save some for later ideally store in the fridge and use the same day.

Breakfast/Snack: Yoghurt, berry and chia pot Serves 1

Preparation time: 5 minutes (35 minutes includes soaking chia seeds)

This makes a great start to the day and can also be used as a healthy dessert. In the winter months you may wish to swap the berries for more seasonal fruits.

Ingredients

100g plain live yoghurt - cow's, sheep's or goat's (I prefer this)

1 tablespoon of chia seeds

250g of fresh or frozen berries of your choice

2 teaspoons of cacao nibs

Pinch of cinnamon

1. Put the yoghurt into a bowl and stir in the chia seeds.
2. Place in the fridge and leave for 30 minutes to enable the chia seeds to sprout and release their nutrients. This also helps to thicken the yoghurt.
3. Add the fruit and cacao nibs, stirring gently.
4. Finally, add a pinch of cinnamon.

Breakfast: Sweet potato, wilted spinach and poached egg Serves 1

Preparation time: 15 minutes

I first came across this very simple meal in a favourite local café called Cocolicious. It is such a delicious combination that I had to put it into the book – thanks Lou-Lou, Ginny and Sarah for this.

Ingredients

1 sweet potatoes washed thoroughly so you don't need to peel

Handful of spinach

1 egg

Olive oil for drizzling

Lemon juice for drizzling

Himalayan salt and freshly ground black pepper

1. Peel the sweet potatoes only if the outer skins are particularly knobbly.
2. Cut the sweet potatoes into 1 cm slices and steam them until they can just be cut easily with a knife.
3. Whilst the sweet potato slices are cooking poach the eggs and steam the spinach. It should take no longer than a minute to wilt.
4. Serve the sweet potato onto warmed plates and drizzle with olive oil.
5. Spoon the spinach over the sweet potatoes and drizzle with lemon juice, which is said to help the absorption of the iron in spinach.
6. Top with the poached egg and season with black pepper and Himalayan salt.

Breakfast: **Smoked salmon and watercress kedgeree** Serves 2

Preparation time: 10 minutes if the rice is already cooked

This is a comforting weekend breakfast and quick to do if you're using leftover cooked rice. If you have a bit more time and need to cook the rice then add 225 ml of fish or vegetable stock with rinsed rice after adding the spices, bring to the boil then reduce the heat, cover with a lid and let it simmer for 12 to 15 minutes until tender.

Smoked salmon replaces the traditional smoked haddock for speed as well as providing omega-3 fats. Watercress brings a refreshing mustardy bite to kedgeree and is one of the most nutritious vegetables rich in minerals such as calcium, iron, potassium and phosphorus.

Ingredients

1 onion chopped

1 knob of butter or coconut oil

1 clove of garlic crushed

1 teaspoon of curry powder

¼ teaspoon of turmeric

100g cooked brown basmati rice

50 g watercress roughly chopped

2 hardboiled eggs sliced

100g of smoked salmon cut into small pieces.

70g fresh peas if in season or thawed frozen peas.

1 tablespoon of lemon juice

Himalayan salt and freshly ground black pepper

1. Melt the butter or coconut oil in a large saucepan.
2. Add the onion and cook gently until it is translucent.
3. Stir in the curry powder, turmeric and garlic.
4. Mix in the rice ensuring each grain is covered with the spices
5. Gently stir in the peas, watercress, eggs and smoked salmon.
6. Season with Himalayan salt and freshly ground black pepper.
7. Serve with lemon wedges

Snacks: **Ultra-quick grab and go avocado** Serves 1

Preparation Time: 1 minute

<u>Ingredients</u>

Avocado

Dash of balsamic vinegar or apple cider vinegar

Ground black pepper and Himalayan salt

Avocados are the ultimate convenience food. A delicious, nutritious, quick and highly portable snack.

1. Cut the avocado in half and remove the stone.
2. Add a dash of balsamic vinegar and sprinkle with the salt and pepper.

The vinegar complements the creaminess of the avocado perfectly. Scoop out the flesh with a teaspoon. No need to serve on a plate to save on washing up!

Snacks: **Lentil Soup** Serves 4

Preparation time: 25 minutes

This is a satisfying and wholesome soup that uses staple store cupboard ingredients. It's much tastier than its simple ingredients would suggest.

Ingredients

1 large onion chopped

15g of butter/coconut oil

225 g red lentils

1 litre of stock or water with a heaped teaspoon of bouillon powder

1 to 2 tablespoons of lemon juice

Himalayan crystal salt and black pepper

1. Rinse the lentils under cold running water until the water runs clear.
2. Gently melt the butter in a saucepan and sauté the onion until soft but not brown.
3. Add the lentils to the onions and stir for about 2 minutes.
4. Add the stock and bring to the boil then half cover the saucepan and leave to simmer for approximately 20 minutes until the lentils are pale and tender.
5. Add Himalayan crystal salt, black pepper and 1 – 2 teaspoons of lemon juice to taste.
6. Use a hand blender if you prefer the soup to be smoother.

5 Variations:

1. When sautéing the onion add a tablespoon of curry powder
2. Just before serving add 1 tablespoon of pea protein powder which has a mild savoury flavour. This not only helps thicken the soup but also makes it a complete protein meal.
3. Replace the lemon juice with orange juice
4. 5 minutes before serving sauté an onion and 2 crushed cloves of garlic. Stir into the soup.
5. Sprinkle with crushed walnuts

Snacks: Crudité

Preparation Time: 5 minutes

Crudité, a traditional French appetizer, are a great way to eat fresh vegetables. You can use whatever you have available. Favourites of mine include celery sticks, carrot sticks, cucumber sticks, bell pepper strips, broccoli florets, cauliflower florets, fennel, asparagus spears and olives. These are delicious dipped into the home-made houmous or mackerel pâté recipes that follow.

Snacks: Houmous

Preparation time: 10 minutes

This makes a great snack to keep in the fridge and graze on either at home or at work and can also make an excellent lunch. You can either buy or make your own houmous. If buying choose organic if possible and check the ingredients to ensure there's no added sugar. It takes minutes to make your own and it has brilliantly nutritious ingredients; all you need is a food processor

<u>Ingredients</u>

1 tin of drained chickpeas

1 tablespoon of tahini

2 crushed garlic cloves

1 tablespoon of extra virgin olive oil

Juice of half a lemon

Freshly ground black pepper

Himalayan salt.

Place all the ingredients into the food processor and blend to a fine paste and you have your houmous. You can experiment and add extra ingredients if you wish. I like to add 50g of walnuts and 200g of steamed beetroot. This really is a great and versatile food and will keep in the fridge for 3 or 4 days.

Snacks: Smoked mackerel pâté

Preparation time: 5 minutes
Serves 2

This is a great pâté for rice cakes and oat cakes or used as a dip for crudités.

Ingredients

2 skinned smoked mackerel fillets

4 tablespoons of plain live yoghurt

2 teaspoons of horseradish sauce

1. Break up smoked mackerel with a fork or place in food blender depending on how coarse or smooth you like the texture.
2. Mix in the yoghurt and horseradish.

Variation:

Replace the mackerel with a cooked salmon fillet and add chopped dill to the yoghurt.

Snacks: Nuts and seeds

A handful of nuts and seeds is a great way of obtaining many important minerals as well as essential fats and protein. They are literally nutritional powerhouses. Taking a small bag with you when out and about can be great if you find your blood sugar dips and to keep the hunger pangs at bay.

Salads: **Beetroot, rocket, apple and cashew nut salad**

Preparation Time: 5 minutes Serves 1

I love salads because they are quick to prepare, offer you an opportunity to bring incredible fresh healthy ingredients, flavours and textures together. They can also be kept in the fridge for later and require a minimum of clearing up!

This salad is so quick to make and has some wonderful flavour combinations as well as great health benefits.

<u>Ingredients</u>

Salad:
1 dessert apple
1 carrot
1 large or 2 small fresh beetroot
Handful of rocket or your preferred salad leaves
25g cashew nuts

Dressing:
1 dessert spoon of extra virgin olive oil
3 dessert spoons of lemon juice
1 dessert spoon of balsamic vinegar
Himalayan salt and freshly ground black pepper.

1. Make the dressing by mixing together the olive oil, lemon juice and balsamic vinegar then season with the salt and pepper.
2. Using a potato peeler 'shave' the carrot and beetroot to create some thick shavings. Alternatively, slice thinly.
3. Toss the rocket with the beetroot and carrot shavings.
4. Sprinkle on the cashew nuts
5. Chop or slice the apple and add to the salad when ready to serve to prevent the apple from turning brown.
6. Drizzle the dressing on the salad and serve straight away.

Salads: **Prawn and avocado salad**

Preparation time: 15 minutes Serves 2

Ingredients

2 avocados

200g cooked prawns

Handful of nuts and seeds

Salad:
- 150 g of mixed salad leaves
- 2 sticks of celery
- 8 cherry tomatoes
- ½ cucumber
- (These are suggestions, use what you have available)

Salad Dressing:
- 2 tablespoons of extra virgin olive oil
- Juice of 2 lemons
- 2 tablespoons of finely chopped basil
- 2 tablespoons of chopped parsley
- Himalayan salt for seasoning
- Freshly ground black pepper for seasoning

1. Make the salad dressing by mixing in all the ingredients together.
2. Rinse the prawns and mix with the salad dressing. If you have time leave in the fridge to allow the prawns to absorb the flavours of the dressing.
3. Wash and chop a selection of green leaves for the base and add any salad vegetables you have available.
4. Scoop out the flesh of the avocados. If you're not serving straight away then mix with the prawns so that the lemon juice in the dressing stops the avocado from discolouring.
5. Sprinkle on some nuts and seeds
6. Season with Himalayan salt and freshly ground black pepper.

Salads: **Salmon Caesar salad**

Preparation: 20 minutes Serves 2

This is a great twist on the classic chicken Caesar salad. Salmon cooks more quickly than chicken and is high in omega 3 fats. This salad is also wheat free, replacing the croutons with potatoes. In the dressing you can use crème fraiche instead of yoghurt, which makes for a thicker consistency. I use yoghurt as it's always in my fridge.

<u>Ingredients</u>

2 salmon fillet

Juice of ½ lemon

12 small steamed new potatoes

1 cos lettuce

Chopped leaves of a sprig of rosemary

<u>Ingredients for the dressing</u>

3 tablespoons of yoghurt

3 tablespoons of extra virgin olive oil

1 tablespoon of lemon juice

20 g Parmesan

1 anchovy fillet

Freshly ground black pepper

1. Pour the lemon juice over the salmon fillets. To preserve and avoid damaging the omega fats and protein in the salmon it is best to steam. If you wish to cook it in the oven so that the flesh is drier keep the temperature at 140 degrees. Cook until it turns a pale pink around 10 to 15 minutes.
2. Chop the steamed potatoes into crouton sized chunks and mix with the chopped rosemary.
3. Make the dressing by smashing up the anchovy fillet with a fork then mixing in the remaining ingredients.
4. Wash the lettuce and spin dry to prevent the dressing becoming too runny. Tear the leaves and arrange on 2 plates.
5. Toss the lettuce with the potatoes and flake the salmon on top.
6. Pour the dressing liberally over the salad.

Salads: **Veggie Caesar salad**

Preparation: 10 minutes Serves 2

This version uses vegetarian pecorino cheese rather than parmesan and capers in the dressing to replace the anchovies.

Ingredients	1 cos lettuce
	12 small steamed new potatoes
	1 cos lettuce
	Leaves of a sprig of rosemary
Ingredients for the dressing	3 tablespoons of yoghurt
	3 tablespoons of extra virgin olive oil
	1 tablespoon lemon juice
	1 tablespoon of capers
	1 very small clove of crushed garlic
	20 g vegetarian pecorino cheese
	Freshly ground black pepper

1. Chop the steamed potatoes into crouton sized chunks and mix with the chopped rosemary.
2. Make the dressing by crushing the capers with a fork then mixing in the remaining ingredients.
3. Wash the lettuce and spin dry to prevent the dressing becoming too runny. Tear the leaves and arrange on 2 plates.
4. Toss the lettuce with the potatoes and pour the dressing on top.

Veggie Nicoise

Preparation: 10 minutes if vegetables are already cooked Serves 4

Large fish like tuna can have a lot of mercury in them so this veggie version is a useful alternative. It's a great way to use up leftover new potatoes and French beans. For a vegan version replace the eggs with white beans such as cannellini.

<u>Ingredients</u>

1 lettuce

500g steamed new potatoes

400g steamed French beans

1 red onion finely sliced

12 cherry tomatoes halved

Handful of olives

1 tablespoon of capers

<u>Ingredients for the dressing</u>

3 tablespoons of extra virgin olive oil

1 tablespoon red wine vinegar

1 teaspoon of Dijon mustard

1 very small clove of crushed garlic

Freshly ground black pepper to season

Himalayan salt to season

1. Make the dressing by mixing all the ingredients together or shake them up in a glass screw topped jar.
2. Toss the potatoes and French beans with a quarter of the dressing. If you are using white beans for the vegan version add here ensuring that each ingredient is coated and shiny with the dressing.
3. Lay the lettuce leaves on a large serving platter or 4 separate plates.
4. Spoon the potato and bean mixture onto the lettuce.
5. Scatter with the sliced onion, cherry tomatoes, olives and capers.
6. Quarter the hardboiled eggs and place evenly over the salad.
7. Trickle the rest of the dressing over the salad and season with freshly ground black pepper.

Meals: **Poached eggs with root veg & crushed seed dressing**

Preparation time: 25 minutes Serves 1

This may sound a bit of a strange combination but it goes together really well. As well as being quick to prepare it tastes delicious, especially if you make your eggs runny so that you can dip your vegetables into the yolk. Use any combination of vegetables you have available.

In this recipe the root veg are steamed rather than boiled as you lose nutrients into the water which are lost when the vegetables are drained. Using a steamer helps to conserve nutrients and the water can be used later for the basis of a soup. If you don't have a steamer rest a metal colander on a large saucepan, with 2 to 3 inches of water in the bottom of the pan. Cover the veg with a lid to stop the steam escaping.

It's tempting to roast root veg as they taste great, but we need to bear in mind that the more heat you apply the more nutrients are destroyed. If steamed veg are a little bland for you, you'll find this tasty and nutritious dressing a great alternative to roasting.

Ingredients

Handful of curly kale

1 sweet potato

2 carrots

1 parsnip

1 potato

2 eggs at room temperature

Dressing ingredients

Pumpkin seeds

Juice of half a lemon water

1 clove of garlic

1 tablespoon of olive oil

½ teaspoon of Himalayan salt

1. Pour 2 to 3 inches of water into the bottom of a steamer saucepan and bring to the boil.
2. Whilst the water is heating chop the washed root vegetables into chunks. Place in the steamer and cover leaving to simmer for around 15 minutes.
3. Make the dressing when the vegetables are steaming. Put all the ingredients in either a blender or food processor and blitz until smooth.
4. Add the curly kale to the steamer to cook with the root vegetables for 5 minutes.

5. When the kale is cooking make the poached eggs. I use a frying pan half filled with water.
    a. When the water is starting to boil, and you can see strings of bubbles forming gently crack in the eggs.
    b. Turn the heat down so they simmer gently for about 2 to 3 minutes.
    c. Use a fish slice to remove from the pan and rest the fish slice on a piece of folded kitchen roll to absorb unwanted water.
6. In a warmed bowl mix the vegetables with the dressing.
7. Serve the vegetables on a warmed plate and top with the poached eggs.
8. Season with some course ground black pepper and Himalayan sea salt.

Meals: **Salmon and quinoa risotto**

Preparation time: 25 minutes Serves 2

This quick and easy recipe is full of great ingredients and can be stored in the fridge for later as it is just as nice to eat cold.

Ingredients

To cook the quinoa:

1 knob of butter or coconut oil

100g quinoa

225 ml of boiling water

Juice and zest of half a lemon

2 salmon fillets

1 knob of butter or coconut oil to sauté the onion and mushrooms

1 red onion

Handful of mushrooms

Juice of half a lemon

Handful of cashew nuts or pine nuts

Pinch of Himalayan salt

Basil infused extra virgin olive oil is excellent for drizzling when the risotto is ready to serve. Alternatively use extra virgin olive oil and add some finely chopped basil.

1. To preserve and avoid damaging the omega fats and protein in the salmon it is best to steam. If you wish to cook it in the oven keep the temperature at 140 degrees. Cook until it turns a pale pink.
2. Whilst the salmon is cooking prepare the quinoa by melting the butter or coconut oil in a saucepan. Add the quinoa and stir-fry gently for about a minute.
3. Add the boiling water, lemon juice and lemon zest. Cover then simmer for 15 minutes until the water has been absorbed and the grains have burst.

4. When the quinoa is simmering gently sauté the onion until translucent but not browned.
5. Add the mushrooms and cook to enable the water to evaporate.
6. Add two cloves of finely sliced or crushed garlic for the last five minutes of cooking once the onions and mushrooms have softened.
7. Fork up the quinoa and add to the onion and mushroom mixture.
8. Mix in a handful of cashews or pine nuts.
9. Flake the salmon and gently mix into the quinoa mixture.
10. Drizzle with lemon juice and the basil infused olive oil. Season with Himalayan salt and freshly ground black pepper.

Meals: **Chickpea curry**

Preparation time: 30 minutes Serves 2

This curry is great if you're looking to include more meat free meals. It's filling, tasty and really nutritious. When time is tight you may prefer to use a jar of organic curry sauce.

Ingredients

- 150 g whole grain rice
- 400g tin of chickpeas
- 2 sliced courgette
- 4 sliced mushrooms

Curry sauce ingredients

- 1 large onion sliced
- 1 knob of butter or coconut oil
- 2 teaspoons of grated root ginger
- 1 clove of garlic, crushed
- 1 teaspoon of ground cumin
- 1 teaspoon of turmeric
- ½ teaspoon of chilli powder
- 225 gram tin of tomatoes
- 1 teaspoon of Himalayan salt

1. Rinse the rice in cold running water. Place in a saucepan with double the amount of water. Bring the boil then cover and simmer gently for 20 to 25 minutes.
2. While the rice is cooking, sauté the sliced onion in the butter or coconut oil until softened
3. Stir in the cumin, turmeric, chilli powder and ginger and cook for a minute.
4. Add the mushrooms and courgette and cook for a further 5 minutes so the vegetables absorb the spices.
5. Mix in the tinned tomatoes and allow to simmer for 5 minutes.
6. Add the crushed garlic and continue to cook the curry for 5 minutes, which should coincide with the rice being ready.
7. Fork up the rice and serve with the curry.

Meals: Rice pasta with feta and sundried tomatoes

Preparation time: 10 minutes Serves 2

Rice pasta was a great find for me when I was trying to reduce wheat and gluten in my diet but still wanted some comfort food. This takes minutes to prepare so is great when you get back home starving and tempted to order a takeaway! I like to use fusilli as there's more surface area for the sauce to stick to the pasta. If you have a bit more time sauté some onions and mushrooms to add with the tomatoes.

Ingredients for cooking pasta	250g brown rice pasta
	1 tablespoon of olive oil
Ingredients to accompany pasta	200g feta cheese cubed or crumbled
	Small jar of sundried tomatoes
	Small bunch of basil
	Freshly ground black pepper.

1. Bring a large saucepan of water to the boil. Add the olive oil, which helps to prevent the pasta sticking together.
2. When the water is boiling vigorously add the pasta a handful at a time.
3. While the pasta is cooking chop the sundried tomatoes and basil.
4. Give the pasta a quick stir then let it boil gently for 6 minutes.
5. Rice pasta has a tendency to suddenly go too soft so it's important to test after 6 minutes by removing one piece of pasta and biting. You're aiming for tender but still a bit of bite to it. I normally find it's perfect between 6 and 8 minutes.
6. Pour the cooked pasta into a colander to drain and shake the colander to remove excess water.
7. Tip the pasta back in the saucepan. Stir in the chopped sundried tomatoes, feta and basil.
8. Pour on some of the oil from the jar of tomatoes and stir heating gently to warm through.
9. Serve the pasta in warmed bowls, sprinkle with pepper.

Meals: **Sea bass fillets with salsa verde, mash and spinach**

Preparation time: 30 minutes Serves 2

This is a great Saturday night supper. Replace the potatoes for the mash with cauliflower, which cooks quicker and is known to cleanse the blood of toxins.

Ingredients	2 seabass or lemon sole fillets
	1 tablespoon of olive oil
	1 small cauliflower broken into florets
	Freshly ground black pepper.
	250g washed spinach
Ingredients for the salsa verde	1 garlic clove crushed
	1 teaspoon of capers finely chopped
	25 g finely chopped walnuts
	20 g parsley finely chopped
	Juice and grated zest of a lemon
	1 tablespoons of extra virgin olive oil.

1. Pre-heat oven to 1400 C.
2. Place the fish on a baking tray lined with grease proof paper and put in the centre of the oven.
3. Steam the cauliflower for 15 minutes until tender.
4. While the cauliflower and fish are cooking make the salsa verde by mixing together all of the ingredients. If you don't fancy chopping the ingredients, then add to a blender or food processor to blitz.
5. Transfer the steamed cauliflower to a large ovenproof bowl.
6. Turn off the heat then add the spinach to the steamer and replace the lid to allow the spinach to wilt in the residual heat.
7. Mash the cauliflower and mix with a knob of butter, a crushed clove of garlic and plenty of Himalayan salt and black pepper. (You could add mustard or horseradish instead of garlic.) Keep the mash warm in the oven.
8. Serve the fish on a bed of spinach with the cauliflower mash on the side. Pour the salsa verde over the fish.

Meals: **Lentil shepherd's pie with sweet potato mash**

Preparation time: 30 minutes Serves 2

This is a comforting lunch for a lazy Sunday. It's even quicker to make if you use leftover mash. Serve with your favourite steamed vegetables.

Ingredients	1 tin of puy lentils drained
	1 large onion
	1 garlic clove crushed
	25 g butter or coconut oil
	6 chestnut mushrooms quartered
	1 teaspoon of mixed herbs
	1 can of chopped tomatoes
	2 tablespoons of soy sauce
	3 tablespoons of chopped parsley
	Freshly ground black pepper
Ingredients for Mash	300 g sweet potatoes peeled
	1 tablespoon of horseradish sauce
	Himalayan salt, freshly ground black pepper

1. Chop the sweet potatoes into 1 cm cubes and steam for 10 minutes.
2. While the sweet potatoes are cooking fry the onion in the butter or coconut fat in a large saucepan until translucent. Add the mushrooms and continue to cook for 5 minutes.
3. Add the garlic, mixed herbs, tomatoes, soy sauce, parsley and lentils. Season with salt and pepper.
4. Transfer the lentil mixture to a shallow oven proof dish.
5. Once the sweet potatoes are cooked, pour the cooking liquid into a jug to use as a base for a soup later.
6. Put the sweet potatoes back in the bottom of the empty steamer

saucepan and mash with a fork or potato masher. Season and stir in the horseradish.

7. Spoon the mash evenly over the lentil mixture and use a fork to make ridges over the surface.
8. Place under the grill for 5 minutes until golden brown.

Health Benefits of Ingredients

I think it's important to link the food we eat more closely with our health. I've therefore included an alphabetical list of the key ingredients in these recipes, so you can see all the health benefits they bring.

Almonds *Recipes:* *Snacks*

Protein Porridge (almond milk)

☺ *Help increase energy levels*

☺ *Decrease the chance of gallstones*

☺ *Help protect the cardiovascular system*

☺ *Increase levels of beneficial (HDL) cholesterol and decreases levels of the bad type of LDL cholesterol*

☺ *Help to control blood sugar*

☺ *Good source of omega 9 and oleic acid*

Apples *Recipes:* *Beetroot, apple and cashew salad*

Protein Porridge

☺ *High in antioxidants*

☺ *Great source of a water-soluble fibre called pectin, which attaches to toxins helping them to be excreted.*

☺ *Help to reduce inflammation*

☺ *Help to cleanse the body*

☺ *Help to encourage healthy bacteria in the gut*

Avocado *Recipes:* *Avocado and chia smoothie*
Ultra-Quick Grab 'n' Go Avocado
Avocado and prawn salad
Smashed avocado, feta on toast

☺ *One of the most nutritionally complete foods you can eat.*

☺ *Contains good levels of almost every recommended vitamin and mineral*

☺ *Contain many beneficial fats*

☺ *Antioxidants*

☺ *Anti- inflammatory nutrients*

☺ *Cardio vascular benefits*

☺ *Anti-cancer benefits*

☺ *Helps the body to absorb antioxidants from salad it is served with*

Balsamic Vinegar *Recipes:* *Ultra-Quick Grab 'n' Go Avocado*
Beetroot, apple and cashew salad

☺ *Helps normalise blood pressure*

☺ *Helps prevent damage to arteries by bad type of LDL cholesterol*

☺ *Contains anti-oxidants*

☺ *Assists in protein digestion*

☺ *A rich source of minerals such as calcium and iron*

☺ *Improves insulin sensitivity which helps control blood sugar*

Beetroot *Recipes: Beetroot, apple and cashew salad*

Houmous – beetroot and walnut

- ☺ *Fights inflammation and anti-carcinogenic*
- ☺ *Rich in nutrients such as vitamin C, folate, potassium*
- ☺ *Helps to increase stamina when exercising*
- ☺ *Helps to support detoxification in the liver*
- ☺ *High in fibre and cleanses the blood*

Black pepper *Recipes: All recipes. I add it to everything!*

- ☺ *Increases the bioavailability of nutrients in food it is served with*
- ☺ *Can help in weight control by blocking the formation of new fat cells*
- ☺ *Enhances digestion of proteins through increasing secretion of hydrochloric acid in the stomach*

Broccoli *Recipes:* Crudité

- ☺ *Enhances detoxification process*
- ☺ *Decreases risk of developing following cancers prostate, colon, breast, bladder and ovarian*
- ☺ *Supports the digestion system, especially in reducing risk of stomach ulcers*
- ☺ *Supports the cardiovascular system*
- ☺ *Beneficial to eye and skin health*

Cacao nibs *Recipes: Yoghurt, berry and chia pot*

If you haven't come across these before, they are broken up cacao beans. As they are then brought to market unprocessed they retain some remarkable health properties. They contain a potent mixture of healthy fats, antioxidants, minerals and numerous other beneficial compounds.

☺ *They have anti-inflammatory properties*

☺ *Anti-carcinogenic*

☺ *Improves gastrointestinal flora (good bacteria)*

☺ *Anti-stress by reducing stress hormones*

☺ *Improve exercise endurance*

☺ *Helps to protect vision*

☺ *Anti-diabetic*

Carrots: *Recipes: Crudité*

Beetroot, apple and cashew salad

Poached eggs with root veg & crushed seed dressing

☺ *Contain good levels of antioxidants and good combination of different types which helps prevent cardio vascular disease*

☺ *Carrots help to prevent degeneration of vision as we get older*

☺ *Have shown to provide protection against colon cancer*

☺ *Good levels of vitamins and minerals*

Celery *Recipes: Crudité*

Prawn and avocado salad

- ☺ *Helps to decrease the risk of stomach ulcers*
- ☺ *Helps to reduce inflammation and blood pressure*
- ☺ *Good source of vitamins including: A,B2, C and K*
- ☺ *Rich in dietary fibre*
- ☺ *Good source of minerals e.g. potassium, manganese, copper, magnesium*

Chia seeds *Recipes: Avocado and chia smoothie*

Yoghurt, berry and chia pot

- ☺ *Great for digestive health due to high soluble fibre forming a gel which aids transit of waste through the digestive tract and help support the growth of healthy bacteria in the gut.*
- ☺ *Improve heart health by regulating cholesterol, lowering blood pressure and helping to prevent inflammation*
- ☺ *Excellent source of complete vegetable protein and minerals that helps to build muscle*
- ☺ *Chia seeds can absorb up to 10 times their own weight in water so provide a feeling of fullness that helps in weight control*
- ☺ *Help to boost your energy due to nutrient dense content*

Chickpeas *Recipes: Chickpea curry*

Houmous

- ☺ *The fibre in chickpeas helps to keep the large intestine healthy*
- ☺ *Contain a unique and powerful mix of antioxidants*
- ☺ *Contain nutrients that support cardiovascular health*

☺ *Help to lower bad type of LDL cholesterol*

☺ *High in iron, calcium, beta-carotene, vitamin C, folic acid + potassium.*

☺ *Neutralise acidity in the body and are anti-inflammatory*

Cinnamon *Recipes:* *Protein porridge*

Avocado and chia smoothie

Yoghurt, berry and chia pot

☺ *Contains a great mix of powerful antioxidant substances*

☺ *Anti-inflammatory*

☺ *Can reduce levels of the bad type of LDL cholesterol and so help to protect against heart disease.*

☺ *Increases sensitivity to insulin helping to control blood sugar*

☺ *Anti-viral and anti-bacterial properties*

Coconut milk/water *Recipes:* *Avocado and chia smoothie*

☺ *Anti-bacterial*

☺ *Helps improve hearth health by lowering blood pressure and bad type of LDL cholesterol.*

☺ *Helps to build muscle and lose fat*

☺ *Contains electrolytes that help prevent fatigue, especially after intense exercise*

☺ *Provide medium chain tri-glycerides that are the preferred energy source for the brain.*

☺ *Coconut milk nourishes the digestive lining due to its electrolytes and healthy fats, improving gut health.*

Eggs *Recipes:* *Sweet potato, wilted spinach and poached egg*

Veggie Nicoise

Poached eggs, root veg, crushed seed dressing

☺ *One of the most nutritious foods you can eat*

☺ *Contain the highest form of bio-available quality protein of any food*

☺ *Contain nutrients beneficial for eye health*

☺ *Contains amino acids that have been shown to help prevent cardiovascular disease and cancer.*

Only consume organic free range pastured eggs if possible. These are laid by hens that roam outside and eat their natural diet. You can tell a free-range egg as the yoke will be bright orange. Eggs from battery farmed caged birds have a dull pale-yellow yoke. Cooking by boiling or poaching is best for nutrition content; frying and scrambling damage the nutrients.

Garlic *Recipes:* *Most of these recipes!*

☺ *Very powerful anti-inflammatory benefits shown to directly provide protection against cardiovascular disease.*

☺ *Anti-viral and anti- bacterial*

☺ *Potent anti-cancer properties if consumed every one to two days*

☺ *Combats bacteria, intestinal parasites and viruses*

☺ *Many anti-oxidants and anti cancer compounds*

☺ *Great for fighting colds as it boosts the immune system*

Ginger *Recipes:* *Chickpea curry*

☺ *Anti-nausea*

☺ *Anti-motion sickness*

☺ *Can help to prevent migraines*

☺ *Anti-biotic, anti-viral and anti-oxidant*

(see chapter 3 on digestion for extra information about ginger)

Horseradish   *Recipes:*   *Smoked mackerel pate*

☺ *Anti-oxidant properties*

☺ *Anti-cancer properties*

☺ *Contains natural antibiotics (shown to be particularly useful for urinary infections)*

☺ *Can provide relief for sinus and respiratory conditions*

Kale   *Recipes:*   *Poached eggs with root veg & crushed seed dressing*

☺ *High in many beneficial antioxidants including vitamin C.*

☺ *Anti-inflammatory properties*

☺ *Helps in detoxification of the body*

☺ *Contains phyto-chemicals that help to reduce the risk of certain cancers (bladder, breast, ovary, colon, prostate)*

☺ *Helps to reduce cholesterol levels, especially when steamed*

☺ *Good levels of minerals including calcium, magnesium and iron*

Lemon juice *Recipes:* *Sweet potato, wilted spinach + poached egg*

Lentil soup

Prawn and avocado salad

Beetroot, apple and cashew salad

Salmon and quinoa risotto

☺ *A powerful anti-bacterial so can kill or slow down growth of bacteria*

☺ *Natural antibiotic so can kill or slow down bacteria, fungi or parasites*

☺ *Antioxidant and anti-carcinogenic*

☺ *Can provide protection from Rheumatoid arthritis*

☺ *High levels of vitamin C*

☺ *Helps balance pH levels making the body less acidic*

☺ *Aids digestion and helps reduce pain in joints*

☺ *Can help the absorption of iron in green leafy vegetables*

Lentils *Recipes:* *Lentil soup*

Lentil shepherd's pie + sweet potato mash

☺ *Helps to reduce the 'bad' type of LDL cholesterol*

☺ *High in fibre (contains both soluble and insoluble types)*

☺ *A good source of vitamins and minerals*

☺ *Shown to have cardiovascular protective properties*

☺ *Great for providing steady continuous energy throughout the day*

Mackerel *Recipes:* *Smoked mackerel pate*

☺ *High in Omega 3 fats*

☺ *Great source of high quality protein*

Mushrooms *Recipes:* *Salmon and quinoa risotto*

Chickpea curry

Feta and sundried tomato pasta

Lentil shepherd's pie + sweet potato mash

☺ *Anti-inflammatory boost the immune system and neutralise toxins*

☺ *High in essential minerals*

☺ *Contain vitamin B and D, selenium and germanium, which can improve energy levels*

☺ *Retain their nutrients after cooking*

Nuts and seeds *Recipes:* *Protein porridge*

Yoghurt + nuts, seeds, cacao nibs

☺ *High in healthy fats*

☺ *Loaded with minerals*

☺ *So nutrient dense that you only need about a handful per day*

Olive Oil (Extra Virgin) *Recipes:* *Most of these recipes!*

☺ *Reduces bad type of LDL cholesterol*

☺ *Rich source of antioxidants and monounsaturated fats*

☺ *Helps protect against cardiovascular disease*

☺ *Helps in weight management*

☺ *Has been found to reduce Rheumatoid arthritis pain*

☺ *Has been linked with reducing risk of breast cancer*

Onions *Recipes: Most of these recipes!*

☺ *Help increase bone density*

☺ *Help strengthen connective tissue, therefore beneficial to joints*

☺ *Anti-inflammatory*

☺ *Reduce the risk of some cancers*

Porridge oats *Recipes: Protein porridge*

☺ *Help lower small, dense LDL cholesterol (there are 2 kinds of LDL cholesterol and only one is bad)*

☺ *Provide a steady and slow energy release which avoids disrupting blood sugar levels and keeps them stable*

☺ *Contain numerous minerals and vitamins*

☺ *Source of protein*

☺ *Help prevent constipation and diarrhoea*

☺ *Remove toxins from the body*

Prawns *Recipes: Prawn and avocado salad*

☺ *Good source of protein*

☺ *Good levels of vitamin B12*

☺ *Good source of healthy fats including Omega 3*

Try to choose prawns that are caught in the coldest water e.g. North Atlantic. If possible, avoid farmed unless organic

Pumpkin seeds *Recipes:* *Poached eggs with root veg & crushed seed dressing*

☺ *Anti-viral and anti-microbial properties*

☺ *High in anti-oxidants*

☺ *Rich in minerals such as magnesium, manganese, copper and zinc*

☺ *Shown to help relieve menopausal symptoms and support the health of men's prostate.*

Quinoa *Recipes:* *Salmon and quinoa risotto*

Pronounced KEEN-WAH it is not strictly speaking a grain but a member of the same family that contains spinach, Swiss chard and beets.

☺ *Contains antioxidants*

☺ *Anti- inflammatory*

☺ *Great source of protein*

☺ *Good source of fibre which helps digestion and blood sugar control*

☺ *Helps lower bad type of LDL cholesterol but maintains good levels of HDL cholesterol*

☺ *Highly nutritious and a good alternative to grains for allergy sufferers*

Rice (brown rice) *Recipes:* *Smoked salmon and watercress kedgeree*

Chickpea curry

Rice pasta with feta and sun-dried tomatoes

☺ *This fibre rich rice can 'brush' out the toxins from the intestines.*

☺ *In comparison to white rice it contains over 2 ½ times the antioxidants and double the iron, magnesium and vitamin B6.*

Rocket *Recipes: Beetroot, apple and cashew salad*

☺ *Good for vision health as it contains beta carotene and lutein*

☺ *Anti-inflammatory and anti-carcinogenic*

☺ *Promotes cardiovascular health*

Salmon *Recipes: Salmon Caesar salad*

Salmon and quinoa risotto

Smoked salmon kedgeree

☺ *Great source of quality protein*

☺ *High in Omega 3 fats*

☺ *Rich in B vitamins*

☺ *Good source of minerals including potassium and selenium*

Try to choose wild salmon and if possible, avoid farmed salmon unless organic

Spinach *Recipes: Sweet potato, spinach and poached egg*

☺ *Rich source of antioxidants including vitamins C and E*

☺ *High in folate - required for protein and sugar metabolism, also lowers blood levels of homocysteine (amino acid associated with coronary heart disease)*

☺ *Anti-inflammatory*

☺ *Contains good levels of vitamin K, calcium and magnesium; all essential for bone health*

Sunflower seeds *Recipes:* *Snacks*

☺ *Increase immune efficiency*

☺ *Anti-inflammatory*

☺ *Great source of Vitamin E and omega-6 linoleic fatty acid*

Sweet potato *Recipes:* *Sweet potato, spinach + poached egg*

Poached eggs, root veg + seed dressing

Lentil shepherd's pie + sweet potato mash

☺ *Contain anti-inflammatory nutrients*

☺ *Rich in antioxidants*

☺ *Helps to regulate blood sugar*

☺ *Rich sources of vitamins A and C*

Tomatoes *Recipes:* *Rice pasta with feta and sundried tomatoes*

Prawn and avocado salad

Lentil shepherd's pie + sweet potato mash

Veggie Nicoise

Chickpea curry

☺ *High source of lycopene an anti-oxidant and anti-cancer agent. Lycopene is thought to increase when tomatoes are cooked.*

☺ *Stimulate the liver to eliminate toxins*

☺ *High in vitamins A and C*

Turmeric *Recipes: Salmon and watercress kedgeree*

Chickpea curry

☺ *Curcumin is the active ingredient in turmeric which is anti-inflammatory - can reduce the symptoms of rheumatoid arthritis*

☺ *Protects the liver from toxins*

☺ *Contains many anti-cancer agents*

Walnuts *Recipes: Lentil soup*

Houmous - Beetroot + walnut

Sea bass with salsa verde

☺ *Abundance of vitamins and minerals*

☺ *Powerful cardiovascular benefits*

☺ *Decrease LDL cholesterol*

☺ *High in omega 3 oil*

☺ *Contain ellagic acid, an antioxidant and cancer fighter*

Yoghurt (plain live) *Recipes: Yoghurt, berry and chia pot*

Protein porridge

Smoked mackerel pate

Salmon and Veggie Caesar salads

☺ *Great source of beneficial bacteria that help boost healthy gut bacteria*

☺ *Good source of protein and vitamins*

☺ *Boosts immune function by stimulating production of gamma interferon.*

A Few Favourite Cookbooks

Since variety is key to eating healthily it's useful to experiment with new recipes. Having lots of recipes to choose from also helps to keep mealtimes interesting. I find that taking some time to flick through cookbooks helps to get some fresh ideas. You probably have your own favourites; here are a few of mine:

New Complete Vegetarian **Rose Elliot**

Any Rose Elliot cookbook is fabulous to have in your collection as she is the queen of vegetarian cooking. All her recipes are straightforward to follow and create delicious meals often from the simplest of ingredients.

A Modern Way to Cook **Anna Jones**

This is a new book to my collection. I love that the recipes are classified in the amount of time they take to cook as it helps me target my search. The recipes are really tasty, easy to follow and include some practical tips to maximise your time. Anna's philosophy also seems to mirror my own approach for eating well without being too self-righteous.

The Green Kitchen **David Frenkiel & Luise Vindahl**

Please don't be put off by another vegetarian cookbook. The inspirational recipes are the result of a combining a health-conscious carnivore and a vegetarian who lived on junk food. There are lots of dairy and gluten free recipes as well. I particularly like the pizza base made from cauliflower rather than wheat – it's really worth a try.

Medicinal Chef Healthy Every Day **Dale Pinnock**

I love the philosophy behind this book that healthy food doesn't need to be bland or boring. There's a great variety of delicious and nutrient rich recipes - something for everyone and every occasion. Each recipe includes symbols to show how you'll be benefitting your body, which I think is a great way to help us link more closely what we eat with our health.

Chapter 5 Review & Ideas for Your Action Plan

1. Which aspects of your diet and supplementation are you happy with?

2. Which aspects would you like to improve upon?

3. Which of the following practices from Section 4 would you like to try?

   Circle the score that best reflects its level of interest to you.

	Not for Me							Give this a go		
a. Food combining	1	2	3	4	5	6	7	8	9	10
b. Fasting	1	2	3	4	5	6	7	8	9	10
c. Detoxing	1	2	3	4	5	6	7	8	9	10

4. In Section 5 are there any areas that could help to supercharge your health?

   Circle the score that best reflects its level of interest to you.

	Low Priority							High Priority		
a. Optimise enzymes	1	2	3	4	5	6	7	8	9	10
b. Control blood sugar	1	2	3	4	5	6	7	8	9	10
c. Reducing inflammation	1	2	3	4	5	6	7	8	9	10

5. Which of the tips in Section 6a would be useful to consider?

☐ 1. Avoid drastic changes	☐ 2. Plan meals	☐ 3. Choose organic
☐ 4. Choose local foods	☐ 5. Storage	☐ 6.Cooking methods
☐ 7. Prep ahead	☐ 8. Juicing	☐ 9.More variety
☐ 10. Avoid over eating	☐ 11. Eat slowly	☐ 12. Read labels
☐ 13. Listen to your body	☐ 14. Flexibility	☐ 15.Avoid eating late
☐ 16. Portion size	☐ 17. Treats	☐ 18. Gradual change
☐ 19. Apps	☐ 20. Raw food	☐ 21. Patience

5. Looking through the Quick Reference Food Table in 6b, are there any foods you're planning to:

a. try that you don't normally eat?

b. eat less of?

6. Reviewing the recipes in 6c, are there any you wish to try?

Chapter 6

Minimise Your Stress to Maximise Your Health

The Impact of Stress on Health as We Get Older

Many chronic illnesses often associated with getting older such as arthritis, late onset diabetes and heart disease are actually more to do with the impact of long-term emotional stress on our bodies and not the number of years we have had on the planet.

The fight/flight response is our inbuilt alarm system designed to quickly prepare our body so that we can protect ourselves from external threats. This automatic response is a complex system of reactions that prime the body for the physical exertion required to either fight the threat or flee from it. The heart rate, for example, will increase when faced with a stressful situation in order to pump more blood to the muscles. Then once the situation is over, the heart rate returns to normal.

However, the stresses of modern living can lead our bodies to be in constant 'pink alert' so our healing mechanisms become compromised. Rather than utilising the fight/flight response for exceptional circumstances it is used far more frequently. Whilst the fight/flight response is incredibly beneficial in the short-term, we are not well adapted biologically to its ongoing use:

Stress Response	Cortisol released from the adrenal glands
Short-Term Benefit	Increases blood sugar levels so the skeletal muscles have the energy to flee or fight Suppresses the immune system to ensure the external threat is prioritised
Potential Long-Term Impact	Foggy thinking, not being able to think straight Reduces the rate at which stem cells in the brain become neurones, which could be linked to the onset of dementia
Stress Response	Heart rate and blood pressure increases
Short-Term Benefit	Pushes blood to the skeletal muscles
Potential Long-Term Impact	High blood pressure Cardiovascular disease
Stress Response	Sugar released into the bloodstream
Short-Term Benefit	Supplies energy in readiness for fleeing from or fighting off the threat

Potential Long-Term Impact	Through overuse can desensitise receptors on the cells to insulin, which can lead to diabetes.
Stress Response	Breathe more rapidly and shallowly
Short-Term Benefit	Gets more oxygen to the skeletal muscles so we can run from the threat or fight it.
Potential Long-Term Impact	Taking between 12 and 30 breaths a minute becomes the norm and restricts breathing, which can lead to heart disease or a chronic respiratory condition. Loss of oxygen to tissues can lead to carcinogenic cells developing. Imbalance between oxygen and carbon dioxide can lead to acidity in the body, which in turn can lead to inflammation.
Stress Response	Skeletal muscles tighten
Short-Term Benefit	Prepares the muscles for action
Potential Long-Term Impact	Muscles stay tight, which reduces flexibility. Rounded shoulders Creates friction around the joints, which can lead to arthritis
Stress Response	Blood diverted from the digestive and immune systems to the adrenal system
Short-Term Benefit	Body has the nutrients it needs to deal with the immediate danger.
Potential Long-Term Impact	Affects the efficiency of the digestive system, which can lead to a diverse range of dis-eases Depresses the immune system so that viruses, bacteria and parasites can take hold more easily.

The body wants to be well, so it does what is necessary to protect itself. When the stress response is activated the body diverts resources from day-to-day healing, maintenance and growth mechanisms like the immune, digestive and elimination systems to the adrenal system in order to deal with the perceived external threat. That is why we tend to be more susceptible to illness when we have been under a great deal of stress.

Back in the 1950's cancerous tumours in rats were found to develop more rapidly when the rats were placed in stressful situations. The stimulation of the fight/flight response diverted blood flow away from the healing mechanisms that would normally be fighting off cancer cells so they were free to proliferate. This is why stress hormones are given to transplant patients as they inhibit the immune system in order to prevent the body rejecting the organ.

Much of the stress we endure in modern life is 'perceived' stress rather than a real threat to our survival. The pressures of target and deadline driven jobs, the anxieties of bringing up children, financial concerns and the demands of looking after ageing parents can all stimulate stress hormones. The body evolved to survive so it will always prioritise external threats and stressors over maintenance and growth systems. Many of us are on the stressed out rather than the chilled out end of the spectrum far more of the time and so make it harder for our bodies to be in optimal health. One of the greatest investments we can make in our long-term health is therefore to minimise stress in our lives.

In this chapter we will look at stress from different angles using my Five Health and Fitness Principles:

Principle 1: Don't underestimate what your body is capable of

Principle 2: Synergy & Balance

Principle 3: Do what you love …..consistently

Principle 4: Listen to your body – be in tune with it

Principle 5: Less is more

Stressed Out to Chilled Out Nurturing Toolkit

A Nurturing Toolkit is included at the end of the chapter with practical tips and ideas to support you in dealing with the inevitable stress of modern life so that 'stressed out' is the rare exception and 'chilled out' can be the norm. To make the Tool Kit more practical the suggestions are grouped into five categories:

1. Stress busting ideas you can do in less than five minutes

2. Stress busting ideas you can do in 5 to 15 minutes.

3. Stress busing ideas for when you can put aside an hour or more.
4. Stress busting habits
5. Stress busting ideas to help you let go and gain a new outlook

Principle 1: Don't underestimate what your body is capable of

"Allopathic medicine treats the body like a machine to fix with drugs. However the new biology, based on perception and epigenetics, reveals that it's not the machine that's wrong, it's the environment and our perception of our environment that's caustic". Bruce Lipton from "The Biology of Belief"

When our bodies aren't working properly we tend to focus on the 'part' that isn't working. Yet when there's something wrong it's rarely our underlying physiology that's to blame. Instead, it is usually our environment and our perception of our environment that are at the root cause. Therefore, when we are not well we need to look at our environment first rather than 'fix' the body. Given the right conditions, our bodies have an amazing capacity to heal and keep healthy. Long-term stress is definitely not required!

At first glance, it's not obvious the impact stress is having on our bodies. Yet when you look at the cellular level, it's far easier to appreciate the detrimental effects stress has on our health; it's also hard not be blown away by what our cells do when they're given the right conditions.

For example, when a cell divides telomeres protect the end of the chromosome (the genetic material). Telomeres are rather like the plastic ends of a shoelace, which prevent the shoelace from fraying. Over time the telomeres shorten – the shorter the telomeres the older we are. Stress causes the telomeres to shorten prematurely so you could say that stress causes us to age! Studies have shown that people who meditate regularly or practise mindfulness techniques preserve the length of their telomeres.

The complex structure of the cell membrane enables the cell to repel what it does not want and absorb what it does. Viruses use the receptors on the membrane to invade the cell. For example, the common cold virus uses the same receptor as an endorphin that is released into the bloodstream when we're happy. If the receptors are attached to this endorphin, the virus has no way of entering the cell, which is why we tend to be less susceptible to colds when we are feeling happy and contented.

The Mind Body Connection

"…attempts to treat most bodily diseases as though the mind were in no way involved must be considered archaic in the light of the new evidence about the way the human body functions." Norman Cousins: The Anatomy of Illness

For centuries, medical doctrine treated the body and mind as separate entities. Yet modern science has shown that they are intrinsically linked. For example, our immune cells make the same chemicals as the ones produced in the brain that control our mood. The brain, heart and gut are an integrated system linked together by the vagus nerve. On a day-to-day basis, we get "butterflies" in our stomach when we feel nervous or blush when embarrassed so we know our emotions affect our physiology. However, we may not consciously think about the influence of our emotions on our physiology and their consequent impact on our long-term health.

Neuroscience, epigenetics and psycho-immunology have demonstrated how intrinsically linked our physical health is with our emotional health. Whilst we previously thought that the genes we are born with determine our fate, it's been found that our life style, our emotions and the food we eat have an impact on which and the extent to which genes are expressed. This, to me, is an incredibly empowering discovery. It also clarifies why the human genome project did not find as many genes as was expected to explain the complexity of the human body. Genes can be switched on and off rather like the dimmer control of a light switch. We can even create genes that we're missing!

With respect to stress, it's important to know that the neurochemistry of how we perceive things tells the DNA how to express itself. It's therefore important that what we recognise as stressful truly warrants our neurochemistry to inform the DNA accordingly. On a day-to-day basis I know I've certainly fallen into the trap of getting stressed with situations that in the greater scheme of things just don't matter and certainly don't justify altering the information that's given to my DNA!.

Our perception creates our reality

"*Consciousness creates reality, mind becomes matter, our thoughts precede our physical bodies*" Candace Pert from "The Molecules of Emotion"

Neuroscience has shown that no action can be stimulated in the brain in the absence of an emotion and so, effectively, emotions energise the brain. Professor Paul Brown, a neuroscientist recommends hyphenating the word 'emotion' (e-motion = energy for action) to remind us of the significance of our emotions. There are eight fundamental emotions, which Professor Brown compares to the three primary colours. In the same way that the primary colours generate all the shades and hues of the rainbow, all our feelings come from these eight basic emotions.

Each emotion stimulates different neurotransmitters and thereby determines whether protective fight/flight mechanisms or healing/maintenance/growth mechanisms are activated. In the case of surprise/startle the neurotransmitters released are determined by the nature of the surprise so the reaction can go either way:

Type of Emotion	Response stimulated	8 Basic Emotions
Survival	The stress response	1. Fear 2. Anger 3. Disgust 4. Shame 5. Sadness
Survival/Delight	Stress or relaxation response	6. Surprise/Startle
Delight	The relaxation response	7. Excitement/Joy 8. Love/Trust

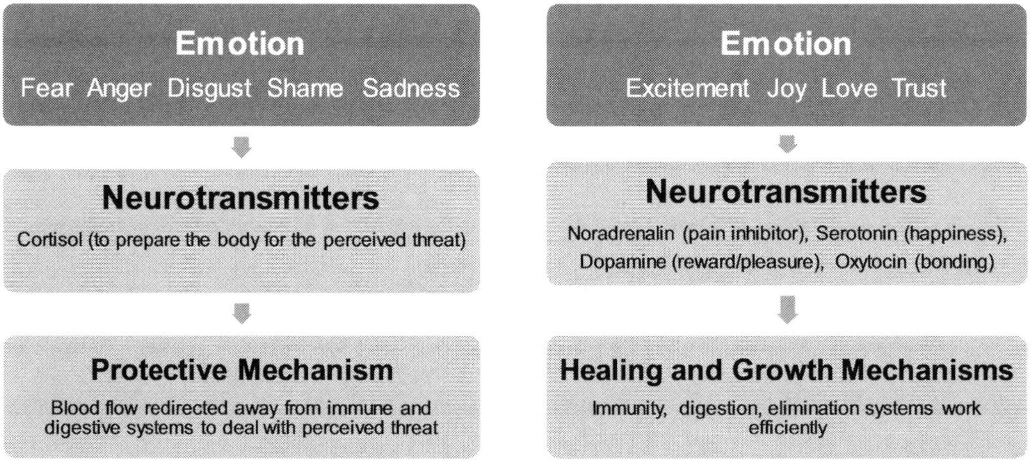

By understanding the interconnection between mind and body, the more we can appreciate the impact our perception of a stressful situation has on us physically. This is not to say that we try to avoid or suppress our feelings; many illnesses are caused by suppressed emotions. We need to express our emotions and let them go. What is extremely important is ensuring that our perception is relevant for the situation. If we misperceive our environment then the wrong information is getting to our cells.

For example, rationally we know that worrying is largely unproductive yet it can easily become habitual, thereby releasing anxiety fuelled cortisol to protect us from the perceived threat. As soon as we notice we are feeling worried we need to remind ourselves that, most of the time, what we worry about turns out to be groundless and that it achieves hardly anything. By changing our perception and the consequent unconscious reactions, we can help to ensure the fight/flight neurotransmitters are reserved for the emergencies they are intended for.

It never ceases to amaze me how incredible our bodies are and what they do to protect us and keep us well. By focusing on minimising the stress in our lives and making sure our perception is appropriate for the situation, we will not be pumping our bodies with jittery molecules and fight/flight hormones that impede our healing and growth mechanisms. By helping our cells to receive the right information, we are effectively investing in our long-term health.

Principle 2: Synergy & Balance

Stressed Out to Chilled Out Spectrum – balance in favour of chilled out!

Stress is not all bad. Brief periods of mild to moderate stress such as when we are feeling nervous can help improve mental and physical performance. Some of us like to have a deadline to spur us into action! This is referred to as "eustress". It can help, for example, musicians and actors to perform. Athletes are better able to reach their full potential with better concentration and focus along with improved reflexes, muscular strength and endurance.

The problems arise when we endure prolonged periods of stress; the body gets out of balance by needing to prioritise the adrenal system at the expense of other vital systems like the immune and digestive systems. This is termed, rather unsurprisingly, "distress". This can be insidious because we can carry on for a long time thinking that we are okay and not notice the detrimental and cumulative effects the stress is having on our health.

The adrenal glands, the pyramid shaped glands that sit on top of the kidneys are often the first glands to suffer. They release the hormones to warn the body of the threat and engage the fight/flight response. If they are stimulated too frequently during intense periods of stress or if there is insufficient time for them to recover between stressful situations, they can become exhausted. Many people are 'tired but wired' these days; stressful working environments and artificial stimulants get them through the day. This is why people can often feel so exhausted at weekends or on holiday when they are not relying on the stress response to fuel their energy.

This, of course, is unsustainable. Rather like a fire alarm alerting us - very useful when we are in danger but if the alarm were to sound continually we would soon become irritated, angry and on edge! If people do not take action to remedy the situation starting with removing sources of stress or changing the way that they respond to situations, eventually their energy levels will plummet and this can even lead to chronic fatigue.

The following list are common symptoms of exhausted adrenals:

- ☹ Feeling "tired but wired"
- ☹ Fatigue and lethargy
- ☹ Feeling hyper
- ☹ Feeling ungrounded
- ☹ Lack of focus or concentration
- ☹ Decline or dips in memory
- ☹ Weight gain or loss
- ☹ Lowered or heightened libido
- ☹ Inability to slow down or take a break
- ☹ The need for frequent caffeine drinks/cigarettes to get through the day
- ☹ Anxiety, fear, depression
- ☹ Allergies and inflammation
- ☹ Aching muscles and joints
- ☹ Low blood pressure
- ☹ Salt and or sugar cravings
- ☹ Reliance on sugary snacks

How to look after your adrenal glands and boost their function

The chances are, even if we have not realised it, that many of us have compromised the health of our adrenals at some time in our lives so it is worthwhile knowing what to do to support them:

- ✓ Follow the lifestyle tips in this chapter that resonate with you to minimise stress.
- ✓ Incorporate foods in your diet that specifically nourish the adrenals. These include aduki beans, asparagus, beetroot, black beans, celery, cranberries, dandelion tea, ginger, seaweed and walnuts.
- ✓ Take a supplement specifically designed to support your adrenal glands or ensure that you take supplements that incorporate the following nutrients: All B vitamins (especially vitamins B5 and B6), Vitamin C, Magnesium, Choline and Inositol, Iodine and essential fatty acids.

Getting back into balance

When life has been stressful for a while, it can be rather overwhelming to know where to start to make the changes we need to make. This burden can often be exacerbated by worrying about the long-term damage the stress might have done to our health – I've certainly been guilty of this!

Our ability to cope with stress depends on many things such as:

☺ Our present state of physical fitness

☺ Our current state of emotional well-being

☺ How supportive our partners, family or friends are

☺ How fulfilled we feel with our life

☺ The quality of our diet

☺ The amount and quality of our sleep

☺ To extent to which we enjoy our work

☺ How much time is available to relax and nurture ourselves

If you feel like you are more on the stressed out than chilled out end of the spectrum, it may be useful to review the above list. For example, you may have a job you love despite it being demanding and you have a loving and supportive partner but perhaps you haven't placed much emphasis on your fitness recently or frequently get to bed too late to re-charge your batteries, so you easily become irritable. Choose which areas of your life are supporting you and which areas may need some work to help you feel calm and centred. Investing time in this will reap amazing benefits for your long-term health.

Thankfully, the cumulative and synergistic effect of integrating small changes can make a huge difference. The body wants to be well so it responds quickly to nurturing and conditions that enable it to thrive.

Principle 3: Do what you love .....consistently

Each cell of our body thrives when it is responding to what it loves and conversely suffers when it needs to react to a threat or toxic environment. We're the same as the trillions of cells that make up our bodies! When we love what's going on around us we respond accordingly whether it's the people we spend time with, the work we do or what we do with our spare time.

Connecting with People

Studies show that in 'Blue Zones' around the world where people live long and healthy lives they live in connected communities where they feel accepted and have a sense of belonging. Conversely, research has shown that loneliness or lacking a sense of belonging can cause many health issues. When people are socially isolated, the nervous system interprets this as a threat so the limbic brain, the primordial and survival focused part of the brain, stimulates the stress response and floods the body with cortisol and adrenalin. Consequently, the self-healing mechanisms in our body that, for example, fight off cancer cells and protect us from heart attacks are constrained. Healthy relationships and a sense of belonging are therefore a crucial part of minimising stress in our bodies to enable the self-healing mechanisms to work effectively.

It's also important that we choose wisely who we spend our time with as this impacts our attitudes, emotions and outlook. We all know that being around happy people makes us feel good and that we can easily find our mood changes when around people who are down or stressed out. This is because mirror neurones in our brains reflect the body language and facial expressions of people around us. We see this clearly when someone yawns, it's almost impossible not to want to yawn yourself. So, if we're surrounded by stressed out people it's no wonder we feel stressed ourselves.

To reduce this "second hand stress" you may wish to see less of negative, cynical naysayers, permanently frazzled people, or those who are hyped up constantly and see stress as some sort of badge of honour.

If this is not possible, just make sure you don't share your goals with them otherwise you may find that you feel less motivated to achieve them or stressed out at the thought of completing them. You may also need to offset the atmosphere they create by doing some extra nurturing to get you back to centre. Focus on spending more time with uplifting people and, if required, developing new relationships.

Loving the work we do

"If our true nature is permitted to guide our life, we grow healthy, fruitful and happy." Abraham Maslow

Why are heart attacks more common early on Monday mornings? Is it the thought of the stressful week ahead? Intuitively it makes sense that if you enjoy your work and it enables you to play to your strengths you are likely to be less stressed than someone who needs to swim against the tide carrying out tasks that don't come naturally to them or having to work in a culture that doesn't suit their working style.

There is now scientific evidence that shows a strong link between our life span and health with the extent to which our work fulfils us. It is therefore worth checking in on a regular basis as to how we feel about our work whether it gives us chance to do what we are good at and what we truly enjoy.

Even if we love what we do, our stress at work might come from the unrealistic targets and deadlines, political culture or simply not feeling valued. So many people put up with jobs that cause them continual stress. Whilst they may not be in a position to change careers completely, making small adjustments can be very effective in reducing stress and increasing their sense of fulfilment.

Being immersed in a project or striving to meet the next deadline can lead us to ignore the impact our work has on us. The following exercises are a starting point to help you gain an objective view of your key motivators and strengths as well as the extent to which your work is in line with to what is important to you.

Exercise: Motivators and Strengths

Motivators: Collate what motivates you at work.

Examples: new challenges, competition, collaboration, security, stability, service, being an expert, taking the lead, autonomy, structure, order, being creative, being entrepreneurial, transparency, openness, variety

Strengths: Collate your innate strengths

Examples: adaptable, assertive, persuasive, supportive, accommodating, empathic, practical, decisive, analytical, lateral thinker, innovative, results oriented, quality focused, efficient, structured, methodical, accurate, diligent.

Quick Audit Exercise– where am I now?

For each of the following statements mark on the arrow where you are now.

Left hand end of the arrow:	This is rarely true
Middle of the arrow:	This is true some of the time
Right hand end of the arrow:	This is true most of the time

My work enables me to play to my strengths and fully utilise my skills

I enjoy working with my colleagues and work contacts

I feel that my contribution is valued

My work is congruent with my work motivators

The culture suits my working style

Today's Date: ________________ Next Review Date: ________________

Are there any areas you want to focus on improving?

Jot down some ideas on how you could move closer to the right hand end of the arrow:

Which ideas can you move forward with easily?

Downtime and Having Fun

"Play is the gateway to vitality. By its nature it is uniquely and intrinsically rewarding. It generates optimism, seeks out novelty, makes perseverance fun, leads to mastery, gives the immune system a bounce, fosters empathy and promotes a sense of belonging and community. Each of these play by-products are indices of personal health." The US National Institute for Play

For many of us living very busy lives it can feel overly decadent to put time aside for simply having fun when there's a list of 'just jobs' to do. "I'll just do this and get this out the way before I ......" When we do put time aside for doing what we love it has a knock-on effect on other aspects of our lives as the sense of fulfilment can re-energise us and gives us fresh perspectives. From a physiology perspective, endorphins are released when we laugh that elevate our mood and enable the self-healing mechanisms in our bodies to do their work.

"Happiness is not something you postpone for the future; it is something you design for the present" Jim Rohn

Whilst it would be ideal for play to be spontaneous, it can be useful to have a plan, so we can make the most of the time we've put aside. Jot down ideas that would be really fulfilling for you. When are you at your happiest? It's easy to be drawn in by what's meant to make us happy. You may want to find a new passion, start a new hobby, rekindle a hobby you gave up when time was tight, start that novel you always wanted to write, or learn something new like another language or a musical instrument.

If this isn't practical for fitting into your life at the moment then consistently do what brings you pleasure - curl up on the sofa with a favourite book, watch a classic film you've never had chance to see, fly a kite on the beach or simply treat where you live as if you're a tourist. The key is to lose yourself so that you're fully engaged in what you're doing and ideally lose a sense of the passage of time. There's some ideas in the Tool Kit at the end of this chapter.

Principle 4: Listen to your body – be in tune with it

"We tend to deal with the physical aspects of keeping ourselves healthy and ignore the emotional dimension – our thoughts and feelings" Candace B. Pert, PH.D.

We can often be the last to notice that we are stressed. We will notice it in others when they are short with us or impatient. Yet we are far less observant of ourselves as stress tends to creep up on us incrementally. We think we are fine and we are coping but don't notice that, for example, feeling anxious or easily irritated has become the norm rather than the exception. We hurl abuse at an inconsiderate driver who has pulled out in front of us or we react disproportionately to something inconsequential that if relaxed and calm would not have bothered us.

I met someone recently in denial that he was on the stressed out end of the spectrum, brushing aside his trigger-happy anger and oblivious to the detrimental impact the stress hormones swimming around his system are having on his health. He put his recent heart attack down to bad luck and did not consider that he needed to do anything differently to restore his health. His tendency to ignore his thoughts and feelings belongs to the outdated paradigm of separating the mind from the body.

Ignore the impact of stress at your peril

"The primary cause of illness is misperception not physiology."

Bruce Lipton from "The Biology of Belief"

I learnt the hard way the impact that stress can have on our health and well-being. I had prided myself in keeping physically fit and endeavoured to back this up with a healthy diet. Not until a nasty bout of shingles did I realise that I needed to become less of a stress-head if I truly wanted to achieve the levels of fitness and vitality I was aiming for. The shingles came at a particularly tough and stressful time in my life. As mentioned earlier, when we're under stress the immune system doesn't receive the support it needs to protect us from pathogens so it's no wonder I contracted such a severe case of shingles.

In my drive to keep going and get on with life despite the stress and pressure I was under, I had fallen into the trap of not listening to my body when it was quietly telling me all was not well. I waited until it shouted and screamed at me with agonising pain and awful sores before I took notice. It was a very high price to pay for not listening! Yet it was an extremely valuable lesson for me to learn. It took me a long time to regain my fitness and build a strong immune system after shingles, much longer than if I had listened to my body earlier and taken the appropriate corrective action.

This is why I am so keen for people to learn from my experience and why I'm so passionate about getting people to listen to what their body is telling them. When we take notice of its messages when it's not at "ease" we'll be able to nip issues in the bud to help prevent "dis-ease" taking hold.

In a world where there is an unwritten rule that life is stressful we tend not to look out for or simply ignore the signs. Yet our body, our mood and our behaviour can provide some useful clues. Here are some of the more common ones:

Clues from our body

Headache, muscle tension or pain, raised blood pressure, increased heart rate, sweating, difficulty in breathing, hyperventilation, nervous tics, tremors, dryness in mouth and throat, weight gain/loss, bruxism (teeth grinding), tight jaw muscles, back ache, neck pain, susceptibility to illness, pounding heart, skin disorders, heartburn or acid stomach, chest pain, fatigue and lethargy, change in sex drive, stomach upsets, sleep problems.

Clues from our mood

Anxiety and feeling fearful, restlessness, lack of motivation or focus, lack of concentration, irritability, anger, sadness, depression, forgetfulness, worrying, feelings of impending doom, low self-esteem, easily distracted, guilt, suspicion, easily frustrated, fear of failure.

Clues from our behaviour

Talking more quickly, overeating or under eating, angry outbursts, drug or alcohol abuse, increased tobacco use, social withdrawal, excessive caffeine intake, impulsiveness, having difficulty with our relationships, less active, avoidance of people or places (social isolation), re-appearance or worsening of phobias, checking and triple checking even the smallest of things.

Quick Audit Exercise:

When you read the above clues, did any ring true for you or do you have other ways of spotting when you are feeling stressed? Being self-aware is a great first step though we must then look at taking steps to minimise the causes of stress in our lives or find ways to perceive them differently. Thankfully, the body is incredibly adaptable and soon responds to being nurtured.

TUNING IN - THE ART OF NOTICING

Being in tune with our bodies gives us the heads up early enough to take action and thereby prevent the destructive effects of stress taking hold. Mastering the art of noticing is therefore critical to being at ease as well as our long-term health.

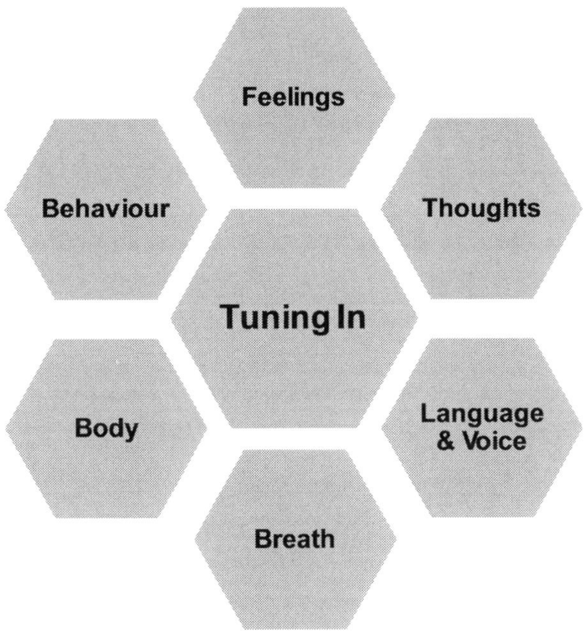

Breath

"When mindfulness of breathing is developed and cultivated it is of great benefit" The Buddha

Our breathing links our body and our mind. In the same way as our thoughts and feelings affect the rhythm and the frequency of our breath, our breathing rate and pattern influences our outlook and emotions. When we're feeling stressed we breathe shallowly and frequently. By consciously breathing more slowly and more regularly, we can feel calmer and settle our thoughts.

A relaxed person's normal rate of breathing is between four and six breaths a minute. Yet many of us breathe far more frequently than that. Even though a person breathing between 12 and 30 times a minute might consider this normal for them, it's actually a sign that the body is distressed. Rapid and shallow breathing means the body is in stress mode. It's therefore useful to get into the habit of noticing your breath and your breathing pattern. When observing your breathing it's important not to judge, just notice with curiosity:

- Is it fast or slow?
- Is it deep or shallow?
- Do you feel your breath more in your chest or more in your abdomen?
- Is it a short breath or a long breath?
- Is it regular or irregular?
- Do you hold it?
- Do you push it out?

The simple practice of following the breath tends to slow it down and consequently reverses the stress response. The following two breathing techniques are great ways to calm us down when we're feeling stressed:

<u>The 4-7-8 Breathing Technique</u>

This technique was developed by Dr Andrew Weil and is based on an ancient yoga breathing practice. It soothes and calms and is worth trying when:

✓ you feel stressed or anxious

✓ you need to feel calmer in response to a sudden stressful situation

✓ you're having trouble getting to sleep

If you find it difficult to hold your breath initially then count more quickly. The 4-7-8 ratio is more important than the pace. When the technique becomes more familiar with practice, count more slowly and focus on breathing more deeply.

1. Find a comfortable position.
   a. If you choose to stand, relax your shoulders, keep your feet hip distance apart and your back straight. Be aware though that some people can feel light headed when they first practice.
   b. If you sit down, keep your feet flat on the floor and your back straight.

   c. If you'd like to utilise this exercise to help you sleep then do this exercise lying down.

2. Rest your tongue on the ridge, just behind and above your top teeth. Please note that you will need to keep your tongue in this position throughout the exercise.
3. Part your lips and exhale through your mouth making a whooshing sound. Close your mouth then inhale quietly through your nose to the count of **4**.
4. Hold your breath for the count of **7**.
5. Exhale for **8** counts, again making a whooshing sound.
6. Repeat the 4-7-8 cycle 4 times.
7. Practice twice a day.

<u>Alternate Nostril Breathing Exercise</u>

This is another breathing technique with yoga origins. It helps to soothe the nerves when we're feeling under pressure or stressed out. Great to do if feeling nervous, for example, before a presentation or an exam.

1. Sit comfortably in a chair ensuring your feet are on the floor. If you prefer, you can kneel or sit cross-legged. Whatever position you choose relax the shoulders and sit upright.
2. Place your right thumb over your right nostril.
3. Place your first two fingers on the bridge of your nose and your next finger over your left nostril.
4. Support your right elbow with your left hand.
5. Lift your right thumb away from your nostril and breathe in for a count of 5.
6. Replace your thumb and hold your breath for 5 counts.
7. Unblock the left nostril and slowly exhale for a count of 5.
8. Breathe in through the left nostril for a count of 5.

9. Replace your finger and hold your breath for 5 counts.
10. Release your thumb from the right nostril and exhale for a count of 5.
11. Repeat this cycle 10 times.

Thoughts

Negative thoughts stimulate stress hormones and place the body in protective fight/flight mode. If you have ever taken the time to tune into your inner dialogue it can be quite surprising how negative many of our thoughts are!

Research has shown that the majority of our 69,000 thoughts a day are fear based. This is probably because our minds evolved to anticipate danger in order to protect us from harm. The research also showed that the vast majority of these negative thoughts never become reality. Hence the acronym for fear:

False **E**xpectations **A**ppearing **R**eal

We need to choose our thoughts carefully to reduce unnecessary stress and trust in ourselves that we have the capacity and resources available to resolve the issue and move forwards. Another useful acronym for fear is therefore:

Faith (in oneself) **E**nables **A**mazing **R**esults

Thoughts are not facts

It's useful to remind ourselves that thoughts are not facts and they can be changed. Our brains are constantly reassessing our experience in order to find meaning. Recognising that we are 'meaning making machines' helps us to acknowledge that it's up to us what meaning we associate with an event. Remember it's only a thought and a thought can be changed!

Writing to declutter unwanted thoughts

Writing is a great way to quieten our 'chattering minds'. Jotting down everything that's currently on our minds and we're getting stressed about can help declutter our minds and help us gain further clarity. We can see the stressful thoughts that have been plaguing our thinking in a new light and gain some new insights and perspectives.

Writing freely, noting down anything that comes to mind without thinking about grammar or punctuation can lead to a thorough spring clean! Just let the thoughts flow without censoring or judging. This can help to switch off our internal 'editor' and allow deeply embedded concerns to be brought to our attention.

If you prefer some structure to collating your thoughts on the page then ask questions instead. Here are some examples:

- What am I concerned about?
- What is scaring me?
- What do I need to let go of?
- What's bothering me?
- What's making my life stressful?

Writing the question with your dominant hand and writing the answer with your non-dominant hand can tap into your unconscious thoughts and bring fresh perspectives.

<u>Focus on the present</u>

We can waste time reliving the past or worrying about the future rather than focusing our thoughts on the present. A useful adage is "forgive the past, accept the present and trust the future".

Feelings

"Emotions are the nexus between matter and mind, going back and forth between the two and influencing both" Candace Pert PhD

As we saw in Principle 1 our emotions have a huge impact on our physiology, it's therefore incredibly valuable to be in tune with our feelings. Please don't be concerned if you have trouble 'feeling your feelings'; it's common these days. We've ignored them for so long we've just got out of the habit of noticing them. Simply checking in at regular intervals throughout the day to get in touch with how you're feeling is a useful habit to adopt. To begin with, it may be difficult to name the emotion. This doesn't matter, just notice the feeling without judgement.

Notice where in the body you're feeling this emotion. Again, this may not be apparent when you first start. In time as you practice you will develop a heightened awareness of your feelings until it becomes second nature. In this way of mindfully getting in touch with your emotions you'll be able to become an objective observer, question their motivation, check their relevance for this particular moment in time and, if required, be in a better position to choose to feel differently about a situation.

So often our feelings are based on past experiences and concerns about the future that we're not really truly tuned into the present moment.

"We re-live past events and re-feel their pain, and we pre-live future disasters and so pre-feel their impact" Mark Williams and Danny Penman

For example, when someone has lived through a stressful period in their lives they can continue to be on edge, irritable or anxious even when there is no longer a reason to be feeling this way. Being in tune with our feelings helps us to recognise these self-protective habits and gives us the opportunity to re-evaluate the present moment and allow other emotions to come to the fore so we can feel calm again and thereby release the neurotransmitters that stimulate our healing, maintenance and growth mechanisms.

Bach Flower Remedies – First Aid Kit for the Emotions

Dr Bach, a medical doctor, bacteriologist and homoeopath developed these remedies in the 1930s. When working with wounded soldiers during the First World War it struck him that there was a strong connection between recovery and the patient's emotional outlook. He was keen to create a simple First Aid Kit that would be easy to use and help people centre themselves when dealing with difficult emotions. There are 38 remedies altogether; the ones I have included in the table on the next page are brilliant ones to have handy for dealing with stressful situations. With the exception of Rescue Remedy where 4 drops are required, you just need to put a couple of drops directly on your tongue or in a drink.

You will find that as you become more familiar with the remedies you will become more attuned with your emotions and know exactly which ones you need. You can use up to six remedies to cover the wide range of emotions you might be feeling at any one time.

Here's an example:

1. Elm to counteract feeling overwhelmed by all the unfinished work.
2. Beech to be more tolerant of a colleague's exceptionally irritating laugh.
3. Impatiens to feel less annoyed with people who are not moving fast enough to get the job done in time and constantly need chasing.
4. White Chestnut to move on from a barbed comment from a colleague that keeps replaying in the mind.
5. Crab Apple to trust quality of work without double and triple checking it.
6. Olive to offset the tiredness and restore some energy after too many late nights at work.

Until you get to know the remedies, Rescue Remedy is a great starting point. It contains five remedies that are typically required in a crisis. It is ideal when you are feeling stressed but don't have the time to pinpoint all the emotions you are feeling!

A Few Bach Flower Remedies Useful When Stressed

Agrimony	When you are feeling really stressed inside but other people would just see a smiley bubbly persona.
Beech	When you're feeling intolerant and getting irritated by people.
Cherry Plum	Those occasions when you are so stressed you don't feel responsible for your actions. You could literally lash out at someone.
Elm	For when you feel overloaded or overwhelmed with your responsibilities or commitments.
Holly	When feeling bad tempered, particularly when the anger comes from jealousy or hatred.
Impatiens	For feelings of irritation and frustration. Particularly useful when you're feeling hyped up and the rest of the world isn't being quick enough!
Rescue Remedy	Great go-to remedy for any stressful situation from feeling hassled after an argument to feeling nervous before a presentation. It contains Rock Rose, Impatiens, Clematis, Star of Bethlehem and Cherry Plum so covers the typical emotions we feel in a crisis.
Sweet chestnut	When you are at your wits end and can't imagine the stress you are under to ever go away.
Willow	When you're feeling resentful inside and when the stressful situation is causing you to ask, "Why me?"

Language & Voice

Watch your language

"Stress" has become such a commonly used word in recent years it's easy to overlook how often we say it.

"I feel so stressed"	*"She's such a stress head"*
"Work is so stressful"	*"I'm completely stressed out"*

It is an incredibly disempowering word as it infers that we have no control over our lives - something that's such an intrinsic part of modern life that we just need to accept and put up with it. It's a useful exercise to notice when you say it and how often you hear it. When I did this, I was flabbergasted how integral it was in my conversations with friends and colleagues.

Our thoughts impact our feelings and therefore determine which neurotransmitters and hormones are circulating in our system. More often than not, the situation does not justify our bodies initiating the fight/flight response! The situation is not life threatening or truly traumatic, the word simply describes our interpretation of a situation as stressful. This can be all manner of things such as confrontation, being late for an appointment or an imminent deadline.

If you notice it's a word that's crept into your vocabulary rather too frequently replace it with more empowering words.

Tune into your voice – check pace and pitch

When we're feeling frazzled, under pressure or irritated we tend to talk faster and as our throat tenses our vocal chords shorten, which can lead to the pitch of our voice to get higher. By tuning into our voice when we're stressed, we'll notice when we may need to lower the pitch and slow down, which will immediately help us to feel more in control and calmer.

Body

Some people naturally produce more of the calming hormone serotonin so tend to have a greater stress tolerance. Others produce more adrenaline, so the stress response is triggered more quickly, and it takes longer for their stress levels to calm down.

It's worth noting here though that our biological makeup is only part of the story in determining how our bodies react to stress. The frequency we have dealt with stressful situations and their intensity have a huge impact on the way we have learnt to deal with stress.

What's important is to be aware of how you tend to react to stress. Think back over times when you've needed to deal with a stressful situation. How quickly did your body click into the stress response and how easy was it for you to feel calm again?

If your cortisol tends to be trigger happy and it takes you a while to feel centred again, you may need to invest more time in nurturing yourself afterwards to minimise the time your body is being subjected to stress hormones.

Exercise is of course the natural antidote to the fight/flight response as the body was set up to run or fight. To get your body back to neutral again, whenever possible do some exercise.

If it's not possible to launch into a full workout then go for a brisk walk, run up the stairs or punch a pillow – anything that's going to enable your body to utilise the changes in its physiology that the stress hormones caused.

Tuning into Tension

When we're stressed we automatically tense our muscles. Ongoing stress can make tense muscles the norm. As this tension builds up gradually we don't notice how tense our muscles are and so are often unaware of the tightness around our joints. Tense muscles shorten the muscle fibres, which constricts blood flow, flexibility around joints and blocks energy.

Stretching and in particular yoga is a fabulous way to help rebalance us. On a day-to-day basis it's worthwhile doing spot checks to notice, for example, how tightly we're holding the steering wheel, or how tense our shoulders are when typing on a computer. Focus on lightening your touch on the keyboard, soften the grip on your steering wheel and allow your muscles to relax.

Tuning into your 'gut feel'

For many people rationality and analytical thinking has taken precedence over our intuition and our 'gut feel'. This leads us to lose touch with our bodies and so we become unaware of their invaluable messages. Taking the time to tune into our bodies provides access to insights into our emotional and physical wellbeing. Learning to trust its cues can be challenging when our mind is saying something different. However, the body does not overthink or have the capacity for denial in the way the mind does. The signs it gives reflect the present moment, unlike the mind, it isn't worrying about the past or the future.

It's therefore important to take notice of its honest feedback. Doing this regularly and learning to trust its inner wisdom can help enormously to nip physical imbalances in the bud. The body scan, a mindfulness technique, is a great way to connect with our body and what it is telling us.

Body Scan

Preparation:

1. Select a time of the day when you can put aside 15 minutes and work up to doing this 5 or 6 times a week. This isn't meant to be a chore, so in busy weeks when there's only chance to do this once, that's fine; do what works for you. I do find, however, that once people start to reap the benefits of the extra clarity, concentration and calmness they feel, they see it as an investment of time rather than just another thing that needs to be fitted in. When it's challenging to break up your day, you may wish to do it when you first wake up – see it as a 15 minute lay in!
2. Choose a quiet place where you won't be disturbed. Leave your mobile phone in another room, turn it off or switch it to silent.
3. You may need a blanket to keep you warm.

Guidelines:

Do:

- ✓ Observe without judgement and be curious.
- ✓ Be aware that it could feel strange as this is new to you.
- ✓ Be patient. Rather like expecting your first few visits to the gym to give you biceps like a body-builder, it can take time to reconnect with our bodies.
- ✓ Focus on being fully aware rather than what you think the experience should be.
- ✓ Concentrate on sensing rather than analysing.

Avoid:

- × Avoid setting objectives for this or having any specific expectations as this creates unnecessary pressure.
- × Don't worry if you don't feel any particular sensations.
- × We have a tendency to 'should all over ourselves' so avoid being self-critical. If, for example, your thoughts wander off then gently and without criticism bring your attention back to the part of the body you were focusing on. -

Getting Started

1. Lie down on a bed, sofa or the floor, wherever feels comfortable.
2. It's up to you whether or not you close your eyes. Do whatever feels right for you.
3. Notice how you're feeling – don't try to change how you're feeling just observe. Let any thoughts pass by without giving them much attention.
4. Take a moment to notice the surface you are lying on. Notice where your body touches it and how it feels – is there any tension or pain?
5. Focus on your breath, follow it in and out of your body and notice any sensations in the chest or abdomen as you breathe. Don't try to change how you're breathing, just observe it.

Things to do or focus on as you work through the body scan

1. As you work through the body scan, notice how each part of the body is feeling:

   Warm or cold? Itchy? Prickly? Painful? Numb? Relaxed? Tense?

2. If there's no feeling then simply notice that. Just let it be.
3. For any sensations you feel, breathe into them and notice any difference this might make.
4. Hold your attention on each part for whatever feels natural to you; most people find 20 to 30 seconds feels about right. Just go at your own pace. Some parts of your body may hold your attention for longer.
5. Move onto the next part of your body on an out breath.
6. If you get an itch scratch it!
7. If you experience any discomfort, adjust your position so you can be comfortable.
8. It's natural for your mind to wander. When you notice your thoughts are elsewhere then bring your attention back to the part of the body you were placing your focus on.
9. If you find you fall asleep, then you may wish to keep your eyes open or sit up.

Scanning the Body

1. Start the body scan by bringing your attention to your feet. Focus on your toes, in between your toes, the soles of your feet, the tops of your feet and your ankles.
2. Move your attention on an outbreath to your legs. Focus on your calves, your shins, your knees then continue to scan upwards to the fronts and backs of your thighs.
3. Transfer your awareness to the pelvic area. Notice any sensations in the groin, genitalia, pubic area, buttocks and hips.
4. Bring your attention to your lower back, your abdomen and your waist. Notice any sensations in your digestive organs and any differences in your abdomen as you breathe in and out.

5. When ready, move your awareness into your chest. Notice any different sensations as you follow your breath.

6. Scan upwards towards your shoulders and your neck, noticing any tension that may be there. Focus your breath on any tension you may find as this can help to dissipate it.

7. Move your awareness from your neck towards your arms. Notice any sensations in your armpits, biceps, triceps, elbows, wrists, palms of your hands, backs of your hands, your fingers and thumbs.

8. Follow your attention up through the arms to the neck again and then take your awareness to your chin, jaw, lips, teeth, tongue, nose, cheeks, eyes, forehead, the crown of your head and then the whole of your head.

9. Finally, on an out breath get a sense of the whole of your body. Notice the feel of the breath as it enters and leaves your body. Then when you're ready stretch and bring your attention back to the room.

You may wish to record yourself reading these steps, so you don't have to remember them. Alternatively, a free audio body scan can be found on the following link: http://franticworld.com/free-meditations-from-mindfulness

Behaviour

"*Finish each day and be done with it. You have done what you could. Some blunders and absurdities have crept in; forget them as soon as you can. Tomorrow is a new day. You shall begin it serenely and with too high a spirit to be encumbered with your old nonsense.*" Emerson

Some of life's major stressors include bereavement, divorce, changing jobs and moving home. It's useful to think back on such times or other prolonged stressful periods to identify any themes you noticed in changes to your behaviour. For example, some people seek comfort in food, others use alcohol to relax, some people find they lose confidence in their abilities, withdraw from social situations, become controlling or find themselves checking and re-checking to gain a sense of certainty and security.

Having an awareness of any tendencies to behave in a certain way can help prevent re-occurrence if faced with another stressful time. It can also help alert us when we are in stress mode!

Responding rather than reacting

When we're stressed we have a tendency to react rather than respond. It can often feel like we don't have control over our reactions, for example, shouting at a driver when we're late for work. However, these reactions are a great barometer as to where we are on the Chilled Out – Stressed Out spectrum. Don't judge yourself when you react in this way, just look at it as your body's way of telling you that it needs some extra nurturing to move closer to the chilled-out end of the spectrum.

The hormonal changes brought on by the fight/flight response cause our behaviour to change. Whilst initially the stress response helps us to concentrate and focus, prolonged stress causes the release of too much cortisol, which can prevent us from thinking straight and in severe cases 'foggy thinking'.

Become Outcome Focused

As we all know the outcome of an event is heavily influenced by our reaction or the response we choose: Event + Response = Outcome

Being mindful of this simple equation can help us to take a breath when a potentially stress induced event happens. Rather than reacting to the situation, focus on the result that you would like to achieve as this can help to determine how you respond, and in turn minimise an undesirable outcome.

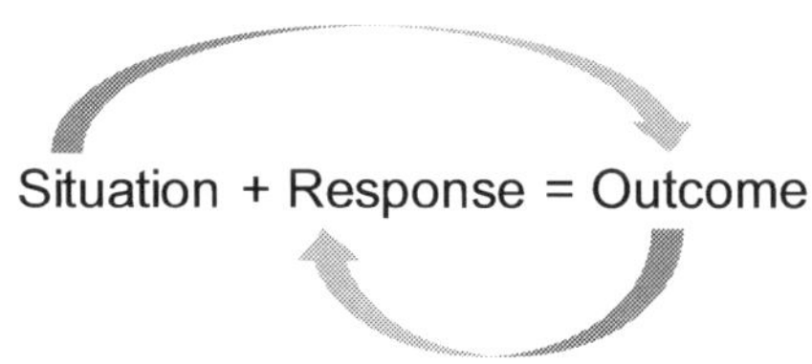

Letting go of the need to be in control

"Misery comes from trying to control things you are powerless to control, and happiness comes from correctly placing your attention on things you can control." Epictetus, a teacher in first century Rome.

One of the biggest causes of stress is uncertainty. In this VUCA world (Volatile, Uncertain, Complex and Ambiguous) it's no wonder that it's easy for us to feel stressed. To counteract the uncertainty we can tend to try to control things. However, control always creates tension. We can become rigid and inflexible, find it difficult to adapt to unexpected circumstances and guess what? We become more stressed!

Whilst we may not be able to control events around us, we do have control over our reactions to these events. The CIA (Control, Influence, Accept) model can help here so when we find we're getting stressed about something we can ask ourselves:

What can I **C**ontrol? What can I **I**nfluence? What do I need to **A**ccept?

Principle 5: Less is more

"Work is not always required. There is such a thing as sacred idleness, the cultivation of which is fearfully neglected." George Macdonald

Modern life moves at such a rapid pace and despite all the labour saving gadgets we have these days we seem to be busier than ever, continually in a rush with many of us suffering from "hurry sickness".

Two doctors, Friedman and Rosenman, whose studies found that there was a strong relationship between stress and heart disease, coined this term. It describes people who sacrifice the present by focusing on the future, what they are working towards and what needs to be done.

When the doctors began their research in the 1950s "hurry sickness" was linked to people in competitive and challenging roles. Now that target driven stressful roles are the norm, hurry sickness and its consequences have become far more widespread.

Modern society tends to place a great deal of emphasis on getting things done quickly; we have become "human doings" rather than "human beings". It is easy to be swept along with this invisible tide, to define ourselves by our achievements, our job title and the brands we buy whether it is the cars we drive or the clothes we wear.

Combined with social media, which has fuelled our tendency to compare ourselves to others, it can lead us to feel lacking or not good enough so we focus on doing more in order to strive to be "more".

This external focus leads us to lose touch with both our bodies and who we are. In striving to achieve our next goal or an imminent work deadline, we don't notice our shoulders are up by our ears, that our muscles are tight and that we're feeling on edge.

This turbo-charged lifestyle can have a huge impact on our long-term health. There is only so long we can rely on the turbo-switch before our batteries run flat. Jon Kabat-Zinn, who introduced mindfulness to the West talks about the importance of non-striving, non-doing and non-judging. When we're busy working through a never ending To Do List and juggling deadlines, the idea of stopping to re-charge can seem like wishful thinking.

The irony is that when we take time to switch off and relax, we gain greater clarity, the ideas flow, our concentration increases and we are more efficient than if we had carried on working! Together with the health benefits of feeling calmer more frequently, it's important to establish a healthy balance between 'being mode' and 'doing mode'.

When we are in "doing mode" we tend to:

☹ Strive towards our next goal

☹ Place more importance on what needs to get done

☹ Ignore how we are feeling in favour of getting the task done

☹ Accept stress as a normal part of achieving timely results

☹ Lose our composure in the face of external pressure

When we are in "being mode" we tend to:

☺ Give attention to the task we are doing and focus on enjoying it.

☺ Pay attention to the present moment

☺ Be mindful of the impact our outlook has on our well-being

☺ Notice our feelings without judgement and choose positive thoughts

☺ Place importance on our inner calm

Breaking the Striving Habit

Step 1: Awareness. Notice with curiosity NOT judgement.

The first step to break the Striving Habit is awareness. As rushing around tends to be the norm these days many of us are unaware that we are running around with jittery molecules playing havoc with our long-term health. The task-at-hand or the looming deadline takes far more precedence than our well-being. So, when you are in the middle of a task or a busy day take a moment to notice how you are feeling. It is important to notice with curiosity and not judgement.

When we realise how stressed we are feeling we can be disappointed and think we should know better than this. People who are achievement oriented can often be tough on themselves! Remind yourself that it's just an old habit that's going to be changed.

Step 2: Gain a new perspective

If you notice you are on the stressed out rather than chilled out end of the spectrum:

- ✓ Observe your breathing and focus on breathing more deeply. Exhale for longer than you inhale. This stimulates the parasympathetic nervous system and calms everything down.
- ✓ If possible, walk away from the task for a few minutes and gain a fresh perspective.
- ✓ Before you continue working on it ensure any feelings of worry, anxiety, frustration or anger are gone. The goal here is to replace any stress response related hormones with calming feel good hormones.

Step 3: Be patient

It's important to be patient. The habit of striving has often developed over a long period of time and doesn't often want to give up without a fight! Keep focused on what you're aiming to achieve, and you'll be amazed at how quickly you can shift to a more chilled out approach to getting things done.

Quick Audit Exercise– where am I now?

For each of the following statements mark on the arrow where you are now.

Left hand end of the arrow: I am rarely like this

Middle of the arrow: I am like this some of the time

Right hand end of the arrow: I am like this most of the time

It is easy for me to switch off and relax

It is easy for me to do nothing without feeling guilty

There is a good balance of work and play in my life

I usually leave work on time and rarely work late

I easily fall asleep at night without worrying about the day's work ahead

Today's Date: ______________ Next Review Date: __________________

Are there any areas you want to focus on improving?

Jot down some ideas on how you could move closer to the right hand end of the arrow:

Which ideas can you move forward with easily?

Stressed Out to Chilled Out Nurturing Toolkit

1. Stress busting ideas you can do in less than 5 minutes

- ✓ Take 2 minutes to breathe and collect your thoughts. Focus on breathing out for longer than breathing in as this stimulates the parasympathetic nervous system and therefore calms you down quicker.
- ✓ Visualise the stress hormones being washed away and being replaced by calming endorphins. The more you can visualise this the more you'll get in touch with your physiology and be in tune with your body.
- ✓ Stretch! When we feel stressed our muscles tense up and blood flow is redirected away from our tissues. Stress also inhibits the lymphatic system, which carries away toxins and fights infection. Stretching helps to reduce the tension in our muscles, stimulates oxygen rich blood to flow to our tissues and enables the lymph to flow freely again.
- ✓ Remove yourself, whenever possible, from the situation that's making you feel stressed. Driving seems to be a common way to stimulate the stress response. If you have been angered by the actions of another driver, why not simply pull over for a few minutes, let that person go on their way and annoy someone else.
- ✓ Put four drops of the Bach Flower Essence Rescue Remedy on your tongue or in a drink to help restore a sense of calm.
- ✓ Sniff calming aromatherapy oils such as lavender or chamomile. Put a couple of drops on a tissue and inhale. Some aromatherapy oil suppliers have specific blends to help create a sense of calm and relaxation. Just make sure you like the smell first! Smell has a strong association with memory so if the oil reminds you of a less than fun time in your life choose another one that gives you a feeling of instant calm.

2. Stress busting ideas you can do in 5 to 15 minutes

✓ If you're feeling stressed at work, try to take a short break. It is amazing how removing yourself from a situation even for 15 minutes helps you to calm down and see things from a different perspective.

✓ Find a quiet spot and perform some deep breathing. This helps to oxygenate your body, lower your heart rate and calm your mind and only takes a few minutes. You may wish to try the 4-7-8 or alternative nostril breathing techniques covered in Principle 4.

✓ Tune into your inner dialogue. Stop stressful thoughts in their tracks by replacing them with more empowering statements. Find ones that work for you. Here are some of the reminders I use to help me to get things back in perspective - "In the greater scheme of things does this really matter?" "I'll be in a coffin one day. Let go and chill out". "How do I want to look back on this in 6 months' time?"

✓ Look out of the window. When we're stressed our thoughts tend to focus inwards, so by standing by a window and focusing our attention on a wider view we can gain a broader perspective.

✓ Put the kettle on. The ritual of making a cup of tea and allowing your thoughts to wander away from what has made you feel stressed can help you unwind. Focus on each step from filling the kettle to choosing a mug and savouring that first sip. Avoid coffee when you're stressed as you don't want to feel even more hyped and jittery! Herbal teas known for their calming effects include chamomile, peppermint, valerian root and lemon balm.

✓ Listen to some relaxing or your favourite music. Quiet and slow paced classical music has been shown to decrease stress hormones, slow the pulse and lower blood pressure. Putting music on the background can help to keep you calm even when you don't have chance to stop for long.

3. Stress busting ideas for when you can put aside an hour or more

✓ Walking in nature, whether it's in the open countryside or strolling through a park is a great way to de-stress. There is a primal instinct to connect with nature yet much of modern life can involve being cooped up indoors. There's something about being around trees that can provide an instant feeling of calm. It's been found that the tiny particles like pollen and fungi when we're walking in nature stimulate something in our system that helps us to re-boot and feel centred.

✓ Spend some time at the beach. A walk along the beach is a great way to blow away the cobwebs and relieve stress. The negative ions in the sea air increase serotonin levels to help calm and relax us.

✓ Watch a favourite film. Films have an incredible ability to transport us away from everyday concerns and change the way we see things. It is amazing how different you can feel afterwards.

✓ Lose yourself in a book. Like films, books have the power to allow us to switch off and relax, even if this is for half an hour. Reading inspirational fictional or true stories can help to change our perceptions on the stresses and strains of life. Rereading a book you loved as a child can transport you back to those stress-free halcyon days.

✓ Treat yourself to a massage. Massage helps us to relax and unwind as it reduces the level of the stress hormone cortisol and can increase the calming neurotransmitters serotonin and dopamine. It can reduce pain and inflammation, boost the immune system and help to improve sleep.

✓ Get colouring! Adult colouring books have become very popular. As well as being fun and creative, colouring takes your mind off your worries and can help you to feel relaxed. Studies have shown that colouring stimulates the areas of the brain related to the senses and creativity as well as helping our minds and bodies to relax.

✓ Get a passion that you can indulge and lose yourself in. Having a passion has been shown to help minimise the effects of stress in life and help people stay healthier e.g. cooking, gardening, drawing, singing, dancing.

✓ Emotions connect us and being with others helps us to feel we are part of something greater so singing groups, book clubs, quiz nights, watching and playing team sports, for example, all help to create a sense of belonging as well as being fun.

4. Stress Busting Habits

- ✓ As you begin each day imagine that you can give up struggling for the whole day. Trust that things will fall into place, your needs will be met and whatever comes along you'll easily deal with it.
- ✓ "Sleep is the best meditation." Dalai Lama. Get enough quality sleep. Even a short nap can have great restorative powers and help you to see stressful situations in a new light. See chapter 2 for tips on how to help you achieve this.
- ✓ Take regular exercise; this is a great way of de-stressing and helps you sleep. This is especially true of yoga. Walking is also a wonderful way of de-stressing. The gentle rhythm of the movement can help to calm us when we've been feeling frazzled. It's also been found that exercising with others significantly reduces stress levels so you may wish to think about starting a new fitness regime with some friends.
- ✓ Stay hydrated; being de-hydrated is one of the biggest physical stresses for your body as every cell under-functions if we get insufficient fluids. Tightness across the forehead that we often relate to feeling stressed can be lack of water. Being hydrated gives the cells what they need, and will then affect our ability to deal with other forms of stress.
- ✓ As we can easily become 'human doings' rather than 'human beings' take time to just be. Rest quietly once or twice a day and quieten your internal dialogue to let your body re-tune itself. Ideally, sit in silence for 10 minutes a day, daydream and just allow your thoughts to wander.
- ✓ Check in regularly with how you're feeling to get in tune with your emotions. Whatever you're feeling express it and then let it go. Explore ways to offset feelings. For example, if you're feeling jittery do some exercise or if feeling overwhelmed then write down everything that's on your mind. This can help to clarify our thinking and prioritise tasks. You may also wish to use the Bach flower remedies that were mentioned in Principle 3.
- ✓ Check in regularly with your body to check it's relaxed. Are your shoulders up by your ears? Do you need to loosen your jaw muscles, lighten the touch on your keyboard or soften your grip on the steering wheel?
- ✓ Mindfulness. There are numerous apps for mobile phones these days to

help us relax when we're on the go, so well worth the investment of time finding one that inspires and nurtures you. Here are some of the popular ones: Calm, Insight, Buddhify and Headspace.

✓ Meditation is a brilliant de-stressor and with ongoing practice helps us to deal with life's stressors more calmly. It lowers blood pressure, supports the immune system, re-conditions breathing patterns and even stimulates anti-ageing effects. Ingrained beliefs such as those that influence the way we handle stress are embedded in our subconscious minds so meditation can be a very effective way to reprogram old thinking. Guided meditations are a great way to start.

✓ *"With every act of self-care your authentic self gets stronger, and the critical, fearful mind gets weaker."* Susan Weiss Berry. It's been found that resilient people take time each day to nurture themselves. Give yourself a cut-off point in the day to switch off and ditch the To Do List.

✓ Take time to have a relaxing bath, light some aromatherapy candles and make sure you won't be disturbed. Putting Epsom salts or Dead Sea salts in your bath can also help to reduce stress as the magnesium in these salts helps to relax our muscles and can help to induce sleep.

✓ A lot of stress these days comes from having too much to do and too many commitments. When we're busy the temptation is to overschedule our day. This can cause us stress when unexpected requests and new priorities arise. Blocking out time in our calendar that is treated as sacrosanct can provide some flexibility as well as valuable 'me time'. It's also useful to block out space in the calendar at weekends.

✓ Mark Forster is his book "Secrets of Productive People" says "*Real work is the work that progresses our goals, visions, career. Busy work is what we do to avoid real work. Another way of putting it is that real work is action, while busy work is merely activity".*

Feeling frustrated with our life can often come from having to spend more time on things that do not contribute to our fulfilment or make us feel that we're making progress. Regularly checking in to ensure that at least some part of your day is focused on what's important to you and enabling you to move forward with your goals can be liberating and reduce stress and frustration.

5. Stress busting ideas to help you let go and gain a new outlook

"Happiness means taking pleasure in what you have" Tom Meyer

- ✓ When we're going through a stressful time it's much easier to focus on the negative, not helped by the fact that our brains have a negative bias! Take the time to look out for good news, think of things that are going well, that you're grateful for or just simple things that made you smile. Apparently, it only takes between 5 and 20 seconds for your brain to absorb positive events, the more you focus on them the more your brain will be able to direct its attention to what's uplifting. In turn, this helps us to gain a new sense of perspective and take things more in our stride.
- ✓ As mentioned in Principle 5 choose 'Being Mode' rather than 'Doing Mode' whenever possible as it helps us sense more clearly the things that support us and those that deplete our resources.
- ✓ *"I release the need to determine how things 'should' be"* Wayne Dyer. Let go of the need to be right! It's amazing how wound up we can get when we focus on upholding our opinions and principles or how things should be. If you find your need to be right impacts on your stress levels then hold your opinions more lightly and remind yourself that feeling calm and contented is far more important than being right!
- ✓ When very busy it is easy to focus on what's yet to be done and so get het up. Remember to acknowledge and congratulate yourself on the tasks you have completed and even the smallest of achievements.
- ✓ *"Out of clutter, find simplicity"* Albert Einstein. When everything is getting on top of us and we're feeling overwhelmed just taking the time to tidy our desk or sort out the inbox of our emails can make us feel clearer. It's also worthwhile investing time in cleaning and tidying our homes. The physical decluttering can be a great de-stressor, can re-energise us and can help us gain more clarity.
- ✓ If you are the sort of person that has grown up with a work ethic that leads you to strive, then experiment with asking yourself "am I trying too hard?" Cut yourself some slack and look if there's a way to take the pressure off and make things easier on yourself. Take a look at the Breaking the Striving Habit in Principle 5.
- ✓ A problem shared is a problem halved. Don't be reluctant to ask for the help of others if you're going through a tough time or seek professional support.

✓ Laughing is one of the best de-stressors because it helps relax your body thereby reducing tension and stress. It triggers endorphins (the body's natural feel good chemicals) which help promote an overall feeling of well-being. It is also thought to be beneficial for the immune system and cardiovascular systems. So, watch funny films, read funny books or listen to comedy on the radio. Laughter definitely is your best medicine when it comes to stress.

Final Thoughts

"The moment you change your perception you can change the chemistry of your body" Dr Bruce Lipton.

Effectively managing stress not only gives us a better quality of life, it can literally save it! Whilst a healthy diet and regular exercise are fundamental to our well-being, we will not be able to attain optimal health if we are frequently stressed.

Stress, in the majority of instances, is a disproportionate reaction to a non-life threatening event. Our perception is absolutely essential, so it's imperative that we achieve a sense of feeling centred and relaxed as our default so we can deal more constructively when those unavoidable pressures of modern life and stressful events occur. Once we are able to do this, we will feel better physically and psychologically. We will also enjoy improved energy, better, more refreshing sleep and a sense of inner peace that allows us to enjoy life to the full.

CHAPTER 6 REVIEW & IDEAS FOR YOUR ACTION PLAN

1. Reflecting on this chapter, are there any areas of your life that may benefit from your attention to help minimise stress.

2. Review the Quick Audit exercises in this chapter to collate any action points that could be useful to you.

3. Which of these would you like to do? Circle the score that best reflects its level of interest to you.

	Not for Me									Give this a go
a. Bach Flower Remedies	1	2	3	4	5	6	7	8	9	10
b. Body Scan	1	2	3	4	5	6	7	8	9	10
c. 4-7-8 Breathing	1	2	3	4	5	6	7	8	9	10
d. Alternate Nostril Breathing	1	2	3	4	5	6	7	8	9	10
e. Balancing Doing/Being Mode	1	2	3	4	5	6	7	8	9	10
f. Break the Striving Habit	1	2	3	4	5	6	7	8	9	10
g. Bach Flower Remedies	1	2	3	4	5	6	7	8	9	10

4. Stress Busting Ideas

Read through the stress busting ideas at the end of the chapter and jot down any ideas or things you could do to nurture you:

Chapter 7

Getting Started & Staying Motivated – You Can Do It!

Motivation is Key to Success

"Knowing is not enough; we must apply. Willing is not enough; we must do."
Johann Wolfgang von Goethe

Moving from knowing what we need to do to actually doing it so that it becomes an integral part of our lives can prove to be a monumental leap! How many of us have joined a gym in January with the best of intentions only to find that later on in the year it's simply a direct debit on our bank statements as other commitments have taken priority?

Therefore, in this chapter we will look at ways to help you keep focused and fired up so that you move your fitness and wellbeing goals forward. Relapsing to old habits is normal as our brains don't like change. Fortunately though, our brains are also brilliant at adapting so we will cover ways to support you to integrate the changes you wish to make to invest in your long-term vitality. It's divided into 3 sections to help you maintain your momentum:

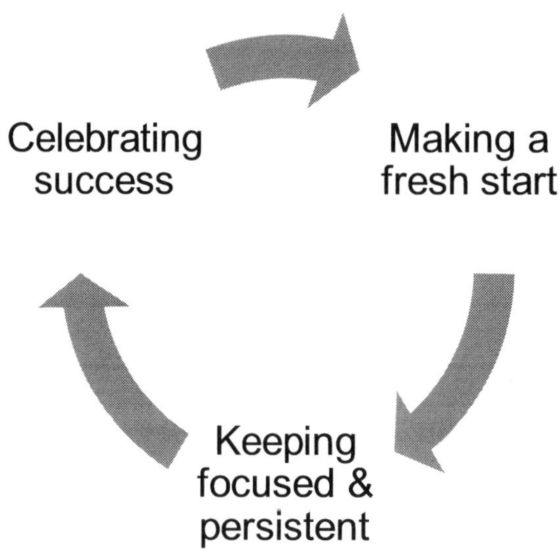

Step 1: Making a Fresh Start

The Power of Clarity

"Your vision of where or who you want to be is the greatest asset you have. Without having a goal it's difficult to score." Paul Arden

Often in our enthusiasm to transform our health we can place a great deal of pressure on ourselves by trying to address too many areas at once. At such times it's worthwhile reminding ourselves of the power of synergy; chipping away at integrating small changes can have a huge impact on our health and can take the pressure off trying to make significant changes too quickly, which can be challenging to sustain.

Being clear on what's most important and what is viable are very important to get started with confidence and focus.

Start by asking:

Where am I now?

Where do I want to be?

What do I need to do?

Regularly putting time aside to review how contented we are with the different aspects of our health and fitness provides us with an at a glance view of what is currently working and can highlight areas that need our attention.

This exercise provides a useful means of assessing which areas of your health and well-being you want to focus on. There's no right or wrong so it's important to be open, honest and non-judgemental. It provides a starting point for change and a means of reviewing your progress over time.

If 1 denotes a real discontentment and 10 denotes feeling fantastic and extremely contented, circle the score that best reflects how you currently feel about your health and wellbeing. If certain categories are not relevant to you, then change them or add in extra ones so that the list represents what fitness means to you.

Health & Wellbeing At-a-Glance View

Date: ______________	Discontented									Fantastic
Energy and vitality	1	2	3	4	5	6	7	8	9	10
Cardiovascular fitness	1	2	3	4	5	6	7	8	9	10
Physical strength/Muscle tone	1	2	3	4	5	6	7	8	9	10
Flexibility	1	2	3	4	5	6	7	8	9	10
Supple joints	1	2	3	4	5	6	7	8	9	10
Refreshing and restful sleep	1	2	3	4	5	6	7	8	9	10
Food/Healthy Recipes	1	2	3	4	5	6	7	8	9	10
Nutritional Supplements	1	2	3	4	5	6	7	8	9	10
Ideal Weight	1	2	3	4	5	6	7	8	9	10
Being calm and relaxed	1	2	3	4	5	6	7	8	9	10
Blood pressure	1	2	3	4	5	6	7	8	9	10
Bowel function	1	2	3	4	5	6	7	8	9	10
______________________	1	2	3	4	5	6	7	8	9	10
______________________	1	2	3	4	5	6	7	8	9	10
______________________	1	2	3	4	5	6	7	8	9	10

What areas could benefit on your focus the most?

Choose an area or areas that you would like to prioritise and work on. Imagine that at some point in the future you will assign a score of 10. What would need to be happening to create this level of satisfaction and fulfilment for you?

Are there any areas that you are contented with that could warrant making some extra enhancements?

The cumulative effect of small changes can make a significant contribution to our overall level of satisfaction and contentment. What do you need to do to increase your scores by two points?

What could you do in the next week to move towards achieving this?

What might you need to take into account that could prevent you from improving your scores in the next 3 months?

The Power of WHY

Doing what we *WANT* to do tends to take precedent over the things that we *HAVE* to do. It's therefore really important to have goals we feel enthusiastic about.

Every decision we make during the course of our day could be simply categorised into either moving towards pain or towards pleasure. Short term moving away from pain can often be at the price of long term pleasure. So when torn between the next episode in the box set and doing some exercise, remind yourself of what you're aiming for.

Often when we set our hearts on being healthier our goals can be so far removed from where we are now that it's hard to imagine if they'll ever be achievable so it's important to set stepping stone goals. It's then easier to feel as if you're making progress and therefore more likely for you to keep the momentum.

For each goal you set for yourself, make sure you understand what it would mean to you to achieve it. It's also essential that you fully understand the cost of not achieving it. Ask:

"If I achieve this, what will it give me?"

"What will happen if I don't take action?"

Jot down all the benefits that achieving your goal will give you and keep your notes handy.

The Power of Positive Goals

It is imperative that you focus on what you want rather than what you don't want. Our brain does not understand the concept of "not" so we'll find we end up moving subconsciously towards what we don't want rather than what we do want to achieve.

For example, if I was to ask you not to think of pink elephants, you have to think about pink elephants before you don't think of pink elephants!! We therefore need to be clear on what we do want. Rather than "I don't want to be tired anymore" you could say "It is fabulous feeling full of energy".

The Power of Setting Goals

"A dream is just a dream. A goal is a dream with a plan and a deadline."

Harvey Mackay

Vague aims are not going to help us when our motivation wanes. Having a specific goal can help enormously, giving us a target to work towards. A timed goal is one of the most effective.

I know lots of people who have wanted to take part in a sporting event and use this as the driving force to stay motivated. Others might want to lose some weight, perhaps for a wedding or a holiday; whatever it is, having a definite date to work towards is a very powerful motivator.

It also has the advantage of establishing habits which benefit your health and fitness so that after you have achieved what you set out to do it is easier to carry on in the same way.

The SMARTER model is a fabulous way to clarify what you want to achieve:

SPECIFIC – Have a specific goal that you wish to achieve, this will make it more real in your mind. So, rather than "I am fit" be more explicit by saying for example "I can walk up the 5 flights of steps to the floor of my office and can talk easily when I get to my desk" or "I can swim 10 lengths of the pool non-stop"

MEASURABLE – Make sure you have an effective way of regularly measuring your progress so that you can see yourself moving towards your goal. This could be by seeing a shrinking waist or improving times during training for a sporting event such a half marathon.

ACTION ORIENTED – Being clear on HOW you'll achieve your goal is key to success. Include what specific actions and behaviours will be required for achievement e.g. get off the bus 2 stops early to integrate more walking into my working day, attend a yoga class on a weekly basis.

REALISTIC – Making your goals overly optimistic can be disempowering when you don't achieve them. For example, wanting to run a first marathon and expecting to train for just one month is clearly unrealistic if you haven't run for a long time. Rather than aiming to run a mile without need to stop for a breath in the first week you might want to run a quarter of a mile at a reasonable pace, then half a mile, building up incrementally each week so you work up to a mile. This approach helps you to work with your body and is more likely to prevent injury and disappointment.

TIMED – Having a timescale gives a goal priority which is why working towards a specific event is so effective. For example, within a month I'd like to swim 12 lengths of the pool. Breaking this down further you could challenge yourself to swim 3 lengths non-stop in the 1st week, 6 lengths in the 2nd week, 9 in the 3rd and then 12 in the 4th.

EXCITING – If a goal doesn't excite you but instead is viewed as a bit of a chore, then it is going to be very difficult to achieve. When you wake up the thought of the goal should give you a buzz of excitement, it has to inspire you! Making your goals 'magnificent obsessions' will have a huge impact on your motivation. Knowing the difference that achieving your goals will make will help you maintain your focus.

RECORDED – Research shows that goals written down are more likely to be achieved. Writing your goal down and displaying it so that you see it every day provides inspiration and motivation; if you share it with people who will motivate and encourage you, so much the better.

The Power of Visualisation

"We are what and where we are because we have first imagined it."

Donald Curtis

Olympic athletes are said to spend 70% of their time visualising their goal. Visualisation is exceptionally powerful when we're making a fresh start or setting new goals. It utilises two characteristics of the mind:

1. The mind thinks principally in pictures
2. The subconscious does not distinguish between real events and thoughts we imagine.

It is important to use all the senses and the more powerful the vision the more convincing it is to your mind. The influence this has on goal achievement can be summed up by the concept:

I × V = R (Imagination mixed with Vividness becomes Reality)

(Canfield/Hansen/Hewitt)

So imagine that you have already achieved your goal. How will you know? What will be different? Visualise, feel, hear, taste, smell – be there!!!!

- What do I see? What do I notice?
- What will others say?
- How do I feel? What will I not feel?
- What am I doing? What am I now able to do?
- What impact has my increased energy levels had on my life?
- How am I utilising my increased levels of strength, cardiovascular fitness and flexibility?
- What is my ideal weight?
- What will I be doing to maintain this level of vitality?

Write this in the present tense and in detail so you are really clear on the benefits it will bring. Having pictures and photos can help to inspire you. Glossy magazines can be useful for cutting out pictures such as an outfit you'd love to wear once you've attained your ideal weight or once you've achieved the flexibility and physical strength you're aiming for perhaps a picture of something you'd like to do like dancing or rock climbing.

The Power of Habits

We are creatures of habit. Up to 90% of our day-to-day behaviour is based on our habits so it's absolutely essential that we're aware of the habits that aren't working for us and introduce new habits that will enable us to yield the results we're aiming for. As the old adage says "if you keep on doing what you've always done you'll keep on getting what you've always got". In order to break bad habits and create good ones we need to **CREATE SPACE FOR ACTION.** This means removing as many obstacles as possible in your life that can deflect you from your goal.

Replacing old habits can feel tough in the first few weeks, particularly those habits that have been part of your life for years. A client of mine had always had dessert after her main meal since a small child. We started by reducing dessert to 6 evenings a week for a couple of weeks, then 5 evenings a week until finally she was able to reduce desserts to weekends only. The benefits of not feeling tired from the sugar dip after the meal and from losing the weight she had wanted to shift for years proved to be a great incentive to integrate this new habit for the longer term.

The secret is to introduce new behaviours one at a time. New habits can be created in as little as 21 days. What's great to know is that after 21 to 30 times of experiencing a new habit, it's harder not to do it than do it.

When we develop the habit of, for example, exercising on a regular basis and establish a new health regime the benefits can start to come very quickly, which in turn helps us to integrate the habit over the long term.

The Power of a Plan

It has been proven that without a written plan our best intentions can so often remain at the "some-day" stage. Rather like an architect producing blue prints for a building, writing down our ideas and plans is crucial to success and has been shown to act as a catalyst for change.

You may like to use the following template to clarify what you want to achieve and translate your ideas into an action plan:

Goal Template Example **Date: 1st May**

Goal	**Target Date**
I have a flat stomach with toned and strong core muscles. I have reduced my waist by 6 inches. I can hold the Yoga Plank Pose for 3 minutes. <u>Interim Goals:</u> Month 1: Waist reduced by 2 inches Hold the Yoga Plank pose for 1 minute Month 2: Waist reduced by 4 inches Hold the Yoga Plank pose for 2 minutes	1st Aug 1st Jun 1st Jul

Benefits of achieving this goal:	1. By improving my core strength I'm: – supporting my lower spine and improving my posture – protecting my lower spine from premature wear and tear – able to exercise more efficiently by transmitting power better able to take up rock climbing and wind surfing 2. I can buy clothes that I feel great in 3. I can go swimming on holiday feeling confident 4. Reducing the fat around my middle reduces my chances of Type II Diabetes

Potential Obstacles to Work Around	1. Out for meals 3 times next week so will choose healthy starter and main course, won't have a dessert and will replace coffee with mint tea. 2. Staying with friends on Bank Holiday Weekend so do Monday's HIIT training the following Friday. 3. Business trip at the end of June with meetings that extend into the evening. As there's no gym at the venue, will therefore need to get up earlier to practise yoga.
Rewards	May: Go window shopping for new clothes Find out about climbing wall classes Investigate wind surfing clubs June: Book up a back massage July: Buy new clothes for holiday August: Sign up for climbing wall classes and wind surfing club
Action Plan	<u>Exercise Plan:</u> 1. Practise yoga after shower every day including the Plank 2. HIIT training Mondays and Wednesdays 3. Resistance training Tuesdays and Thursdays 4. Swimming on Fridays <u>Nutrition Plan:</u> 1. Reduce daily croissant with coffee to once a week 2. Replace daily 2nd cappuccino at work with a green tea 3. Cut out potatoes from evening meal 3 times a week

Goal Template Date: ____________

Goal		Target Date
Benefits of achieving this goal:		
Potential Obstacles		

Action Plan	Review Date	Target Date:

Step 2: Keeping Focused and Persistent

"No one keeps his enthusiasm automatically. Enthusiasm must be nourished with new actions, new aspirations, new efforts, new vision." Papyrus

When we're keen to get started it's easy to bound ahead. Then, when obstacles get in the way of our plans we can get demotivated and even give up. By investing time in putting firm foundations in place will help to ensure you keep on track with your plans and reap the benefits for the rest of your life. This means having strategies in place to work around the inevitable obstacles and minimising the effects of motivation thieves.

Top 10 Motivation Thieves

Everyone is inspired in different ways and once we are able to identify those things or people that truly inspire and motivate us, we can achieve whatever we put our minds to. Motivation is bound to falter from time to time so being resourceful in how we keep fired up is key to success. What gets in the way of your motivation? Outlined below are 10 common Motivation Thieves. Tick the ones that apply to you and review the tips further on to help you minimise their impact:

1. Procrastination. ❑
2. Perfectionism. ❑
3. Lack of time ❑
4. Feeling overwhelmed or overloaded ❑
5. Lack of self-belief ❑
6. Influence of others - naysayers, pessimists, cynics ❑
7. Impatience – not making progress quickly enough ❑
8. Setbacks ❑
9. Boredom ❑
10. Over commitment – leading to demotivating injuries! ❑

Motivation Thief 1: Procrastination

"Things which matter most must never be at the mercy of things which matter least." Goethe

Most of us have mastered the art of procrastination and we can be very creative in finding excuses and justifying ourselves! All of a sudden, many other low priority tasks become super urgent! "I'll just open this email", "I'll just make this call", "I'll just make a cup of tea and read this article then I'll definitely get started!"

This can be especially true of exercising. If we are a bit tired or feel that we don't quite have the time, it is amazing how quickly we can create avoidance tactics or find excuses why we should not exercise that day.

As well as stopping us from achieving our health and fitness goals, procrastination has a huge impact on our motivation in that it can make us feel guilty, dispirited and self-critical. Whilst putting things off once in a while is unlikely to have a significant impact on our long term health and fitness, we need to ensure that procrastination doesn't become a habit and get in the way of our progress. It's worth reminding ourselves that we usually have plenty of energy for the things we want to do!!

Tips for Dealing with Procrastination

- ✓ When you're considering your next task ask: "Will it move me closer towards or further away from my ultimate goal? This can prove to be a practical way of keeping focused on what's most important.
- ✓ Refer back to your notes as to the benefits of achieving your goal and the price of not achieving it.
- ✓ Refer back to the section of The Power of Why in Step 1. Remind yourself in a little more detail of the benefits of improved health and well-being:
    - ☺ Improved longevity with reduced chances of suffering from a disease or health condition.
    - ☺ The ability to remain active for the rest of your life
    - ☺ A sense of life long wellbeing and being able to enjoy life through all of your senses and faculties with the minimum of degeneration.

☺ The knowledge and experience to be able to inspire family and friends so that they may follow your example and also enjoy long and healthy lives.

Useful quotes to help you keep focused:

"Action may not always bring happiness; but there is no happiness without action." Benjamin Disraeli

"The pain of discipline weighs ounces whereas the pain of regret weighs tons." Jim Rohn

"If you do the things you have to do when you have to do them, you'll have the time to do the things you want to do when you want to do them." Zig Ziglar

"Of all the sad words of tongue and pen, the saddest are these – it might have been." John Greenleaf Whitier

Motivation Thief 2: Perfectionism

It's easy not to get started or to be put off when the exacting standards we've set for ourselves are not achieved. When we're new to something there's lots of trial and error, which does not fit well with the mind-set of perfectionists as they want to get things right!

The good news is that if you tend to be a perfectionist you are achievement oriented, so you can utilise this strength to maintain your motivation! The secret is setting a benchmark of success that will encourage action.

Tips for Dealing with Perfectionism

- ✓ Set yourself stepping stone goals. The achievement of each will act as a catalyst to your ultimate goal.
- ✓ Be patient with yourself
- ✓ Resist any temptation to be overly self-critical.
- ✓ Focus on what you have achieved rather than what you've not yet achieved.
- ✓ Refer to section in Step 1 on setting achievable and realistic goals.

Useful quotes when perfectionism is getting in the way:

"Too many people spend too much time trying to perfect something before they actually do it. Instead of waiting for perfection, run with what you've got, and fix it as you go." Paul Arden

"Embrace being perfectly imperfect. Learn from your mistakes and forgive yourself, you'll be happier." Roy Bennett

"Don't let perfectionism become an excuse for never getting started." Marilu Henner

"When you aim for perfection, you discover it's a moving target." Geoffrey Fisher

"A certain type of perfection can only be realized through a limitless accumulation of the imperfect." Haruki Murakami

Motivation Thief 3: Lack of Time

"Time is our most valuable asset, yet we tend to waste it, kill it, and spend it rather than invest it." Jim Rohn

All of us have 24 hours in the day and 168 hours in a week so we need to be focused on how we want to utilise our time. Often lack of time is linked to a lack of direction. Clear direction creates time and in turn the motivation we feel from utilising our time wisely creates more energy.

Tips to help you maximise your time

✓ Review how you spend your 24 hours in your day and the 168 hours in your week. I've often found when I'm working with my clients that when we start to review how they spend their time we identify things that move them away from rather than towards their goals.

  For example, when we start to add up how many hours we spend in front of the TV, we can reassign that time to our fitness. If you don't wish to reduce the time you spend watching TV then use the adverts to do some exercise! If you were to choose to do some stretching each time there's a commercial break, you'll soon be super supple!!

✓ Rather than fitting exercise around other commitments, it can be useful to put exercise as an appointment in your diary so it doesn't get relegated down the priority list.

- ✓ Prioritise which activities can be moved, scaled down or stopped in order to make the time available. This is not always easy but freeing up a definite, fixed amount of time to exercise is the only way if you want to make serious progress. If you try and squeeze it in on top of all your other commitments the chances are that it will be the first thing to be dropped when a problem crops up.
- ✓ If you find it hard to put a half hour or an hour slot aside in your day to exercise, integrate individual slots of 5 or 10 minutes at a time. This will help to energise you as well as improve concentration levels!
- ✓ Use daily activities to integrate fitness into your day:
    - When you're waiting for the kettle to boil, do some warm up exercises then perhaps some lunges or some squats.
    - Walk up the stairs instead of using lifts
    - Rather than stand on escalators walk up instead.
    - Get off the bus at least 1 stop early and walk the rest of the way.
    - If you have a desk job rather than sit for the majority of the day, stand up for a few hours.
    - When you're on the phone walk around or take the time to do some stretching.
    - Park your car the furthest from the entrance to the car park so you're walking more.
    - When you're walking home from the shops with some food shopping do some bicep curls on your way back.

Useful quotes to reframe when time feels short

"This constant, unproductive preoccupation with all the things we have to do is the single largest consumer of time and energy." Kerry Gleeson

"Life is what happens while you are busy making other plans." John Lennon

"For everybody in their busy lives, you need to invest in sharpening your tools, and you need to invest in longevity." Ryan Holmes

"It is not enough to be busy. So are the ants. The question is: What are we busy about?" Henry David Thoreau

Motivation Thief 4: Feeling Overwhelmed or Overloaded

In the modern world with the volume of information that bombards us and mobile devices that mean we can be contacted anytime and anywhere; it is easy to feel overloaded and that there simply is not enough time to get things done. We can lose sight of what is important to us as we worry about all of the things we have to do.

Constantly juggling priorities and dealing with the unexpected can deprive us of the energy and drive we need to keep on top of things. When our minds are full of everything that we think we should be doing we cannot give the focus and attention to the task in hand. This can be very disheartening if it prevents us from achieving or even starting to work towards our goals.

Tips to support you when feeling overwhelmed

- ✓ Set yourself realistic targets. So for example, try out at least one new healthy recipe a week rather than be overly ambitious as this can easily make you feel overwhelmed and therefore more likely to give up. Making incremental steps are far more likely to stand the test of time than making monumental leaps.

- ✓ Stephen Covey in his book "The 7 Habits of Highly Effective People" talks about putting first things first. He uses the analogy of pebbles and rocks that you need to fit in a jar. If you put the pebbles in first you'll struggle to fit in the rocks, whereas if you put the rocks in first, you will be able to fit the pebbles around the rocks. In the same way when managing our time, we need to focus on prioritising the rocks. Since without our health and fitness we can't live life to the full, we need to prioritise those tasks that will contribute to our ongoing health.

- ✓ Whatever you're doing – immerse yourself completely. Our bodies respond very quickly when they feel nurtured. If you've put 10 minutes aside for some yoga try to forget about everything else. If you're switching off to a favourite film, lose yourself completely. You'll be amazed at how different you feel afterwards.

- ✓ Avoid being too optimistic about what you can achieve in one day. It's a very common mistake to put too many tasks on the To Do list. This can result in frustration and self-criticism when you fall behind schedule. I find it works much better to focus on completing the most important and urgent tasks. Then any additional tasks you get chance to do feels like a bonus.

The important thing to do is to congratulate yourself for what you have achieved rather than berating yourself for what you haven't yet done. Remember to delegate tasks in order to free up your time to achieve what's most important to you.

- ✓ It is easy to feel so overwhelmed by all the things we have to do that we lose sight of what is important to us. Our minds become so full of recurring thoughts and worries about everything we haven't yet done, that we cannot be fully focused on the task in hand.

  If you ever feel that your commitments are getting on top of you, take the time to write down everything that is currently playing on your mind. This simple task acts like the save key on a computer, freeing you to focus on your priorities. It can create the space and clarity to identify what is urgent, what is important as well as to develop an action plan to enable you to feel in control again.

- ✓ When we're feeling overwhelmed we can feel stressed and our energy levels can plummet. This creates a vicious circle because by having less energy we get less done, then of course feel even more overwhelmed! A simple trick to break this cycle is to breathe more deeply to reenergise our cells and to stretch.

  Tension prevents the flow of energy in the body, so by stretching everyday you'll find your energy levels restored. In turn, as you start to feel more energised you will have more clarity about what needs prioritising as well as the energy to drive your goals forward.

- ✓ Remember that eating healthily and exercising are energising so by including sitting down to a nutritious meal and exercise on your priority list you will find you will feel more energised to complete the remaining tasks.

- ✓ The Bach Flower Remedy Elm is great when you feel overwhelmed by too much work or too many responsibilities. It helps to restore reassurance and gain a new perspective to the way forward.

Useful quotes when you're feeling overloaded

"The secret of getting ahead is getting started. The secret to getting started is by breaking your complex, overwhelming tasks into small manageable tasks, then starting on the first one." Mark Twain

"Often I feel that projects overwhelm us when we look at how many hours are involved until completion. But just getting started is usually not that difficult." Emily Giffin

Motivation Thief 5: Lack of Self-Belief

When I first start working with people one of the first things I focus on is identifying if there are any self-limiting beliefs that could get in the way of their enthusiasm to maintain the momentum. It's amazing the impact such beliefs can have when we're still working towards our goals. "I've always been chubby" can be used to justify giving up too soon.

We don't tend to recognise our self-limiting beliefs as they're such an integral part of our lives. They come from a wide variety of sources: family, friends and social conditioning. The ones that originate from childhood can be so indoctrinated we don't even question them, so they can be tougher to replace with more empowering beliefs. Here are some common self-limiting beliefs:

"I'm not a naturally flexible person"

"That level of fitness is for athletes not for me"

"I can expect my knees to ache at my age"

All of which I hasten to add I've managed to dispel once people follow the tips and guidance I give. They are amazed at what is possible for them to achieve!

Tips to build your inner confidence

✓ When your motivation is lacking, tune into your inner dialogue to notice if there's a self-limiting belief that's getting in your way. A belief is simply a thought we have thought over and over again. So, by thinking different thoughts, we can create new and more empowering beliefs. Remind yourself that it's just a thought and a thought can be changed!

✓ We always get what we focus on. If we focus on not being sporty then we will find all the evidence to prove ourselves right when we're not making the progress we would ideally like. Focusing on your strengths can be a brilliant way to build your self-belief.

For example, "I was never any good at sport at school" is a common belief. By focusing on a strength instead, such as self-discipline, "Being disciplined I have attended Parkrun every Saturday for the last month and achieved by personal best time". Such self-talk is far more inspiring!

- ✓ Make incremental changes as these will lead to long-term benefits and in so doing build your self-belief.
- ✓ Be nurturing and supportive rather than self-critical if you find yourself lapsing back to old habits.

Useful quotes when you lack self-belief, or your confidence is low

"Believe you can and you can. Belief is one of the most powerful of all problem dissolvers. When you believe a difficulty can be overcome, you are more than halfway to victory over it already." Norman Vincent Peale

"*They are able who think they are able.*" Virgil

"Go confidently in the direction of your dreams! Live the life you've imagined." Henry David Thoreau

Motivation Thief 6: Influence of others - naysayers, pessimists, cynics

"Just don't give up trying to do what you really want to. Where there is love and inspiration, I don't think that you can go wrong." Ella Fitzgerald

When it comes to motivation some people can be very encouraging and others can be, shall we say, less so. It is unfortunate that there are always those who may knowingly or unknowingly demotivate us with their opinions or views. Quite often this can be well meaning friends and family. The media can also be a source of negativity with respect to perceived ideas of what is possible and socially conditioned views on ageing.

When we're feeling a bit down about our progress the last thing we need to hear is someone saying, "I told you that you wouldn't be able to do it" or "you should have listened when I said that you are too old".

Obviously, everyone is entitled to their views, but it does not mean that you have to be around all the time to hear them! It has been found that the 5 people in our lives we spend the most time with will determine our outlook, so we need to choose our friends wisely.

When working towards your health and fitness goals spend time with likeminded people who you can perhaps train with and provide encouragement to each other when our motivation is waning or obstacles are getting in the way of progress.

Tips for countering the naysayers and optimising likeminded people

- ✓ Only share your aspirations and goals with likeminded people
- ✓ Find and surround yourself with people who have similar aspirations as you. It helps hugely to have the support of other likeminded individuals and with their inspiration and encouragement you are much more likely to stay motivated. Join a Facebook group or create one yourself.
- ✓ Conversely avoid sharing your goals with people who may try to undermine what you want to achieve. It is often the case that their limiting belief in their own potential leads them to want to keep you where you are now.
- ✓ Find a fitness buddy. You can then spur each other on. Partnering someone in the gym can be great for encouragement or committing to a fitness class together can help to ensure frequent attendance.
- ✓ Joining clubs can also be a brilliant way to maintain your enthusiasm. Parkrun has proven to be a fabulous way to improve fitness for people at all different levels of ability. People are very welcoming and provide a great deal of moral support to each other. For more details: www.parkrun.org.uk
- ✓ Set up a Healthy Supper Club with your friends. It's a great way to be with likeminded people and to share healthy recipes.
- ✓ Use role models to inspire you:
  - Finding inspiration and therefore motivation in role models is a great way to help you to achieve your goals. I have read biographies of people who I admire and very often their stories are ones of overcoming huge challenges to make their dreams a reality; very inspiring stuff!
  - Role models might also be people that you know personally. Perhaps someone who has achieved the same goals that you are working towards or a person who has managed to reach and maintain an outstanding level of health and fitness. I have been extremely lucky to have trained and studied with people who are role models to me and who I often think of when I need some extra motivation.

Motivation Thief 7: Impatience/Not making progress quickly enough

It's really easy to lose heart when we aren't seeing any benefit from the effort we're putting in. On occasions when the body is busy getting rid of toxins, we can even feel worse before we feel better. Sometimes the perceived effort required to achieve something can put us off doing it. Even the most dedicated souls have times when they lack the motivation to do the right thing, whether it is preparing a healthy meal or doing some exercise.

WHY POWER is crucial when your motivation has disappeared through perceived lack of progress. Constantly remind yourself why you are making these changes and what you're aiming to achieve. Although this sounds a blindingly obvious thing to do, it's so easy to place our focus on the lack of progress rather than the benefits of achievement.

Tips when you don't feel you're making progress quickly enough

- ✓ Break long-term aims into stepping stone goals. Each time you achieve one of the interim goals you will feel motivated and such successes are a fantastic way to demonstrate the progress you're making.
- ✓ If weight loss is your primary goal remind yourself that this must be done gradually. It's natural to get a bit disheartened if, after three or four weeks, you are not losing weight at the rate you expected to. However, you need to bear in mind that if too much is lost too quickly as is so often the case with a lot of fad diets, there is a good chance that you will immediately regain it after you finish your diet.

  This is because losing weight quickly puts the body into survival mode and it uses an enzyme called lipoprotein lipase to collect and store fat once you come off the diet. If you then eat a little more than you should, this is immediately retained and stored as fatty tissue putting back on all the fat you have just lost and frequently a bit more besides.

  Most diets also reduce your body's ability to use fats in body tissue as an energy source. Restrictive diets reduce the basal metabolic rate. So, don't "go on a diet", change it to a healthy one you can stick with, be patient and wait for nature to take off the fat gradually.
- ✓ Giving some thought as to why we wish to improve our health and wellbeing as well as what the consequences will be if we don't, really helps to change our perspective. It enables us to fully commit in the

knowledge that the benefits will justify the effort and commitment required. Rather than simply looking at the pros and cons it can be far more powerful to use this matrix:

If I **DO** continue working towards my goal what **WILL** happen?	If I **DON'T** continue working towards my goal what **WILL** happen?
If I **DO** continue working towards my goal what **WON'T** happen?	If I **DON'T** continue working towards my goal what **WON'T** happen?

Example: Eating more nutritious foods

If I **DO** continue working towards my goal what **WILL** happen? ☺ Have more energy ☺ Achieve my ideal weight ☺ Have more confidence in how I look ☺ Wear the clothes I've always wanted to wear ☺ Feel healthier ☺ Have clear skin	If I **DON'T** continue working towards my goal what **WILL** happen? ☹ Susceptible to more illness ☹ Gain more weight ☹ Joints will continue to ache ☹ Continue to feel bloated ☹ Spotty skin ☹ Feel guilty for not making the best of myself
If I **DO** continue working towards my goal what **WON'T** happen? ☺ Won't feel tired ☺ Joints won't hurt ☺ Won't feel fat ☺ Won't feel bloated ☺ Won't get so many colds ☺ Won't wear clothes that hide my shape	If I **DON'T** continue working towards my goal what **WON'T** happen? ☹ Won't achieve my ideal weight ☹ Won't feel healthier ☹ Won't be able to buy nice clothes that make me feel good ☹ Won't feel comfortable just wearing swimwear on the beach

Motivation Thief 8: Setbacks

Inevitably, there are all manner of setbacks that we can experience in life and these can be one of the biggest de-motivators of all. We may have prioritised our commitments to make room for our new healthy regime and surrounded ourselves with motivational people but at some stage events beyond our control will halt our progress.

Common examples of setbacks that threaten to derail our ambitions are injury, family problems, losing our job and bereavement. I have experienced bereavement of close family members a number of times over the last 10 years. Although it is one of the inescapable things in life, it can of course be extremely stressful and disruptive, negatively affecting our physical and emotional health. I certainly found that as life had literally been turned upside down, it was incredibly difficult to maintain my regular exercise regime.

Tips to work around the effects of setbacks

✓ Cut yourself some slack. Accept that you'll need to adapt your plans for a while. Try as much as possible not to give up on your goals completely as this will be demoralising, and it can be much harder to get back in the flow once life has returned to some sort of normality. Even the smallest of steps will have benefits in the longer term and help to minimise the effects of the setback on your motivation.

✓ Bear in mind that supporting your health and exercising can help to alleviate the negative effects of stress and assist in coping more effectively with the setback.

✓ Illness can of course be frustrating. However, it's paramount that any illness including colds, coughs and flu should be treated with good nutrition and rest. You should desist from your exercise program until you feel strong enough to continue. Forcing yourself to exercise when you're ill will weaken you and most likely result in the illness lasting longer and be counterproductive.

  If you feel weakness during illness your body is certainly not in a position to benefit from exercise, listen to what your body is telling you and be patient. Of course, if you suffer from any kind of medical condition or are on prescribed medication it is vital that you get your doctor's approval before beginning a program.

Motivation Thief 9: Boredom

If you find that you get bored easily it may be because you're someone who loves variety, gets excited by new things or someone who loves a new challenge. Therefore, regimented, mundane and repetitive fitness regimes are not going to keep your levels of motivation high.

Tips for overcoming boredom

- ✓ Variety is the spice of life so it's important when you set your goals in Step 1 to find innovative ways and lateral approaches to keep things as varied and interesting as possible.
- ✓ As far as nutrition is concerned, challenge yourself to introduce new recipes and try different foods. Organic veg box schemes can be a useful way for trying less run of the mill vegetables and for ensuring that what's in your cupboards is different every week. Organic recipe box schemes are also a fabulous way to add variety to your meals. (See Useful Websites at the back of the book)
- ✓ In terms of fitness, find as many different types of exercise to keep your levels of interest high. Choose exercises that really fire you up or perhaps introduce an element of competition. So rather than a weekly game of squash, join a league so there's new targets to aim towards.
- ✓ When exercising use different music to motivate you. We all have our favourite music that makes us feel good though it's easy for it to feel a bit stale if we stick to the same tracks. Plan ahead and have a number of different track lists to keep you fired up.

Motivation Thief 10: Over-commitment leading to injury!

Being too motivated can become a motivation thief as it can lead to injury, which is very dispiriting! When we're fired up to get started it's easy to overdo it as we're so keen to make progress. Remember that you're not looking for a quick fix (however tempting that is), you're looking for long-term optimal health and vitality that you will be reaping the benefits from for the whole of your life.

As far as exercise is concerned, it is possible to be over-committed to maintaining and enhancing your fitness levels. I know many people, me included, who enjoy keeping fit so much and get such a great sense of fulfilment from a challenging workout that it's easy to ignore those twinges or feeling under the weather.

I've certainly paid the price of ignoring my body's warning signs then ended up really demotivated by not being able to exercise at all in order to treat an injury. So, the rules of thumb are:

Don't:

- × Exercise when you're feeling unwell
- × Exercise when you're injured
- × Exercise through pain
- × Rush into a level of intensity that your body is not ready for.
- × Exercise in worn out trainers that no longer support your muscles and joints.
- × Start on a punishing programme without getting your posture checked first
- × Set yourself goals in an unrealistic timeframe
- × Change your diet too quickly. As it can make it harder to maintain and it can cause unpleasant detoxification reactions.

Do:

- ✓ Listen to your body
- ✓ Some stretching or gentle yoga poses if you're feeling below par
- ✓ Invest in the right footwear.
- ✓ Incorporate rest days into fitness regimes to give your muscles chance to recover
- ✓ Get your posture checked regularly to ensure that your body is in optimal alignment and balanced.
- ✓ Set achievable goals. Break aspirational and challenging goals into manageable chunks.
- ✓ Introduce healthy recipes gradually so your body has chance to adapt to new nutrients.

Step 3: Celebrating Success –

Celebrate each step towards your goal

"There is no high on earth like the high of realizing even one part of one's dream." Lauren Bacall

This stage encourages celebrating milestones along the way to provide motivation towards the next step. It reminds us to enjoy the journey as well as focus on the destination. It provides welcome support and encouragement when the going gets tough.

The sense of accomplishment that comes from completing a short-term goal provides the motivation for the next goal, inspiring you to continue to expand your comfort zone and propel you towards your long-term goal.

Take notice of how you feel and look

We all want to feel and look our best in life and when we do it makes life richer and more fulfilling. As your health and fitness improve and you have more energy, better physical abilities, improved mood and physical appearance you will be spurred on to maintain this improved state.

Learning to tune into how you feel physically and mentally and also taking note of how you look is a powerful motivator. It can also be useful to keep a journal making notes on how you feel on a daily basis which you can use to chart and measure improvements in your health and fitness.

Rewarding yourself helps you to stay motivated

"Pleasure is the object, duty and goal of all rational creatures." Voltaire

The great sense of fulfilment in achieving our goals cannot be underestimated. At the same time, extra rewards to acknowledge even the smallest of successes can prove to be a valuable motivator. They don't necessarily need to be extravagant, just something that makes you feel good.

When you feel good, your mood is good, you're motivated and your determination, focus and productivity increase! Focusing on what you want will fuel your motivation.

I'll leave the final word to Marcus Aurelius: *"What the mind of man can conceive, he can achieve."*

CHAPTER 7 REVIEW & IDEAS FOR YOUR ACTION PLAN

Step 1: Making a Fresh Start - Clarifying Your Focus

1. In the Health & Wellbeing At-a-Glance View exercise which areas did you identify that you would like to focus on?

- ☐ Energy and vitality
- ☐ Cardiovascular fitness
- ☐ Physical strength/muscle tone
- ☐ Flexibility
- ☐ Supple joints
- ☐ Refreshing and restful sleep
- ☐ Food/healthy recipes
- ☐ Nutritional supplements
- ☐ Ideal weight
- ☐ Being calm and relaxed
- ☐ Blood pressure
- ☐ Bowel function, digestive system

2. Goal setting check list.

- ☐ I'm excited about my goals
- ☐ I've created stepping stone goals
- ☐ I'm clear on why I want to do this
- ☐ My goals follow SMARTER
- ☐ I can visualise achieving my goals
- ☐ They're worded in a positive way
- ☐ The photos that help me visualise the goal are in a place I see every day
- ☐ I've a plan to create new habits and know which behaviours to target first
- ☐ I've collated ideas for rewards to celebrate the achievements of my goals

Step 2: Keeping Focused and Persistent

- Top 10 Motivation Thieves

Which of the common motivation thieves could get in the way of your progress?

- ☐ Procrastination
- ☐ Perfectionism
- ☐ Lack of time
- ☐ Feeling overwhelmed
- ☐ Lack of self-belief
- ☐ Influence of pessimists/cynics
- ☐ Impatience
- ☐ Setbacks
- ☐ Boredom
- ☐ Over commitment

Step 3: Celebrating Success – Rewarding yourself along the way

You may wish to keep a journal to chart your progress and of course remember to reward yourself when you reach each stepping stone goal!

A Few Final Words

First of all, I would like to thank you for reading this book. I truly hope it proves to be a valuable resource to help you invest in your long-term health. I'm passionate about helping people transform their health and fitness. Having witnessed loved ones lose their health I know the devastating effect it has. It does not matter who we are, our lives will be immeasurably poorer without our health and well-being.

Social conditioning is very powerful and seems to continue to give us a broadly pessimistic view on ageing, something to be fearful of rather than something to embrace.

The prime message that I wanted people to appreciate is the amazing strength and resilience of the human body and its ability to self-heal and thrive throughout our lives.

Age need not be the inevitable barrier it is often portrayed as with a constant barrage of negative messages. Ideally getting older simply means being young for a very long time!

If you'd chosen to read this book, you probably already know this! You're unlikely to take your well-being for granted and you recognise the importance of taking responsibility for your health.

I do hope this book has given you some new insights and plenty of practical tips to help you make the most of your health. I also hope the Five Principles prove to be a useful way to keep your approach to health and fitness on track.

My next plan is to set up a community on Facebook to enable people to share tips on what's worked for them, share in their successes and simply benefit from engaging with likeminded people.

I'll be adding fitness videos and updates on health and fitness so please check out Older Fitter, which I hope will help you maintain momentum in your commitment to your health.

OLDER FITTER

DON'T LET AGE BE A BARRIER

sturoberts@olderfitter

If you do have any thoughts or feedback then I would really appreciate you leaving a review on

Amazon, or alternatively you can get in touch via the following email address

sturoberts@olderfitter.co.uk

Thank you again for reading this book. I wish you every success with your health and fitness and many years living a healthy, happy and fulfilling life.

Stuart Roberts

September 2018

Further Reading & Useful Websites

Please note the following information was to the best of our knowledge accurate when we published. References are provided for informational purposes only and do not constitute endorsement of any websites or other sources. It is not meant to be an exhaustive list though we hope it provides a useful resource for you as a basis of your own research.

Chapter 2

Further Reading

Oil Pulling Therapy by Dr. Bruce Fife	www.credence.org

Useful Websites

Just Stand	www.juststand.org
Natural Light Alarms	www.sad-lighthire.co.uk/
	www.lumie.com
	www.BioBrite.com
Homocysteine Test	www.yorktest.com
Non-toxic household cleaning products	www.methodproducts.co.uk
	www.uk.ecover.com/
Non-toxic personal care products	www.greenpeople.co.uk
	www.nealsyardremedies.com.

Chapter 3

Suppliers of supplements to support the digestive system

Please refer to suppliers in chapter 5 for digestive enzymes, probiotics, glutamine and aloe vera juice.

Useful Websites

Squatty Potty www.squattypotty.com

Examples of places that test for leaky gut, allergies and food intolerances

Genova Diagnostics Europe www.gdxuk.net

Higher Nature www.highernature.co.uk

York Test Laboratories www.yorktest.com

Chapter 4

Further Reading

Body by Science Doug McGuff and John Little.

Quick check for body fat www.calculator.net/body-fat-calculator

Chapter 5

To find a nutritional therapist: www.bant.org.uk

British Association for Nutrition and Lifestyle Medicine

UK organic vegetable box schemes www.riverford.co.uk

www.abelandcole.co.uk

Himalayan salt www.credence.org

Further Reading

Detox Handbook	Dr Jennifer Harper
The 9 Day Liver Detox	Patrick Holford
All New Sports Nutrition Guide	Michael Colgan
Fats that Heal Fats that Kill	Udo Erasmus
Collins Gem Guide GL (Glycaemic Load)	Kate Santon

Recipe Books

New Complete Vegetarian	Rose Elliot
A Modern Way to Cook	Anna Jones
The Green Kitchen	David Frenkiel & Luise Vindahl
Medicinal Chef Healthy Every Day	Dale Pinnock

Nutritional Supplement Suppliers

Archturus Healthcare	www.archturus.co.uk/
Higher Nature	www.highernature.com
Lamberts Healthcare	www.lambertshealthcare.co.uk
Nutrigold	www.nutrigold.co.uk
Solgar	www.solgar.co.uk
Vitamin D Test	www.vitamindtest.org.uk/
Food Analysis App Example:	www.cronometer.com

Chapter 6

Further Reading

Molecules of Emotion	Candace Pert
Biology of Belief	Bruce Lipton
Reinventing the Body Resurrecting the Soul	Deepak Chopra
Every Breath You Take	Rose Elliot
The Art of Effortless Living	Ingrid Bacci
The 38 Flower Remedies	Judy Howard

Flower Essences for Emotional Support

The Dr Edward Bach Centre www.bachcentre.com

Mindfulness Apps:

Examples include: Aura, Buddhify, Calm, Headspace, and Insight Timer.

Chapter 7

Further Reading

These are not health and fitness books. However, the concepts and techniques they cover I've found are useful for keeping focused on health and fitness goals.

The Power of Focus	Canfield, Hansen and Hewitt
The Compound Effect	Darren Hardy
The 7 Habits of Highly Effective People	Stephen Covey

Useful Websites Park Run - www.parkrun.org.uk

Studies, Articles and Further References

Chapter One

Counter Clockwise Professor Ellen Langer

Book that describes her 1979 Harvard University study

2010 BBC documentary "The Young Ones" replicating Professor Langer's original experiment

Chapter Two

Health Consequences of shift work and insufficient sleep.

British Medical Journal (BMJ) 2016 Nov Kecklund G1, 2, Axelsson J3.

Siesta in Healthy Adults and Coronary Mortality in the General Population 2007

Naska A., Oikonomu E., Trichopoulou A., Psaltopoupou T., Trichopoulos D.

European Commission Regulation Introducing Changes to the Conditions and Levels of Use for Food Additives Containing Aluminium

Food Standards Agency Northern Ireland Consultation

Diesel engine exhaust is carcinogenic 2012 Dr Chris Portier

World Health Organisation (WHO) International Agency Research Cancer IARC

Air Pollution and Optimal Health

Colgan Institute News feature article March 2003

Health Consequences of Diesel Engine Omissions 2002

U.S. Environment Protection Agency (EPA) 10-year study

www.juststand.org/facts/scientificresearch

The Hordaland Homocysteine Study. A community-based study of homocysteine, its determinants, and associations with disease. Journal of Nutrition. 2006 Jun; 136 (6 Suppl): 1731S - 1740S. H. Refsum, et al.

The Role of Homocysteine in the Development of Cardiovascular Disease:

Paul Ganguly, Sreyoshi Fatima Alam

Chapter Three

Confirmed, your digestive system dictates whether you're sick or well

articles.mercola.com/sites/articles/archive/2013/01/.../digestive-system-gut-flora.aspx

Bowel flora as therapy (Probiotics)

Dr Lawrence G Plaskett B.A. Ph.D., C.Chem., F.R.I.C.

Gliadin, zonulin and gut permeability: Effects on celiac and non-celiac intestinal mucosa and intestinal cell lines.

Drago. S, et al Scand J Gastroenterol. 2006 Apr; 41 (4):408-19. PMID: 16635908

Digestive Enzymes – The key to optimal health

Nutrigold Education News – issue 18

Aloe Vera – The Health Benefits

Dr Lawrence G Plaskett B.A. Ph.D., C.Chem., F.R.I.C.

Chapter Four

Natural News – Ground breaking study reveals High Intensity Interval Training may be the key to slowing ageing: Earl Garcia April 16th, 2017

http://fitness.mercola.com/sites/fitness/archive/2012/02/10/phil-campbell-interview aspx

Peak Fitness – reap the benefits of high intensity interval training

articles.mercola.com/peak-fitness.aspx

Eight weeks of a combination of high intensity interval training and conventional training reduce visceral adiposity and improve physical fitness: a group-based intervention. GIANNAKI C D et al

The Journal of Sports Medicine and Physical Fitness 2016 April; 56(4):483-90

High Intensity Intermittent Exercise and fat loss

Stephen H. Boucher J Obes. 2011; 2011; 868305: 2010 Nov 24th

Impact of exercise intensity on body fatness and skeletal muscle metabolism. Metabolism Tremblay, A., Simoneau, J., & Bouchard, C. (1994), 43 (7), 814-818

American College of Sports Medicine, High Intensity Interval Training (PDF)

fitness.mercola.com/sites/fitness/archive/2016/05/.../super-slow-weight-training.aspx

Chapter Five

articles.mercola.com/sites/articles/archive/.../food-nutrients-vitamin-supplements.aspx. Why Widespread Nutritional Deficiencies Are a Reality That Must Be Reckoned With. 0. January 20, 201

www.patrickholford.com/advice/supplements-healthy-pregnancy

Chow CK, Thacker RR, Changchit C, Bridges RB, Rehm SR, Humble J, Turbek J.

Lower levels of vitamin C and carotenes in plasma of cigarette smokers.

J Am Coll Nutr. 1986; 5 (3):305-12.

www.patrickholford.com/advice/the-truth-about-alcohol

www.unm.edu/~lkravitz/Article%20folder/TartCherryJuicee.htm

Fall prevention and vitamin D in the elderly: an overview of the key role of the non-bone effects

Cedric Annweiler, 1 Manuel Montero-Odasso, 2 Anne M Schott, 3 Gilles Berrut, 4 Bruno Fantino, 1 and Olivier Beauchet 2010 Oct 11

Vitamins for chronic disease prevention in adults: clinical applications. Fletcher RH1, Fairfield KM Journal of the American Medical Association JAMA. 2002 Jun 19; 287 (23):3127-9.

www.mreassociates.org/pages/ama_speaks_out.html

American Medical Association Acknowledges the Role of Vitamins for Chronic Disease Prevention in Adults.

www.medscape.com/viewarticle/500874_1

Vitamin D and the Elderly - Medscape

Lisa A. Barker, 1, * Belinda S. Gout, 1 and Timothy C. Crowe, 2, Hospital Malnutrition: Prevalence, Identification and Impact on Patients and the Healthcare System Int J Environ Res Public Health. 2011 Feb; 8 (2): 514–527

(PDF) Undernutrition in the UK - British Nutrition Foundation www.nutrition.org.uk/.../153_Undernutrition%20in%20the%20UK.pdf by S Schenker - 2003

Health Benefits of Krill Oil. Nutrigold Newsletter.

Dr Lawrence G Plaskett B.A. Ph.D., C.Chem., F.R.I.C.

www.updates.nutrigold.co.uk/nutritional_newsletters updates.nutrigold.co.uk/assets/pdf/newsletters/NG-Education-Newsletter-VitaminD.pdf Vitamin D – More than a ray of sunshine

Are You Sabotaging Your Health and Longevity by Eating Too Much Protein?

articles.mercola.com/sites/articles/archive/2015/12/21/excessive-protein-intake.aspx21 Dec 2015 -

Increasing fruit and vegetable consumption to reduce the risk of noncommunicable diseases. World Health Organisation (WHO)

www.who.int/elena/titles/bbc/fruit_vegetables_ncds/en

Burning Fat for Fuel Increases Quality and Quantity of Life, Apr 24th 2017

articles.mercola.com/sites/articles/.../04/.../burning-fat-for-fuel.aspx

Sugar: Killing us Sweetly. Staggering Health Consequences of Sugar

www.globalresearch.ca/sugar-killing-us-sweetly/5367250

High-Fibre Diet for Stroke Prevention - Health Notes BioCare

www.biocare.co.uk/default.aspx?...%2Fassets%2Ffeature%2Fhigh-fiber-diet... stroke.

Dietary fiber intake in relation to coronary heart disease and all-cause mortality over 40 y: the Zutphen Study. 2008 American Society for Clinical Nutrition. 1, 2, 3 Martinette T Streppel, Marga C Ocké, Hendriek C Boshuizen, Frans J Kok, and Daan Kromhout

Vegetable, fruit, and cereal fiber intake and risk of coronary heart disease among men. Rimm EB1, Ascherio A, Giovannucci E, Spiegelman D, Stampfer MJ, Willett WC. 1996 Feb 14; 275 (6):447-51

The Many Health Benefits of MCT Oil

articles.mercola.com/sites/articles/.../mct-oil-health-benefits.aspx

The effect of physical activity on the brain derived neurotrophic factor: from animal to human studies. Zoladz JA1, Pilc A. J Physiol Pharmacol. 2010 Oct; 61 (5):533-41.

https://www.ncbi.nlm.nih.gov › NCBI › Literature › PubMed Central (PMC) Brain-Derived Neurotrophic Factor.

Prog Neurobiol. 2001 Jan; 63 (1):71-124. Brain-derived neurotrophic factor in the control human brain, and in Alzheimer's disease and Parkinson's disease.

Murer MG1, Yan Q, Raisman-Vozari R.

Jeffrey S. Bland, Deanna Minich, Robert Lerman, Gary Darland, Joseph Lamb Matthew Tripp, Neile Grayson Isohumulones from hops (Humulus lupulus) and their potential role in medical nutrition therapy

updates.nutrigold.co.uk/assets/pdf/newsletters/NG_Newsletter_Pain.pd (PDF) alpha acids and natural pain relief - Nutrigold Update Service

The Alkaline Diet: Is There Evidence That an Alkaline pH Diet Benefits ...https://www.ncbi.nlm.nih.gov › NCBI › Literature › PubMed Central (PMC) by GK Schwalfenberg - 2012

Https://draxe.com/balancing-act-why-ph-is-crucial-to-health/

updates.nutrigold.co.uk/assets/all/Nutrigold_PH_Newsletter_-_for_web.pdf PDF The importance of balancing body pH - Nutrigold Update.

16671762R00209

Printed in Great Britain
by Amazon